A COMPARISC

LANGUAGES:

FROM MÉXICO TO GUATEMALA

MATEO G.R. 'NIM B'AJLOM' &

SANDRA CHIGÜELA

B'AJLOM II NKOTZ'I'J PUBLICATIONS

(2020)

FIRST EDITION

A COMPARISON OF FOUR MAYAN LANGUAGES:

FROM MÉXICO TO GUATEMALA

©B'AJLOM II NKOTZ'I'J PUBLICATIONS & KDP PUBLISHING

Guatemala C.A. & U.S.A.

This Book is dedicated to my wife, Sandra, and my children – Cristel, Emilio, Alejandra, Camila & Galilea.

Brief History of the Author

Mateo Russo and his wife Sandra founded 'Bajlom ii Nkotz'i'j Publications' in 2018. The organization was named using two words of Mayan origin from the Tz'utujiil Language of Guatemala. The two words tell the love story of Mateo and Sandra. 'B'ajlom' means 'Jaguar' and the word 'Nkotz'i'j' means 'My flower' which is the loving name that Mateo gave to his wife. This love story of the Jaguar and his beloved flower gave birth to the mission of Mateo to preserve indigenous languages of Guatemala and southern Mexico and to create linguistic texts that can provide a written record of specific dialects and the stories of people who are collaborators with this project. The goal is to preserve all of the indigenous languages of Guatemala and others from southern Mexico; not only through a text book or grammar book, but through poetry, songs, and many other forms of literary art and artistic expression. The goal is to give a voice to the highly marginalized indigenous people who have been highly discriminated against in all societies of Latin America. Mateo has hopes in expanding this project through time, one language at a time. Mateo's philosophy is founded in the philosophy of EZLN (The Zapatista Army of National Liberation) and through the teachings of Subcomandante Marcos the original spokesperson for EZLN. The fight of EZLN has inspired Mateo to create another front in the fight that continues: The battle to preserve and protect the remnants of our past and our perception of the world around us, our own words and those words being of our ancestors. Our indigenous linguistic history is very beautiful and it needs to be preserved, because it is our linguistic inheritance. Despite that many indigenous languages are moribund... Mateo and his wife have joined together with the fight to preserve the most important facet of the cultures of the indigenous people: Our linguistic inheritance (our mother tongues). Mateo passionately supports Indigenous Human Rights and the preservation and protection of every indigenous language of Guatemala and southern Mexico. Mateo will not rest until every indigenous language has a written literary archive and until the voice of the indigenous people is not forgotten but is permanently marked in human history.

Contact Information:

'B'ajlom ii Nkotz'i'j Publications'

biinpublications@gmail.com

biinpublications@facebook.com

If you would like to donate to our cause and give your support or if you would like to donate your time or be a literary collaborator with us, please, contact us by e-mail.

Introduction

Vocabulary Lists & Phrasebooks

Introduction:

Although Mayan Languages are one of the most well-documented groups of Amerindian Languages from Mesoamerica, they still remain quite a bleak and obscure topic to the World at large; except for a small group of Anthropologists, Archaeologists and Mayanists. The many Mayan cultures of southern Mexico and Guatemala remain in obscurity within the hustle and bustle of the Post-modern widely-globalized world. For the most part, resources for Mayan Language Acquisition are very few and at some times they are non-existent. We hope that with this academic work, we may shed some light on the topic of the common similarities between modern-day Mayan Languages within the much broader Mayan Language Linguistic Family Tree.

Although people in the Post-modern Era may think that Mayan Cultures are an archaic and long-gone part of early human history, Mayan people are indeed alive and well; and their languages are even more so spoken by several million individuals who inhabit Guatemala, Belize, Honduras, El Salvador and southern Mexico. There is not only one specific Mayan Language, but over 25 different languages spoken by Mayan communities that all have their own history, culture, and customs that differ from one another to many varying degrees. For every language or cultural group, there are multiple dialects and sub-dialects that can vary from region to region, or even from village to village. Although, it would be a mistake to generalize all Mayan Languages as Mayan as Anthropologists have done for many years, for many groups do not identify as 'the Maya' as do the Yucatec-speaking peoples of the Península de Yucatán of México. 'Maayat'aan' is the name of the Yucatec Language spoken in Belize, Mexico and in sparse areas of Guatemala (especially Péten). 'Maayat'aan' literally means 'The Speech of the Maya' and therefore, the Yucatec speakers refer to themselves as 'the Maya.' Other cultural groups do not identify as such, but only by the name they give themselves to distinguish themselves from other nearby cultural groups. For example, the Tz'utujil people from el Departamento de Sololá, Guatemala refer to themselves as 'the Tz'utujil People' and the Ch'ol of Tumbalá, Chiapas, Mexico refer to themselves simply as 'The Ch'ol'. Many Mayan cultural groups refer to themselves as 'the people' using whichever dialectal variant for this word to describe themselves as a unified group. The same goes for their individual languages; as many may refer to their language as 'the Speech' or 'Our Speech.' The Tz'utujil people use the word 'Ajtz'utujil' when they refer to themselves individually. 'Ajtz'utujil' simply means 'a Tz'utujil person' or 'speaker of Tz'utujil.' 'Aj-' in Tz'utujil is a prefix that is used to show that a trait or action belongs solely to the individual [even more specifically; a person]. A speaker of Tz'utujil would call a speaker of another language accordingly; in this manner a speaker of Mam would be called 'Ajmam'.

Within this academic article we will show examples of how Tz'utujil, K'iche', Ch'ol and Yucatec compare and contrast between themselves.

Tz'utujil and K'iche' both come from the Eastern Branch of Mayan Languages and are closely related to Kaqchikel. Ch'ol Maya is part of the Western Branch of Mayan Languages and it is closely related to Chontal, Ch'orti' and Ch'olti' [extinct]. Yucatec, also known as 'Maayat'aan', formed its own branch many years ago and stems from the Classical Mayan. The Yucatecan Branch of Mayan Languages also includes: Lakantun, Itza' and Mopan.

8

*Proto-Maya < Huastecan Branch, Yucatecan Branch, Western Branch & Eastern Branch

Huastecan Branch –

WASTEK [ISOLATE]

CHICOMUSELTEC [EXTINCT]

Yucatecan Branch –

YUCATEC

LAKANTUN

ITZA'

MOPAN

Western Branch < *Ch'olan & **Q'anjobalan –

*Ch'olan < Ch'ol Proper & Tzeltalan

Ch'ol Proper --	*Tzeltalan* –
CH'OL	TZ'ELTAL
CHONTAL	TZOTZIL
CH'ORTI'	
CH'OLTI' [EXTINCT]	

**Q'anjobalan < Chujean, Q'anjobalan Proper & Mocho'

Chujean --

CHUJ

TOJOLAB'AL

Q'anjobalan Proper --

Q'ANJOB'AL

AKATEK

JAKALTEK

Mocho' –

MOCHO' [ISOLATE]

Eastern Branch < *Quichean & **Mamean

*Quichean < Quichean Proper, Poqom, Q'eqchi' & Uspantek

Quichean Proper --

K'ICHE'

TZ'UTUJIL

KAQCHIKEL

ACHI

SAKAPULTEK

SIPAKAPENSE

Poqom --

POQOMCHI

POQOMAM

Q'eqchi'--

Q'EQCHI

Uspantek –

USPANTEK

Mamean < *Mamean & **Ixilean

***Mamean** –*

MAM

TEKITEKO

***Ixilean** –*

IXIL

AWAKATEK

THE FOLLOWING CHAPTERS WILL BE A CONCISE AND DETAILED CONTRAST AND COMPARISON OF:

1) TZ'UTUJIL [QATZIJOB'AL]

2) K'ICHE' [QATZIJOB'AL]

3) CH'OL [LAK T'AN / TY'AÑ]

4) YUCATEC [MAAYAT'AAN]

I) Common Similarities and Differences

There are three ways that Mayan Language Vocabulary can compare and contrast between Languages:

1) All Languages share a common root word (very similar)

   Ex.

   Tz'utujil: TZ'IJB' (Writing)

   K'iche': TZ'IB' (Writing)

   Ch'ol: TS'IJB' (Writing)

   Yucatec: TZ'IIB' (Writing)

2) Several Languages share a common root while others do not (varying similarity)

   Ex.

   Tz'utujil: TZ'I' (Dog)

   K'iche': TZ'I' (Dog)

   Ch'ol: TS'I' (Dog)

   Yucatec: PÉEK (Dog)

3) All Languages compared use a different root word that may be specific to only the individual Language (no similarity)

Ex.

Tz'utujil: JAB'ELIIL (Beauty)

K'iche': JE'LAL (Beauty)

Ch'ol: ITY'OJOLEL (Beauty)

Yucatec: JATZ'UTZIIL (Beauty)

The following will be a list of charts comparing and contrasting common root words in these four Mayan Languages:

CORN:

Tz'utujil: IXIIM
K'iche': IXIIM
Ch'ol: IXIM
Yucatec: XI'IM / IXIM

JAGUAR:

Tz'utujil: B'AJLOM
K'iche': BALAAM
Ch'ol: BAJLÄM / BO'LAY
Yucatec: BAALAM / BAALAN / CHAKMO'OL

AVOCADO:

Tz'utujil: OOJ
K'iche': OOJ
Ch'ol: OON
Yucatec: OON

SWEET POTATO:

Tz'utujil: IIS

K'iche': IIS / IXQ'ANAJOY / KAMOT

Ch'ol: AJKUM

Yucatec: IIS

CHILE PEPPER:

Tz'utujil: IIK

K'iche': IIK

Ch'ol: ICH [*consonant shift*]

Yucatec: IIK

WOMAN:

Tz'utujil: IXOQ / Q'AAPOJ

K'iche': IXOQ / Q'APOJ

Ch'ol: X'IXIK

Yucatec: XCH'UUP

PERSON:

Tz'utujil: WINAQ

K'iche': WINAQ

Ch'ol: WINIK

Yucatec: WIINIK / MÁAK

QUETZAL [BIRD]:

Tz'utujil: K'UK'

K'iche': K'UK'

Ch'ol: XMANK'UK' / XKENZAL

Yucatec: K'UK'

MAN:

Tz'utujil: AACHI

K'iche': ACHI

Ch'ol: WINIK

Yucatec: MÁAK / WIINIK / XIIB

GOD / LORD:

Tz'utujil: AJAAW / DYOS
K'iche': AJAW / QAJAW / DIOS
Ch'ol: CH'UJUTAT
Yucatec: K'U / YUUM / DYOS

TO CROSS:

Tz'utujil: Q'ATOJ
K'iche': Q'AXIK
Ch'ol: K'AXEL / K'AXTAN
Yucatec: K'AATEL

TO DO:

Tz'utujil: B'ANOJ
K'iche': B'ANOJ
Ch'ol: TUMBEN / MEL / CHA'LEN
Yucatec: BEETIK

TO GO [root]:

Tz'utujil: -B'E
K'iche': -B'EK
Ch'ol: MAJLEL
Yucatec: BINEL

TO ENTER [root]:

Tz'utujil: OOK
K'iche': OOKIK
Ch'ol: OCHEL
Yucatec: OOKOL

TO ARRIVE [HERE]:

Tz'utujil: UUL
K'iche': UUL
Ch'ol: JULEL
Yucatec: K'UCHUL

MOON:

Tz'utujil: IIK' / QATI'T
K'iche': IIK'
Ch'ol: UW
Yucatec: UW

SUN / DAY:

Tz'utujil: Q'IIJ
K'iche': Q'IJ
Ch'ol: K'IIN
Yucatec: K'IIN

NIGHT:

Tz'utujil: AQ'A'
K'iche': AQ'AB'
Ch'ol: AK'ÄLEL
Yucatec: AK'AB

TO DIE:

Tz'utujil: KAMIK
K'iche': KAMIK
Ch'ol: CHÄMEL
Yucatec: KIIMIL

TO SAY:

Tz'utujil: -B'IIJ / -B'IX
K'iche': -B'IJ
Ch'ol: AL
Yucatec: A'AL

TO EAT:

Tz'utujil: -WA'
K'iche': -WA'IK
Ch'ol: K'UX
Yucatec: JANAAL

TORTILLA:

Tz'utujil: WAAY

K'iche': WA / LEEJ

Ch'ol: WAJ

Yucatec: WAAJ

PUMPKIN:

Tz'utujil: K'UUM

K'iche': K'UUM

Ch'ol: CH'UJM [*consonant shift*]

Yucatec: K'UUM

BLOOD:

Tz'utujil: KIK'

K'iche': KIK'

Ch'ol: CH'ICH' [*consonant shift*]

Yucatec: K'IK'

HAND / ARM:

Tz'utujil: Q'AB'AJ
K'iche': Q'AB'AJ
Ch'ol: K'ÄBÄL
Yucatec: K'AB

BUTTERFLY:

Tz'utujil: MARIPÓOSA [*original word lost*]
K'iche': PEMPEN
Ch'ol: PEJPEM
Yucatec: PEEPEM

BOY:

Tz'utujil: AK'AL
K'iche': AK'AL / AL
Ch'ol: ALOB
Yucatec: PAAL / XI'IPAL

GIRL:

Tz'utujil: XTAN / XTEN
K'iche': CH'UCH' / ALI
Ch'ol: XCH'OK
Yucatec: XCH'UUPAL

TREE:

Tz'utujil: CHE'
K'iche': CHE'
Ch'ol: TE' [*consonant shift*]
Yucatec: CHE'

WHAT?:
[*No similarity*]
Tz'utujil: ¿NAQ?
K'iche': ¿JAS?
Ch'ol: ¿CHUKI?
Yucatec: ¿BA'AX?

WHERE?:

[Tz'utujil & Ch'ol similarity]

Tz'utujil: ¿B'AAR / B'AARKII' / B'AAKII'?

K'iche': ¿JAWI' / JAWICHI'?

Ch'ol: ¿BAK / BAKI?

Yucatec: ¿TU'UX?

HOUSE:

Tz'utujil: OOCHOOCH / JAAY

K'iche': OCHOCH / JA

Ch'ol: OTOT

Yucatec: OTOCH / KAJTAL

MOTHER:

Tz'utujil: -TAAN / -TEE'

K'iche': CHUCH

Ch'ol: ÑA'

Yucatec: NA' / MAAM

LAND:

Tz'utujil: ULEEW / ULEEP
K'iche': ULEEW
Ch'ol: LUM / LUMAL
Yucatec: LU'UM / KAAB

WATER:

Tz'utujil: YA'
K'iche': JA'
Ch'ol: JA'
Yucatec: JA'

RAIN:

Tz'utujil: JAB'
K'iche': JAB
Ch'ol: JA'AL
Yucatec: CHAAK / JA'

STONE:

Tz'utujil: AAB'AJ
K'iche': ABAJ
Ch'ol: TUN / XAJLEL
Yucatec: TUUNICH

CACAO:

Tz'utujil: KOKOP, KAKAW, KAKOW, KOKOW
K'iche': KAKAW, KAKOW
Ch'ol: KÄKÄW
Yucatec: KAKAW

COFFEE:
[from Spanish]
Tz'utujil: KAPE
K'iche': KAPE
Ch'ol: KAJPE' / KAJWE' / KAPE
Yucatec: BOXJA' / KAAPE

BEANS:

Tz'utujil: KINAQ'

K'iche': KINAQ'

Ch'ol: BU'UL

Yucatec: BU'UL

ATOL (DE ELOTE):

Tz'utujil: Q'OR AJ

K'iche': Q'OR AJ

Ch'ol: UL

Yucatec: SA' / SAKSA'

LIFE:

Tz'utujil: K'ASLEEM / K'ASLEEMAAL

K'iche': K'ASLEMAL

Ch'ol: KUXTÄLEL

Yucatec: KUXTAL

CHICKEN:

Tz'utujil: EK' / AK'
K'iche': EK' / AK'
Ch'ol: BI'TI MUT / CH'ITON MUT
Yucatec: KAAX

FIREWOOD:

Tz'utujil: SI'
K'iche': SI'
Ch'ol: SI'
Yucatec: SI'

BOOK / PAPER:

Tz'utujil: WUUJ
K'iche': WUUJ
Ch'ol: JUN
Yucatec: JU'UN

FOOD:

Tz'utujil: RIKIIL
K'iche': RIKI'L
Ch'ol: WAJ
Yucatec: WAAJ / O'OCH

SALT:

Tz'utujil: AATZ'AAM
K'iche': ATZ'AM
Ch'ol: ATS'AM
Yucatec: TA'AB

BAT [animal]:

Tz'utujil: SOOTZ'
K'iche': SOTZ'
Ch'ol: SUTS'
Yucatec: SOOTZ'

COYOTE:

Tz'utujil: UUTIIP
K'iche': UTIW
Ch'ol: MATE'EL TS'I'
Yucatec: CH'AMAK / CH'OMAK

BIRD:

Tz'utujil: TZ'IKIN
K'iche': TZ'IKIN
Ch'ol: TSUNKAY
Yucatec: CH'IICH'

FISH:

Tz'utujil: CH'UU'
K'iche': CH'U'
Ch'ol: CHÄY
Yucatec: KAY / LU'

A SUMMARY OF THE MOST PROMINENT CHARACTERISTICS THAT ALL MAYAN LANGUAGES SHARE:

1) ALL MAYAN LANGUAGES SHARE A SELECTION OF VOCABULARY THAT CAN BE TRACED BACK TO CLASSICAL MAYA; SOME LANGUAGES MAY SHARE MORE ROOT VOCABULARY WITH CLASSICAL MAYA THAN OTHERS.

2) MAYAN LANGUAGE VERBS ARE STRUCTURED IN THE SAME MANNER WITH VARYING COMPONENTS DEPENDING ON THE LANGUAGE. ALL LANGUAGES HAVE A VERBAL STRUCTURE THAT IS MADE UP OF THREE PARTS: [ASPECT / TENSE PREFIX] + [PERSON INFIX] + [VERBAL ROOT]. THIS STRUCTURE IS CONSISTENT WITH ALL MAYAN LANGUAGES. VERBS ARE COMPLEX AND CAN HAVE PREFIXES AND SUFFIXES ADDED THAT CAN CHANGE THE OVERALL MEANING OF THE CONJUGATED VERB.

3) MANY MAYAN VERBS RECEIVE ERGATIVE PRONOUNS; MOSTLY WHEN THE VERB STEM BEGINS WITH A VOWEL AND ALL VERBS ARE SEPARATED BETWEEN INTRANSITIVE AND TRANSITIVE VERBS. EVERY VERBAL ROOT HAS TWO SEPARATE FORMS; WITH SOME EXCEPTIONS DEPENDING ON THE LANGUAGE.

4) ALL MAYAN LANGUAGES HAVE AN ERGATIVE SET OF PRONOUNS.

5) ALL MAYAN LANGUAGES LACK A TRUE INFINITIVE VERBAL FORM; VERBAL ROOTS IN SOME LANGUAGES MAY HAVE A BASIC FORM FROM WHICH CONJUGATED VERBAL FORMS MAY STEM FROM OR SOME MAYAN LANGUAGES MAY HAVE A VERBAL FORM WITH A SUFFIX ATTACHED THAT INDICATES THE DIFFERENCE BETWEEN INTRANSITIVE AND TRANSITIVE VERBS.

6) THERE ARE SOME VERBS THAT ARE USED WITHIN EVERY MAYAN LANGUAGE THAT CAN BE TRACED BACK TO CLASSICAL MAYA.
7) VERBAL ROOTS CAN BE EASILY CHANGED WITH A SUFFIX IN ORDER TO CREATE A VERBAL NOUN.
8) ALL LANGUAGES TEND TO HAVE THREE ASPECTS / TENSES: PRESENT, PAST & FUTURE [WITH SOME EXCEPTION DEPENDING ON THE LANGUAGE]. ALL LANGUAGES HAVE A PASSIVE FORM FOR EVERY VERB.
9) ALL ADJECTIVES ARE PLACED BEFORE THE NOUN.
10) ALL MAYAN LANGUAGES HAVE GLOTTAL STOPS ['] AND LETTERS THAT ARE GLOTTAL CLICKS [K' / Q / Q'] IN THE BACK OF THE THROAT.
11) ALL MAYAN LANGUAGES HAVE POSSESSIVE PREFIXES THAT ARE ATTACHED TO THE FRONT OF THE NOUN IN ORDER TO SHOW POSSESSION.
12) ALL MAYAN LANGUAGES HAVE PREPOSITIONS THAT CAN BE BLENDED WITH A PRONOUN [WHETHER PREFIX, INFIX OR SUFFIX] OR THE PREPOSITION CAN STAND ALONE IN SOME CASES.
13) ALL MODERN-DAY MAYAN LANGUAGES HAVE LOANWORDS BORROWED FROM SPANISH IN ORDER TO FILL GAPS IN THE LANGUAGE WHERE SOME VOCABULARY MAY NOT EXIST OR MAY HAVE BEEN LOST OVER TIME DUE TO CONSTANT EXPOSURE TO SPANISH.
14) ALL MODERN LANGUAGES MAY IN SOME WAY AND FORM HAVE VERBAL CONSTRUCTIONS THAT ALLOW FOR THE USE OF SPANISH VERBS THAT MAY NOT BE PART OF MAYAN VOCABULARY.
15) ALL MAYAN LANGUAGES HAVE SIMILAR [PERSON INFIX] FORMS THAT ARE USED WITH VERBAL CONJUGATION.

16) ALL MAYAN LANGUAGES MAKE USE OF PARTICLES [WHETHER LOCATIVE, DIRECTIONAL OR EMPHATIC] THAT ENHANCE THE MEANING OF A SENTENCE [ESPECIALLY IN A VERBAL PHRASE].

17) ALL MAYAN LANGUAGES MAY HAVE VARYING ALPHABETS DUE TO THE DIVERSE AND COMPLEX PHONOLOGIES OF EACH INDIVIDUAL LANGUAGE AND THEREFORE, THERE IS NOT A SINGLE WIDELY-USED UNIFORM ALPHABET USED AMONG MODERN-DAY MAYAN LANGUAGES.

18) ALL MAYAN LANGUAGES HAVE A WIDE ARRAY OF VOWELS; WHETHER LONG OR SHORT. SOME LANGUAGES MAY BE TONAL; SUCH AS YUCATEC MAYA. MOST LANGUAGES MAY USE 'J' [PRONOUNCED LIKE IN SPANISH IN SOME CASES] AFTER A VOWEL TO INDICATE A LONG-STRESSED VOWEL OR IT MAY BE PRONOUNCED AS A ROUGH THROATY 'H'.

19) ALL MODERN-DAY MAYAN LANGUAGES ARE WRITTEN IN LATIN-BASED ALPHABETS [PRIMARILY FROM SPANISH]. LITERACY IS AN ISSUE AMONG POVERTY STRICKEN COMMUNITIES IN GUATEMALA AND MEXICO AND MANY MAYAN PEOPLES ARE MONOLINGUAL, WHICH MAKES ACCESS TO INFORMATION VERY DIFFICULT FOR MAYAN LANGUAGE-SPEAKING COMMUNITIES.

20) ALL MAYAN LANGUAGES ARE DIVIDED INTO GROUPS [HUASTECAN, YUCATECAN, WESTERN & EASTERN] BASED ON THEIR SIMILARITY TO ONE ANOTHER; SOME LANGUAGES ARE MORE CLOSELY RELATED THAN OTHERS, BUT ALL MAYAN LANGUAGES' SHARED CHARACTERISTICS CAN BE TRACED BACK TO CLASSICAL MAYA. PROTO-MAYA IS THE HYPOTHETICAL ANCESTOR OF ALL MODERN-DAY MAYAN LANGUAGES AND IT IS BELIEVED

THAT THE MOST COMMON ROOT VOCABULARY STEMS FROM THIS HYPOTHETICAL LANGUAGE.

21) ALL MAYAN LANGUAGES HAVE MANY SIMILARITIES WITHIN THEIR NUMERICAL SYSTEM; ESPECIALLY WITH NUMBERS 1-10, WHICH ARE NEARLY UNIFORM AND CAN BE TRACED BACK TO CLASSICAL MAYA. ALL MAYAN LANGUAGES SHARE NOT ONLY SIMILARITIES BETWEEN EACHOTHER WITH NUMBERS 1-10, BUT THEY ALSO TEND TO FOLLOW A COMMON PATTERN WITH NUMBERS 11-100 [CONSIDERING OCCASIONAL ODDBALL DIFFERENCES].

II)   Common Root Vocabulary from Classical Mayan

Many root words used in modern-day Mayan Languages can be traced back to Classical Maya which is the group of Mayan Languages spoken during the Classical Period. The Languages of that Period of History are reflected through the Mayan glyphs [Logograms] that cover the many surfaces of the Mayan Temples, Ruins, Stelae and Ochre-covered walls [those that did stand the test of time]. Many of the root words used at that time are still being used in modern-day Mayan Languages. With plenty of study, one will find that both Yucatecan and Ch'olan Languages tend to have preserved the highest quantity of vocabulary words from Classical Maya. Evidence of such a notion can clearly be seen through consonant shifts from [K < CH] in which 'K' is used by Yucatec with many words, and 'CH' will be used with those same words…thoroughly replacing 'K'.

The following chapter will show examples of Classical Maya vocabulary and how it compares to the four languages being compared in this book:

This will be the format throughout this chapter:

[Classical Maya word] = [English Translation]:

Tz'utujil: ----

K'iche': ----

Ch'ol: ----

Yucatec: ----

36

NAL = CORN; MAIZE:

[No equivalent word used]

Tz'utujil: IXIIM

K'iche': IXIIM

Ch'ol: IXIM

Yucatec: XI'IM / IXIM

B'ALAM; JIX = JAGUAR:

Tz'utujil: B'AJLOM

K'iche': BALAAM

Ch'ol: BAJLÄM / BO'LAY

Yucatec: BAALAM / BAALAN / CHAKMO'OL

IXIK = WOMAN:

Tz'utujil: IXOQ / Q'AAPOJ

K'iche': IXOQ / Q'APOJ

Ch'ol: X'IXIK

Yucatec: XCH'UUP

WINIK = PERSON:

Tz'utujil: WINAQ

K'iche': WINAQ

Ch'ol: WINIK

Yucatec: WIINIK / MÁAK

K'UK' = QUETZAL [BIRD]:

Tz'utujil: K'UK'

K'iche': K'UK'

Ch'ol: XMANK'UK' / XKENZAL

Yucatec: K'UK'

WINIK; XIB' = MAN:

[Chol and Yucatec similarity]

Tz'utujil: AACHI / WINAQ

K'iche': ACHI / WINAQ

Ch'ol: WINIK

Yucatec: MÁAK / WIINIK / XIIB

AJAW; K'U / K'UJ = GOD / LORD:

Tz'utujil: AJAAW / DYOS

K'iche': AJAW / QAJAW / DIOS

Ch'ol: CH'UJUTAT

Yucatec: K'U / YUUM / DYOS

CH'UL, CH'UJUL; K'UL, K'UJUL = HOLY, SACRED [adj.]:

[Ch'ol and Yucatec similarity]

Tz'utujil: LOQ'OLAJ

K'iche': LOQ'OLAJ

Ch'ol: CH'UJUL

Yucatec: K'UJUL

TAL = TO COME:

Tz'utujil: PEJTEEM

K'iche': PEJTEM

Ch'ol: TILEL / TÄLEL / TAL

Yucatec: TAAL / TAALEL

XAN = TO GO [root]:

[no similarity; see note below]

Tz'utujil: -B'E

K'iche': -B'EK

Ch'ol: MAJLEL / SAMI

Yucatec: BINEL

*The Classical Maya verb 'XAN – to go' only bears a resemblance to Yucatec's Imperative Form of 'to go.'

"XEN! = GO! [Yucatec]

OCH = TO ENTER [root]:

Tz'utujil: OOK

K'iche': OOKIK

Ch'ol: OCHEL

Yucatec: OOKOL

JUL = TO ARRIVE [HERE]:

Tz'utujil: UUL

K'iche': UUL

Ch'ol: JULEL

Yucatec: K'UCHUL

K'IN = SUN / DAY:

Tz'utujil: Q'IIJ
K'iche': Q'IJ
Ch'ol: K'IN / CH'UJUTAT
Yucatec: K'IIN

AK'AB' = NIGHT:

Tz'utujil: AQ'A'
K'iche': AQ'AB'
Ch'ol: AK'ÄLEL
Yucatec: AK'AB

CHAM, CHAMIL = TO DIE:

Tz'utujil: KAMIK
K'iche': KAMIK
Ch'ol: CHÄMEL
Yucatec: KIIMIL

ALIY / JAL = TO SAY:

Tz'utujil: -B'IIJ / -B'IX

K'iche': -B'IJ

Ch'ol: AL

Yucatec: A'AL

WE' = TO EAT:

Tz'utujil: -WA'

K'iche': -WA'IK

Ch'ol: K'UX

Yucatec: JANAAL

WA / WAJ = TORTILLA:

Tz'utujil: WAAY

K'iche': WA / LEEJ

Ch'ol: WAJ

Yucatec: WAAJ

K'AB' = HAND / ARM:

Tz'utujil: Q'AB'AJ

K'iche': Q'AB'AJ

Ch'ol: K'ÄBÄL

Yucatec: K'AB

TE' / CHE' = TREE:

Tz'utujil: CHE'

K'iche': CHE'

Ch'ol: TE' [*consonant shift*]

Yucatec: CHE'

SAK = WHITE [adj.]:

Tz'utujil: SAQ

K'iche': SAQ

Ch'ol: SÄK, SÄSÄK, SÄKWA'AN

Yucatec: SAK

NA / NAJ / OTOT = HOUSE:

Tz'utujil: OOCHOOCH / JAAY

K'iche': OCHOCH / JA

Ch'ol: OTOT

Yucatec: OTOCH / KAJTAL

NA / NAJ = MOTHER:

[Ch'ol and Yucatec similarity]

Tz'utujil: -TAAN / -TEE'

K'iche': CHUCH

Ch'ol: ÑA'

Yucatec: NA' / MAAM

JA' = WATER:

Tz'utujil: YA'

K'iche': JA'

Ch'ol: JA'

Yucatec: JA'

CHAAK / JA' = RAIN:

Tz'utujil: JAB'

K'iche': JAB

Ch'ol: JA'AL

Yucatec: CHAAK / JA'

TUN = STONE:

[Ch'ol and Yucatec similarity]

Tz'utujil: AAB'AJ

K'iche': ABAJ

Ch'ol: TUN / XAJLEL

Yucatec: TUUNICH

KAKAW = CACAO:

Tz'utujil: KOKOP, KAKAW, KAKOW, KOKOW

K'iche': KAKAW, KAKOW

Ch'ol: KÄKÄW

Yucatec: KAKAW

B'UL = BEANS:

Tz'utujil: KINAQ'

K'iche': KINAQ'

Ch'ol: BU'UL

Yucatec: BU'UL

SA / UL = ATOL (DE ELOTE):

Tz'utujil: Q'OR AJ

K'iche': Q'OR AJ

Ch'ol: UL

Yucatec: SA' / SAKSA'

K'AK' = FIRE:

Tz'utujil: Q'AAQ'

K'iche': Q'AAQ'

Ch'ol: K'AJK'

Yucatec: K'AAK'

JUN = BOOK / PAPER:

Tz'utujil: WUUJ

K'iche': WUUJ

Ch'ol: JUN

Yucatec: JU'UN

SUTZ' = BAT [animal]:

Tz'utujil: SOOTZ'

K'iche': SOTZ'

Ch'ol: SUTS'

Yucatec: SOOTZ'

B'ATZ' / MAX = MONKEY:

Tz'utujil: K'OOY

K'iche': BATZ' / K'OY

Ch'ol: BATS'

Yucatec: BAATZ'

AYIN = LIZARD; CAIMAN:

[Tz'utujil and K'iche' similarity]

Tz'utujil: AAYIN

K'iche': AYIN

Ch'ol: P'OK / XYÄX P'OK / XMANCHAJK

Yucatec: JOOJ / IXMECH / TOOLOK

CHAK = RED [adj.]:

Tz'utujil: KAQ

K'iche': KAQ

Ch'ol: CHÄKWA'AN

Yucatec: CHAK

KAB'A = NAME:

Tz'utujil: BII'AJ

K'iche': BII'

Ch'ol: K'AB'A

Yucatec: K'AB'A

EK' = BLACK [adj]:

Tz'utujil: Q'EQ

K'iche': Q'EQ

Ch'ol: I'IK'

Yucatec: EEK' / BOX

MAM = ANCESTOR; GRANDFATHER

Tz'utujil: MAMA'

K'iche': MAM

Ch'ol: TATUCH

Yucatec: MAAM / NOJOCH TAAT / NOJOCH TAATA

NIKTE' / NICHIM / NICHIL / NIKIL = FLOWER:

Tz'utujil: KOTZ'I'J / SI'J

K'iche': KOTZ'I'J

Ch'ol: BOB / NICHIM

Yucatec: LOOL / NIKTE'

YAX = GREEN [adj.]

Tz'utujil: REX / RAX

K'iche': RAX

Ch'ol: YÄXMULAN / YÄJYÄX / YÄXEL

Yucatec: YA'AX

WITZ = MOUNTAIN:

Tz'utujil: JUYU'

K'iche': JUYUB'

Ch'ol: WITS

Yucatec: WITZ

CHI = MOUTH:

Tz'utujil: CHII'

K'iche': CHI'

Ch'ol: EJÄL / YEJ

Yucatec: CHI'

MA = NOT; NO:

Tz'utujil: MA'

K'iche': MAN / NA

Ch'ol: MA' / MACH'

Yucatec: MA' / M- [*auxiliary*]

B'E / B'I = ROAD; PATH; WAY:

Tz'utujil: B'EEY

K'iche': B'E

Ch'ol: BIJ

Yucatec: BEEL

IL = TO SEE [verb]:

[K'iche' and Yucatec similarity]

Tz'utujil: TZ'ATOJ / TZ'ETOJ / TZU'UJ

K'iche': ILOJ / TZU'UJ

Ch'ol: K'EL

Yucatec: ILIK

AJTZ'IB' = SCRIBE; WRITER:

[uniformity]

Tz'utujil: AJTZ'IJB'

K'iche': AJTZ'IB'

Ch'ol: AJTS'IJB

Yucatec: JTZ'IIB'

TZ'IB' = WRITING:

[uniformity]

Tz'utujil: TZ'IJB'

K'iche': TZ'IB'

Ch'ol: TS'IJB

Yucatec: TZ'IIB'

KAAN / CHAAN = SNAKE; SERPENT:

[Ch'ol and Yucatec similarity]

Tz'utujil: KUMATZ

K'iche': KUMATZ

Ch'ol: CHAN / LUKUM

Yucatec: KAAN

KAAN / CHAAN = SKY:

Tz'utujil: KAAJ

K'iche': KAJ

Ch'ol: CHAN

Yucatec: KA'AN

TI / TA = TO; ON; AT; IN [prep.]:

Tz'utujil: PA / PAN / -PAN

K'iche': PA / PAN / -PAN

Ch'ol: TI' / TYI'

Yucatec: TI'

YETE' = WITH [prep.]:

[only Yucatec; and maybe Ch'ol]

Tz'utujil: K'IIN / -K'IIN

K'iche': -UK'

Ch'ol: YIK'OT / YIT'OK

Yucatec: YETEL

B'AK = BONE:

[uniformity]

Tz'utujil: B'AAQ

K'iche': B'AQ

Ch'ol: BAK'

Yucatec: BAK

CHAMIY = IT DIES:

Tz'utujil: NKAM

K'iche': KAKAMIK

Ch'ol: MI CHÄMEL

Yucatec: TUN KÍIMIL

LUM = LAND:

Tz'utujil: ULEEW / ULEEP

K'iche': ULEEW

Ch'ol: LUM / LUMAL

Yucatec: LU'UM / KAAB

III)   Verb Structure and Verbal Roots

All Mayan Languages share the same complex verbal structure and they all share common characteristics with "verbal clusters" and how they are formed.

We will use the verb 'to write' from each of the four Mayan Languages being compared within this book to show the basic construction of modern-day Mayan verbs.

Tz'utujil: TZ'IJB'ANEM [*intransitive*]; TZ'IJB'AXIK [*transitive*]

K'iche': TZ'IJB'ANEM [*intransitive*]; TZ'IJB'AXIK [*transitive*]

Ch'ol: TS'IJBUJEL [*intransitive*]; TS'IJBUÑ [*transitive*]; TS'IJBAÑ [*transitive*]

Yucatec: TZ'IIB [*intransitive*]; TZ'IIBTIK [*transitive*]

*ALMOST ALL VERBS ARE SEPARATED BETWEEN TRANSITIVE AND INTRANSITIVE; EXCEPT WITH SOME VERBS THAT ONLY HAVE AN INTRANSITIVE VERBAL FORM

The Construction of the Verbal Cluster is one of the key facets that all Mayan Languages share. It is one of the most common characteristics among Mayan Languages.

The basic construction of the Verbal Cluster is as follows:

(Tense) + (Person) + (Verbal Root)

The following examples will use the previously show verbs for 'to write' and all four will be displayed in the 1st Person Singular Present Tense Form. The following examples will be used to compare the basic construction of Maya Verbs.

Tz'utujil:

N-IN-TZ'IJB'AN(I) = NINTZ'IJB'ANI (I WRITE);

N-IN-TZ'IJB'AJ = NINTZ'IJB'AJ (I WRITE SOMETHING)

K'iche':

K-IN-TZ'IB'ANIK = KINTZ'IB'ANIK (I WRITE);

K-IN-TZ'IB'AJ = KINTZ'IB'AJ (I WRITE SOMETHING)

Ch'ol:

MI-K-TS'IJBUJEL (I WRITE)

MI-K-TS'IJBUÑ (I WRITE [SOMETHING])

MI-K-TS'IJBAÑ (I WRITE [SOMETHING])

Yucatec:

K-IN-TZ'IIB = KINTZ'IIB (I WRITE [*habitually*]);

K-IN-TZ'IIBTIK = KINTZ'IIBTIK (I WRITE SOMETHING [*habitually*])

Most Mayan Languages have three Verbal Tenses: Present, Past & Future.

K'iche' used to have a Future Tense Construction during the Classical Quiché Period, but the usage of the Future Tense fell out of style and now has been entirely replaced by the Present Tense. Therefore, modern-day K'iche' only uses two distinct Verbal Tenses: Present & Past Tense.

Tz'utujil:

PRESENT TENSE PREFIX: N- / T- [only with Negation]

PAST TENSE PREFIX: X-

FUTURE TENSE PREFIX: XK-...NA / XT-...NA [only 3rd Person Sing.]

K'iche':

PRESENT TENSE PREFIX: K-

PAST TENSE PREFIX: X-

Ch'ol:

PRESENT TENSE PREFIX: M- / MI-

PAST TENSE PREFIX: TS-

FUTURE TENSE PREFIX: MI KAJ -

Yucatec:

[Yucatec primarily uses Auxiliaries that blend with the Person Infix]

PRESENT TENSE PREFIX: K- [Habitual Present]; T- [Simple Present Tense]

PAST TENSE PREFIX: [TZOK + Person] = TZ'- [Past Tense]

Ex. TZOK IN… / TZ'IN…

FUTURE TENSE PREFIX: H- [Future Tense]

SPECIAL NOTE:

Ch'ol is the only Language out of the four Languages being compared in this book to have a Present Progressive Verb Conjugation:

Ch'ol (Present Progressive Aspect):

WOLI- [PERSON AFFIX] + VERB STEM

WOLI-K MAJLEL = I AM GOING

WOLA' MAJLEL = YOU ARE GOING

WOLI' MAJLEL = HE IS GOING

ETC.

Now we will show the same verb for 'to write' with the Past Tense Forms between the four Languages:

Tz'utujil:

X-IN-TZ'IJB'AN(I) = XINTZ'IJB'ANI (I WROTE);

X-IN-TZ'IJB'AJ = XINTZ'IJB'AJ (I WROTE SOMETHING)

K'iche':

X-IN-TZ'IB'ANIK = XINTZ'IB'ANIK (I WROTE);

X-IN-TZ'IB'AJ = XINTZ'IB'AJ (I WROTE SOMETHING)

Ch'ol:

TSA-K-TS'IJBUJI = TSAK TS'IJBUJI (I WROTE)

TSA-K-TS'IJBU = TSAK TS'IJBU (I WROTE [SOMETHING])

TSA-K-TS'IJBA = TSAK TS'IJBA (I WROTE [SOMETHING])

Yucatec:

TZ'-IN-TZ'IIB = TZ'IN TZ'IIB (I WROTE);

TZ'-IN-TZ'IIBTIK = TZ'IN TZ'IIBTIK (I WROTE SOMETHING)

Now we will demonstrate the Future Tense [except with K'iche'] with the following examples:

Tz'utujil:

XK-IN-TZ'IJB'AANI NA = XKINTZ'IJB'AANI NA (I WILL WRITE);

XK-IN-TZ'IJB'AJ NA = XKINTZ'IJB'AJ NA (I WILL WRITE SOMETHING)

K'iche': *[only Present Tense used]*

Ch'ol:

MI KAJ K TS'IJBUJEL = MI KAJ K TZ'IJBUJEL (I WILL WRITE)

MI KAJ K TSIJBUÑ = MI KAJ K TS'IJBUÑ (I WILL WRITE SOMETHING)

MI KAJ K TS'IJBAÑ = MI KAJ K TS'IJBAÑ (I WILL WRITE SOMETHING)

Yucatec:

H-EN TZ'IIB-E = HEN TZ'IIBE (I WILL WRITE);

H-EN TZ'IIBTIK-E = HEN TZ'IIBTIKE (I WILL WRITE SOMETHING)

The following charts will show the Person Infixes used with Verbs in all four Mayan Languages in order to display both comparisons and differences between them.

Tz'utujil:

1   -IN- / -INW-   -OQ-/-OJ- [before 'K']

2   -AT- / -AW-   -IX-

3   --- / -UU-*   -EE-

*Only with some verb types

B'ANOJ < XUUB'AN [he did it]

VS.

KAMIK < XKAM [he died]

K'iche':

1   -IN- / -INW-   -UJ-

2   -AT- / -AW-; -LA* [polite]   -IX-; -ALAK* [polite]

3   -A- *[schwa]* / -UU-**   -E-

*K'iche' has two polite forms when addressing someone; one singular and one plural. The verb is conjugated in the 3rd Person and 'LA [sing.]' or 'ALAK [pl.]' follows after the verb.

XKAMIK LA / ALAK = YOU [polite sing. / polite pl.] died

**Only with some verb types

B'ANOJ < XUUB'ANO [he did it]

VS.

KAMIK < XKAMIK [he died]

Ch'ol:

1   -K / J- [before 'K']   -K / -J...LOJON [excl.] & -LAK- [incl.]*

2   -A   -LA'- / -LA W-

3   -I / -IY-   -I...-OB / -IY...-OB

*Ch'ol has two forms to express the 1st person plural; one exclusive and one inclusive.

MIK MAJLEL LOJON = We go [Us not you]

VS.

MI LAK MAJLEL = We go [all of us together]

Yucatec:

1   -IN-; -EN- / -INW-; -ENW-   -Q / -K

2   -A- / -AW-   -A-...E'EX / -AW-...E'EX

3   -U- / -UY-   -U-...O'OB / UY-...O'OB

NOTE: All Yucatec Person Affixes are usually blended with Auxiliaries.

Verb – ANTIK = to Help

K'AAT IN WANTIKEECH = I want to help you

NOTES: One should notice that with all four Languages there are Ergative Pronouns that are affixed to Verb Stems that begin with a vowel; the most commonly used are 'W' for 1st Person and 2nd Person or a 'Y' for 3rd Person. The primary Pronoun Affix is used with a verb stem that begins with a consonant.

There are multiple suffixes, infixes and particles that can be added to different parts of the Verbal Structure in order to change the meaning of the conjugated verb. Mayan Languages are quite complex, but this is one of the most common traits that all Mayan Languages share between themselves.

Examples from Tz'utujil & K'iche' of particles and how they change the overall meaning of a conjugated verb:

Tz'utujil:

NINTZ'IJB'ANI KAAN = I remain writing…

NINTZ'IJB'AJ KAAN = I remain writing it…

NINTZ'IJB'ANI CHIK = I am writing again…

NINTZ'IJB'AJ CHIK = I am writing it again…

NINTZ'IJB'ANI PONA = I ought to write…

NINTZ'IJB'AJ PONA = I ought to write it…

XA / XER NINTZ'IJB'AANI = I am only writing…

XA / XER NINTZ'IJB'AJ = I am only writing something…

NINTZ'IJB'AANI NA = I have to write…

NINTZ'IJB'AJ NA = I have to write it…

RAJWAAJ NINTZ'IJB'AANI = It is necessary that I write…

RAJWAAJ NINTZ'IJB'AJ = It is necessary that I write it…

K'iche':

KINTZ'IB'ANIK KAAN = I remain writing…

KINTZ'IB'AJ KAAN = I remain writing it…

KINTZ'IB'ANIK CHIK = I am writing again…

KINTZ'IB'AJ CHIK = I am writing it again…

XA KINTZ'IB'ANIK = I am only writing…

XA KINTZ'IB'AJ = I am only writing something…

RAJAWAXIK CHI KINTZ'IB'ANIK = It is necessary that I write…

RAJAWAXIK CHI KINTZ'IB'AJ = It is necessary that I write it…

Ch'ol:

MUX MIK TS'IBUJEL = I am still writing…

MUX MIK TS'IJBUÑ = I am still writing it…

MUX MIK TS'IJBAÑ = I am still writing it…

YOM MIK TS'IJBUJEL = I ought to write…

YOM MIK TS'IJBUÑ = I ought to write it…

YOM MIK TS'IJBAÑ = I ought to write it…

Yucatec:

K'AABEET IN TZ'IIB = I need to write…

K'AABEET IN TZ'IIBTIK = I need to write it…

YAAN IN TZ'IIB = I have to write…

YAAN IN TZ'IIBTIK = I have to write it…

KIN TZ'IIB BEYO' / BEYA' = I write like that / this…

KIN TZ'IIBTIK BEYO' / BEYA' = I write it like that / this…

SAAM TEN TZ'IIB = I am still writing…

SAAM TEN TZ'IIBTIK = I am still writing it…

NOTE: Mayan Languages tend to use many particles [whether prefix or suffix] and auxiliaries to change the meaning of verb constructions.

TRANSITIVE VS. INTRANSITIVE

All Mayan Languages have dual Verb Stems. They are all split between Transitive and Intransitive Verbs, which will all have the same Verbal Root; only with a slightly different ending when conjugated. Intransitive verbs tend to show that the action is being done by the Subject of the sentence and that it may be an ongoing process [incomplete process]. Transitive verbs specify that the action is being done by the Subject of the sentence to an object, person or animal.

Tz'utujil:

TZIJONEM [*intransitive*] < -TZIJONI (TO SPEAK)

TZIJOB'EXIK [*transitive*] < -TZIJOB'EJ (TO SPEAK TO SOMEONE)

K'iche':

SLABEM [*intransitive*] < -SLABIK (TO MOVE)

SLABAXIK [*transitive*] < -SLABAJ (TO MOVE SOMETHING)

Ch'ol:

CH'ÄKOJEL [*intransitive*] (TO CURSE)

CH'ÄK [*transitive*] (TO CURSE SOMEONE)

Yucatec:

JANAAL [*intransitive*] (TO EAT)

JANTIK [*transitive*] (TO EAT SOMETHING)

As we have shown in the previous Chapter, there are several Verbs that stem from Classical Maya that are still used today in many modern-day Mayan Languages. This final section of this Chapter will display similarities with certain verbal roots between the four Mayan Languages being compared.

*All conjugated verbs will be shown in the 3rd Person Conjugated Form.

CHAM / CHAMIL [TO DIE]:

Tz'utujil: KAMIK

K'iche': KAMIK

Ch'ol: CHÄMEL

Yucatec: KÍIMIL

Present Tense --

Tz'utujil: NKAM(I)

K'iche': KAKAMIK

Ch'ol: MI CHÄMEL

Yucatec: TUN KÍIMIL

Past Tense --

Tz'utujil: XKAM(I)

K'iche': XKAMIK

Ch'ol: TS'I CHÄMI

Yucatec: TZ'U KÍIMIL

JUL [TO ARRIVE]:

Tz'utujil: UULEM

K'iche': UULEM

Ch'ol: JULEL

Yucatec: K'UCHUL

Present Tense --

Tz'utujil: NUUL(I)

K'iche': KUULIK

Ch'ol: MI JULEL

Yucatec: TUN K'UCHUL

Past Tense –

Tz'utujil: XUUL(I)

K'iche': XUULIK

Ch'ol: TS'I JULI

Yucatec: TZ'U K'UCHUL

OCH [TO ENTER]:

Tz'utujil: OOKEM
K'iche': OKEM
Ch'ol: OCHEL
Yucatec: OOKOL

Present Tense --
Tz'utujil: NOOK(I)
K'iche': KOOKIK
Ch'ol: MI OCHEL
Yucatec: TUN OOKOL

Past Tense –
Tz'utujil: XOOK(I)
K'iche': XOOKIK
Ch'ol: TS'I OCHI
Yucatec: TZ'U OOKOL

IL [TO SEE]:

Tz'utujil: TZ'ATOJ; TZ'ETOJ; TZU'UJ

*K'iche': ILOJ / TZU'UJ

Ch'ol: K'EL

*Yucatec: ILIK

Present Tense --

Tz'utujil: NUUTZ'AT; NUUTZ'ET; NUUTZU'

K'iche': KARILO / KUUTZU'

Ch'ol: MI K'EL

Yucatec: KU' YILIK

Past Tense –

Tz'utujil: XUUTZ'AT; XUUTZ'ET; XUUTZU'

K'iche': XARILO / XUUTZU'

Ch'ol: TS'I K'ELE

Yucatec: TZ'U YILIK

ALIY / JAL [TO SAY]:

Tz'utujil: -B'IJ / -B'IX

K'iche': -B'IJ / -B'IX

Ch'ol: AL

Yucatec: A'AL / A'ALIK

Present Tense --

Tz'utujil: NUUB'IJ / NUUB'IX

K'iche': KUUB'IJ / KUUB'IX

Ch'ol: MI YÄL

Yucatec: KU' YA'AL / KU' YA'ALIK

Past Tense --

Tz'utujil: XUUB'IJ / XUUB'IX

K'iche': XUUB'IJ / XUUB'IX

Ch'ol: TS'I YÄLÄ

Yucatec: TZ'U YA'AL / KU' YA'ALIK

TZ'IB' [TO WRITE]:

Tz'utujil: TZ'IJB'ANEM
K'iche': TZ'IB'ANEM
Ch'ol: TS'IJBUJEL
Yucatec: TZ'IIB

Present Tense --
Tz'utujil: NTZ'IJB'AAN(I)
K'iche': KATZ'IB'ANIK
Ch'ol: MI TS'IJBUJEL
Yucatec: TUN TZ'IIB

Past Tense --
Tz'utujil: XTZ'IJB'AAN(I)
K'iche': XTZ'IB'ANIK
Ch'ol: TS'I TS'IJBUJI
Yucatec: TZ'U TZ'IIB

WE' [TO EAT]:

Tz'utujil: WA'IM

K'iche': WA'IM

Ch'ol: K'UX

Yucatec: JANAL

Present Tense --

Tz'utujil: NWA'(I)

K'iche': KAWA'IK

Ch'ol: MI K'UX

Yucatec: TUN JANAL

Past Tense --

Tz'utujil: XWA'(I)

K'iche': XWA'IK

Ch'ol: TS'I K'UXU

Yucatec: TZ'U JANAL

WAY [TO SLEEP]:

Tz'utujil: WAREEM
K'iche': WAREEM
Ch'ol: WÄYEL
Yucatec: WENEL

Present Tense --
Tz'utujil: NWAR(I)
K'iche': KAWARIK
Ch'ol: MI WÄYEL
Yucatec: TUN WENEL

Past Tense --
Tz'utujil: XWAR(I)
K'iche': XAWARIK
Ch'ol: TS'I WÄYI
Yucatec: TZ'U WENEL

NOTE: These several Verbs are the Key Verbs that compare with Verbs from the four Mayan Languages being compared within this Book. Some of the Mayan Languages within this sample may not have the particular Verbal Root that stems from Classical Maya. There are other Verbs from Classical Maya that may be used in other Mayan Languages that are not in this Comparison Sample.

IV) Comparison of the Use and Placement of Direct Objects with Verbs

Mayan Languages tend to have both the Subject [Person] and the Direct Object attached or infixed into or onto the Verbal Cluster. Tz'utujil and K'iche' use specific blended forms [Infixes] to indicate both the Subject and Direct Object [one primary pronoun along with one ergative pronoun] within the Verbal Cluster opposed to Yucatec and Ch'ol which attach the Direct Object to the end of the Verbal Structure while the rest of the Verbal Structure is unchanged.

The Examples below demonstrate the placement of the Direct Object 'You' in Tz'utujil & K'iche' opposed to the placement of the Direct Object 'You' in Yucatec & Ch'ol:

Tz'utujil:

N-**AT**NW-AJOB'EEJ = [I LOVE YOU]

K'iche':

K-**AT**W-AJ = [I LOVE YOU]

VS.

Yucatec:

K-IN YAKUNTIK-**EECH** = [I LOVE YOU]

Ch'ol:

MI-K K'UXBIÑ-**ET** = [I LOVE YOU]

The following Charts will show the placement and implementation of Person Infixes and Direct Objects within all four Mayan Languages in this sample.

TZ'UTUJIL SUBJECT / DIRECT OBJECT FORMS:

	Consonant	Vowel
I / you	-ATIN-, -ATNU-	-ATNW-
I / him	-IN-	-W-, -INW-
I / you all	-IXIN-, -IXNU-	-IXINW-, -IXNW-
I / them	-EEN-	-EENW-
You / me	-INA-	-INAW-
You / him	-A-	-AW-
You / us	-OQA-	-OQAW-
You / them	-EE'A-	-EE'AW-
*He / me	-INR-	-INR-
*He / you	-ATR-	-ATR-
*He / us	-OQR-	-OQR-
*He / you all	-IXR-	-IXR-
*He / them	-EERU-	-EER-
We / you	-ATQA-	-ATQ-
We / him	-OQ-	-OQ-
We / you all	-IXQA-	-IXQ-
We / them	-EEQA-	-EEQ-

You all / me	-INE-	-INEW-
You all / him	-E-	-EW-
You all / us	-OQE-	-OQEW-
You all / them	-E'E-	-E'EW-
Them / me	-INKI-	-INK-
Them / you	-ATKI-, -ATKEE-	-ATK-
Them / us	-OJKI-	-OJK-
Them / you	-IXKI-, IXKEE-	-IXK-
Them / them	-EKE-	-EK-

K'ICHE' SUBJECT / DIRECT OBJECT FORMS:

	Consonant	Vowel
I / you (Yo/te)	-ATIN-, -ATNU-	-ATW-, -ATINW-
I / him (Yo/le)	-IN-	-W-, -INW-
I / you all (Yo/uds)	-IXIN-, -IXNU-	-IXW-, -IXINW-
I / them (Yo/los)	-EN-	-EW-, -ENW-
You / me (Tú/me)	-INA-	-INAW-
You / him (Tú/le)	-A-	-AW-
You / us (Tú/nos)	-UJA-	-UJAW-
You / them (Tú/los)	-A'-	-A'-
*He / me (Él/me)	-INU-	-INR-
*He / you (Él/te)	-ATU-	-ATR-
*He / us (Él/nos)	-UJU-	-UJR-
*He / you all (Él/uds)	-IXU-	-IXR-
*He / them (Él/los)	-U'-	-U'-
We / you (Nos./te)	-ATQA-	-ATQ-
We / him (Nos./le)	-UJ-	-UJ-
We / you all (Nos./uds)	-IXQA-	-IXQ-
We / them (Nos./los)	-EQA-	-EQ-
You all / me (Uds/me)	-INI-	-INIW-
You all / him (Uds/le)	-I-	-IW-
You all / us (Uds/nos)	-OJI-	-OJIW-

You all / them (Uds/los)   -I'-   -I'-

Them / me (Ellos/me)   -INKI-   -INK-

Them / you (Ellos/te) -ATKI-   -ATK-

Them / us (Ellos/nos)   -UJKI-   -UJK-

Them / you all (Ellos/uds) -IXKI-   -IXK-

Them / them (Ellos/los) -EKI-   -EK-

CH'OL SUBJECT / DIRECT OBJECT FORMS:

Yo a tí, I / you

K-…-ET / *J-…-ET

Yo a él, I / him

K-… (#) null / *J-… (#) null

Yo a Ustedes, I / you all

K-…-ETLA / *J-…-ETLA

Yo a ellos, I / them

K-…-OB / *J-…-OB

Tú a mí, You / me

A-…-ON / A-…*¹W-…-ON

Tú a él, You / him

A-… (#) null / A-…*¹W-… (#) null

Tú a nos, You / us

A-…-ON LOJON / A-…*¹W-…-ON LOJON

Tú a ellos, You / them

A-…-OB / A-…*¹W-…-OB

Nosotros a tí, We / you

K- LOJON…-ET / *J- LOJON…-ET

Nosotros a él, We / him

K- LOJON… (#) null / *J- LOJON… (#) null

Nosotros a Ustedes, We / you all

K- LOJON…-ETLA / *J- LOJON…-ETLA

Nosotros a ellos, We / them

K- LOJON…-OB / *J- LOJON…-OB

Ustedes a mí, You all / me

LA'-…-ON / LA'-…*[1]W-…-ON

Ustedes a él, You all / him

LA'-… (#) null / LA'-…*[1]W-… (#) null

Ustedes a nos, You all / us

LA'-…-ON LOJON / LA'-…*[1]W-…-ON LOJON

Ustedes a ellos, You all / them

LA'-…-OB / LA'-…*[1]W-…-OB

Ellos a mí, They / me

I-…-ONOB / I-…*[1]Y-…-ONOB

Ellos a nos, They / us

I-…-ONOB LOJON / I-…*[1]Y-…-ONOB LOJON

Ellos a Ustedes, They / you all

I-…-ETLAJOB / I-…*[1]Y-…-ETLAJOB

Ellos a ellos, They / them

N/A

Él a mí, He / me

I-…-ON / I-…*¹Y-…-ON

Él a tí, He / you

I-…-ET / I-…*¹Y-…-ET

Él a nos, He / us

I-…-ON LOJON / I-…*¹Y-…-ON LOJON

Él a Ustedes, He / you all

I-…-ETLA / I-…*¹Y-…-ETLA

Él a ellos, He / them

N/A

(*) El infijo de primera persona 'k' se hacen 'j' cuando inicia una raíz verbal que ya tiene una 'k' inicial / The first-person infix 'k' becomes a 'j' when it precedes a verbal root that already begins with a 'k'

(*¹) Estas formas se implementan cuando una raíz verbal comienza con un vocal / These forms are implemented when a verbal root begins with a vowel.

Ejemplo: / Example:

Mij k'uxbinet –Te amo / I love you (Mik + K'uxbin = Mij K'uxbin)

Ma' wäk' – Das / You give (äk' = to give; Ma' w + äk')

YUCATEC SUBJECT / DIRECT OBJECT FORMS:

I/YOU   IN (W-)…-EECH

I/HIM   IN (W-)…-I / <small>TRANSITIVE VERB ENDING</small>

I/YOU ALL   IN (W-)…-E'EX

I/THEM   IN (W-)…-O'OB

YOU/ME   A (W-)…-EEN

YOU/HIM   A (W-)…-I / <small>TRANSITIVE VERB ENDING</small>

YOU/US   A (W-)…-O'ON

YOU/THEM   A (W-)…-O'OB

HE/ME   U (Y-)…-EEN

HE/YOU   U (Y-)…-EECH

HE/US   U (Y-)…-O'ON

HE/YOU ALL   U (Y-)…-E'EX

HE/THEM   U (Y-)…-O'OB

WE/YOU   K…-EECH

WE/HIM   K…-I / <small>TRANSITIVE VERB ENDING</small>

WE/YOU ALL   K…-E'EX

WE/THEM   K…-O'OB

YOU ALL / ME   A (W-)…-E'EX TEEN

YOU ALL / HIM   A (W-)…-E'EX TI'E / LEETI'

YOU ALL/ US   A (W-)…-E'EX TO'ON

YOU ALL / THEM   A (W-)…-E'EX TI'O'OB

THEY/ME	U (Y-)…O'OB TEEN
THEY/YOU	U (Y-)…-O'OB TEECH
THEY/US	U (Y-)…-O'OB TO'ON
THEY/YOU	U (Y-)…-O'OB TE'EX

V)   Common Root Similarities and the Consonant Shift

Although each Mayan Language is quite different from other Mayan Languages; with the exception of Sister Languages within their own linguistic group [that may share a broader amount of similarities to each other than to other Mayan Languages outside of their own group], there are word roots that are carried throughout every Mayan Language that stem from Proto-Maya [hypothetical Language] from which all Mayan Languages originally developed.

One feature that constantly comes up, as one compares vocabulary from one Mayan Language to another, is the apparent Consonant Shift that is present with all modern-day Mayan Languages. This Chapter will show several examples of the 'Consonant Shift' that has occurred; especially with the Western Branch [Ch'olan] Languages.

From the previous Chapters one can easily surmise through the many comparisons of the four Mayan Languages in this book that Ch'ol tends to use 'CH' opposed to 'K' with many common vocabulary words that stem from Classical Maya. Through the Classical Maya Glyphs [Logograms], Anthropologists were able to see that there was a clear difference between two separate dialects projected in the stelae and few remaining Mayan Codices. These differences were separated between the Yucatecan and Ch'olan dialects. These same differences can be seen today with modern Mayan Languages; especially the modern dialects of Yucatec and Ch'ol.

CONSONANT SHIFT [K >< CH]:

CHAM; CHAMIL (CH#M-) = TO DIE:

Tz'utujil = KAMIK [K#M-]

K'iche' = KAMIK [K#M-]

Ch'ol = CHÄMEL [CH#M-]

Yucatec = KÍIMIL [K#M-]

CHAAN / KAAN (CH#N / K#N) = SKY

Tz'utujil = KAAJ [K#J]

K'iche' = KAJ [K#J]

Ch'ol = CHAN [CH#N]

Yucatec = KA'AN [K#N]

CHA / KA (CH# / K#) = TWO [*numerical*]

Tz'utujil = KA'

K'iche' = KEB'

Ch'ol = CHA'

Yucatec = KA'A

OCH [#CH] = TO ENTER

Tz'utujil = OOKEM < -OOK- [#K]

K'iche' = OOKEM < -OOK- [#K]

Ch'ol = OCHEL < OCH- [#CH]

Yucatec = OOKOL < OOK- [#K]

CONSONANT SHIFT [K' >< CH']

CH'UUM / K'UUM [CH'##M / K'##M] = SQUASH; PUMPKIN

Tz'utujil = K'UUM [K'##M]

K'iche' = K'UUM [K'##M]

Ch'ol = CH'UJM [CH'##M]

Yucatec = K'UUM [K'##M]

In addition, other words project further consonant shifts:

CONSONANT SHIFT [T >< CH]

OTOT [#T#T] = HOUSE; HOME:

Tz'utujil: OOCHOOCH [#CH#CH

K'iche': OCHOCH [#CH#CH]

Ch'ol: OTOT [#T#T]

Yucatec: OTOCH [#T#CH]

TE' / CHE' [T#' / CH#'] = TREE:

Tz'utujil: CHE' [CH#']

K'iche': CHE' [CH#']

Ch'ol: TE' [T#']

Yucatec: CHE' [CH#']

NOTE: The Consonant Shifts become quite evident when comparing modern-day Mayan Languages with one another. Many of these Consonant Shifts are quite common with Western Branch Ch'olan Languages.

VI)   Noun Classifiers

Another common trait with many Mayan Languages is the usage of Noun Classifiers. This is also a common trait of Mandarin Chinese, where a particle is added to the numeral when counting nouns. Each Classifier describes different objects or it can specify if the things being counted are humans, animals, trees, or objects with specific shapes, sized or dimensions. Altogether it is a very complicated system and there are many Mayan Languages that have dropped the usage of this system entirely. Besides the complex phonology and pronunciation of Mayan Vocabulary, this is another feature that makes Mayan Languages difficult to learn for non-native speakers.

Tz'utujil and K'iche' have dropped this complicated system entirely and simply use numbers without Noun Classifiers. Yucatec and Ch'ol, however, have maintained a portion of this system.

The following example will use the number '1' or 'Juun' with the common non-specific Noun Classifier that is used with counting objects that do not fit in any of the other criteria for certain Classifiers:

Tz'utujil: JUUN WUUJ [a Book / one Book] *No Classifier*

K'iche': JUUN WUUJ [a Book / one Book] *No Classifier*

Ch'ol: JUMP'EJL JUN [a Book / one Book]; *-p'ejl / -p'ej* *[non-specific classifier]*

Yucatec: JUMP'ÉEL JU'UN [a Book / one Book]; *-p'éel* *[non-specific classifier]*

We will demonstrate Noun Classifiers that exist with Yucatec and Ch'ol with numbers one through five.

Ch'ol Noun Classifiers:

-p'ejl / -p'ej [alt.] = en general / in general

-wejt = taza (de) / cup or glass (of)

-kojt = animales / animals

-k'ojl = objetos redondos / round objects

-ejk = platos de comida / servings of food (plates)

-i = usado cuando números se cuentan solos; ningún objeto / for real numbers in counting; not with objects

-jojp = puñazos con el puño / punches with one's fist

-lajm = pasos [con pie] / steps [with foot]

-lejb = pedazos [de algo] / pieces [of something]

-pojch = con ropa / with clothing

-tejk = árboles / trees

-tejm = rollos de algo / rolls of something

-tikil = con personas / with people

-ts'ijt = con lapices y boligrafos / with pencils or pens

-wox = objetos esféricos [huevos, piedras] / spherical objects [eggs, rocks]

-yajl = veces [que algo se hizo; repetición] / times; times things done repetitively

Yucatec Noun Classifiers:

-P'EL = IN GENERAL; CAN BE USED WITH ANYTHING

-P'IIT = A LITTLE OF SOMETHING OR A SMALL QUANTITY OF THE FOLLOWING NOUN

-KUUL = TREE

-TUUL = PERSON OR ANIMAL; ANIMATE

-TZ'IIT = SOMETHING LONG; OR THIN AND LONG

NOTE: As can be seen, Ch'ol has maintained many more Noun Classifiers than Yucatec.

Examples with Numbers 1-5:

CH'OL:

JUNWEJT KAJPE' = ONE COFFEE; A COFFEE

CHA'WEJT KAJPE' = TWO COFFEES

UXWEJT KAJPE' = THREE COFFEES

CHÄNWEJT KAJPE' = FOUR COFFEES

JO'WEJT KAJPE' = FIVE COFFEES

JUNEJK WAJ = ONE PLATE OF FOOD; A PLATE OF FOOD

CHA'EJK WAJ = TWO PLATES OF FOOD

UXEJK WAJ = THREE PLATES OF FOOD

CHÄNEJK WAJ = FOUR PLATES OF FOOD

JO'EJK = FIVE PLATES OF FOOD

JUNTIKIL X'IXIK = ONE WOMAN; A WOMAN

CHA'TIKIL X'IXIK = TWO WOMEN

UXTIKIL X'IXIK = THREE WOMEN

CHÄNTIKIL X'IXIK = FOUR WOMEN

JO'TIKIL X'IXIK = FIVE WOMEN

JUNTEJK TE' = ONE TREE; A TREE

CHA'TEJK TE' = TWO TREES

UXTEJK TE' = THREE TREES

CHÄNTEJK TE' = FOUR TREES

JO'TEJK TE' = FIVE TREES

JUNKOJT B'AJLÄM = ONE JAGUAR; A JAGUAR

CHA'KOJT B'AJLÄM = TWO JAGUARS

UXKOJT B'AJLÄM = THREE JAGUARS

CHÄNKOJT B'AJLÄM = FOUR JAGUARS

JO'KOJT B'AJLÄM = FIVE JAGUARS

YUCATEC:

JUMP'ÉEL KAPE / BOXJA' = ONE COFFEE; A COFFEE

KA'AP'ÉEL KAPE / BOXJA = TWO COFFEES

OOXP'ÉEL KAPE / BOXJA = THREE COFFEES

KAMP'ÉEL KAPE / BOXJA = FOUR COFFEES

JO'P'ÉEL KAPE / BOXJA = FIVE COFFEES

JUMP'IIT O'OCH = A LITTLE BIT OF FOOD; SOME FOOD
[Can only be used with the number '1' / 'Juun']

JUNKUUL CHE' = ONE TREE; A TREE

KA'AKUUL CHE' = TWO TREES

OOXKUUL CHE' = THREE TREES

KANKUUL CHE' = FOUR TREES

JO'KUUL CHE' = FIVE TREES

JUNTUUL B'AALAM = ONE JAGUAR; A JAGUAR

KA'ATUUL B'AALAM = TWO JAGUARS

OOXTUUL B'AALAM = THREE JAGUARS

KANTUUL B'AALAM = FOUR JAGUARS

JO'TUUL B'AALAM = FIVE JAGUARS

JUNTUUL XCH'UUP = ONE WOMAN; A WOMAN

KA'ATUUL XCH'UUP = TWO WOMEN

OOXTUUL XCH'UUP = THREE WOMEN

KANTUUL XCH'UUP = FOUR WOMEN

JO'TUUL XCH'UUP = FIVE WOMEN

JUNTZ'IIT CHE' = ONE STICK (FROM TREE); A STICK (FROM A TREE)

KA'ATZ'IIT CHE' = TWO STICKS (FROM TREE)

OOXTZ'IIT CHE' = THREE STICKS (FROM TREE)

KANTZ'IIT CHE' = FOUR STICKS (FROM TREE)

JO'TZ'IIT CHE' = FIVE STICKS (FROM TREE)

NOTE: As can be seen, the Noun Classifiers used by Ch'ol and Yucatec do not have much similarity despite having similar Classifiers for common objects [such as trees, people, animals; cups (of) liquid, etc.]. Ch'ol for the most part has maintained many of its original Noun Classifiers and Yucatec, for the most part, has maintained Classifiers for certain criteria.

VII) Numbers 1-10

In this final Chapter, we will compare one of the most common similarities between Mayan Languages that stems directly from Classical Maya and, for the most part, is one of the most uniform aspects of Mayan Languages: The Numerical System. Numbers in Mayan Languages are one of the most common characteristics that all Mayan Languages share and usually only contrast slightly; while maintaining the original root word from Classical Maya.

In addition, this similarity is usually the most prevalent with numbers 1-10. This Chapter will show the original Classical Maya Numbers and then compare them to the four modern-day Mayan Languages being compared within this book.

NOTE: One should keep in mind that these similarities usually only exist with numbers (1-10) and the Classical Maya Numbers beyond the Number (10) differ from modern-day Mayan Languages. Later in this Chapter, examples will be shown for [11-20] and how they compare and contrast between Tz'utujil, K'iche', Yucatec and Ch'ol.

Classical Maya (1-10)

●   (1) JUN

●
●   (2) CHA / KA

●
●
●   (3) OX

●
●
●
●   (4) CHAN / KAN

| (5) JO

●| (6) WAK

●●| (7) WUK

●●●| (8) WAXAK

●●●●| (9) B'OLON

‖   (10) LAJUN

Tz'utujil (1-10):

1 - JUN   6 - WAQ

2 - KA'   7 - WUQ

3 - OX'   8 - WAJXAQ

4 - KEJI'   9 - B'ELEJEE'

5 - JO'   10 - LAJUUJ

K'iche' (1-10):

1 - JUUN   6 - WAAQIB'

2 - KEB'   7 - WUQUB'

3 - OXIB'   8 -WAJXAQIB'

4 - KAJIB'   9 - B'ELEJEB'

5 - JO'OB'   10 - LAJUUJ

Ch'ol (1-10):

1 - JUN	6 – WÄK
2 – CHA'	7 - WUK
3 - UX	8 - WAXÄK
4 – CH'AN	9 - BOLON
5 – JO'	10 – LUJUN

Yucatec (1-10):

1 - JUN	6 - WAAK
2 - KA'A	7 - UK
3 - OOX	8 - WAXAK
4 - KAN	9 - BOLON
5 - JO'	10 - LAJUN

*As can be seen from the examples compared to Classical Maya, despite minor differences [different vowels, added consonant, differing consonant, etc.] the root word for each Mayan Number remains the same. Numbers (1-10) are another similarity that all Mayan Languages share and for the most part remain uniform.

Classical Maya [11-20]

11 - B'ULUK

12 - CHALAJUN / KALAJUN

13 - OXLAJUN

14 - CHANLAJUN / KANLAJUN

15 - JOLAJUN

16 - WAKLAJUN

17 - WUKLAJUN

18 - WAXAKLAJUN

19 - B'OLONLAJUN

20 - K'AL

Tz'utujil [11-20]

11 - Ju'lajuuj

12 - Kab'lajuuj

13 - Oxlajuuj

14 - Kajlajuuj

15 - Jo'lajuuj

16 - Waqlajuuj

17 - Wuqlajuuj

18 - Wajxaqlajuuj

19 - B'eleejlajuuj

20 - Junwinaq

K'iche' [11-20]

11 - Ju'lajuuj

12 - Keb'lajuuj

13 - Oxlajuuj

14 - Kajlajuuj

15 - Jo'lajuuj

16 - Waqlajuuj

17 - Wuqlajuuj

18 - Wajxaqlajuuj

19 - B'eleejlajuuj

20 - Junwinaq

Ch'ol [11-20]

11 - Buluch / Junlujun

12 - Lajchän

13 - Uxlujun

14 - Chänlujun

15 - Jo'lujun

16 - Wäklujun

17 - Wuklujun

18 - Waxäklujun

19 - Bolonlujun

20 - Junk'al

Yucatec [11-20]

11 - BULUK

12 - LAJKA'A

13 - OOX LAJUN

14 - KAN LAJUN

15 - JO' LAJUN

16 - WAK LAJUN

17 - UK LAJUN

18 - WAXAK LAJUN

19 - BOLON LAJUN

20 - JUN K'AAL

NOTE: With Numbers 11-20, it is clearly evident that Yucatec and Ch'ol closely resemble the numerical pattern of Classical Maya, and Tz'utujil and K'iche' are very similar with only minor differences. Despite this, one can clearly see the pattern that exists between all four languages. Usually these patterns are quite consistent except for the one or two numbers here and there that do not quite fit the patterns of the others.

20-100 follow a specific pattern in all four languages, but the patterns followed differ from language to language.

Vocabulary Lists & Phrasebooks

A) Tz'utujil
B) K'iche'
C) Ch'ol
D) Yucatec

A) TZ'UTUJIL

Language name: TZ'UTUJIL, TZ'UTUJIIL, TZIJOB'AL TZ'UTUJIL, QATZIJOB'AL, TZ'UTUJIL TZIIJ, TZ'UTUJIIL TZIIJ

Region / Country: SOLOLÁ, GUATEMALA; ESPECIALLY ON THE SOUTHERN COAST OF LAKE ATITLÁN; SANTIAGO, SAN PEDRO LA LAGUNA, ETC.

Quantity of native speakers: 47,000+

TZ'UTUJIL VOCABULARY:

Food / Riikiil

Apple = Mansa'n

Avocado = Ooj

Banana = Saq'ujl

Beans = Kinaq'

Beer = K'uyaa'

Bread = Kaxlanwaay

Cacao / Cocoa = Kokop

Cactus = Noxti'

Chicken = Ek' / Ak'

Chile = Iik

Chocolate = Chaqijya'

Chorizo = Choríiso

Coffee = Kape

Corn = Ixiim

Fruit = Raxamuuniil

Garlic = Anxux

Ginger = Xiipla

Guava = Ikaq'

Guineo Majunche (Type of small banana) = Majúunche

Güisquil (Regional Vegetable in Guatemala) = Ch'imay

Icecream = Xb'ajb'oj

Jocote (Regional fruit in Guatemala) = Q'inom

Lobster = Cho'm

Mango = Máanko

Milk = Léeche

Orange = Araanxex

Papaya = Papáaya

Peach = Kaxlan K'uum

 Peanut butter = Maníiya

Pineapple = Ch'oob'

Repollo (very similar to coleslaw) = Repo'l (Repóoya)

Rice = Aróosa

Salt = Aatz'aam

Shrimp = Kamaroon [Kah-mah-rohn]

Squash = K'uum

Sugar = Askol

Sweet Potato / Yam = Iis

Tamale with meat = Katamal

Tomato = Xkooyaa'

Tortilla = Waay

Water = Ya'

Watermelon = Sandíiya

Animals / Chikop

Bat = Sootz'

Beast = Keej

Bird = Tz'ikin

Butterfly = Maripóosa

Cat = Me's

Cat = Miix

Cow = B'áaka

Coyote = Uutiip

Crab = Tap (Top)

Deer = Masaat

Dog = Tz'i'

Eagle = Nima xijk

Female Turkey = Xtu'x

Fish = Ch'uu'

Fly = Jaan

Frog = Pujtzin

Grasshopper = Saak'

Head lice = Uk'

Jaguar = B'ajlom

Lice = Uk'

Lizard = Aayiin

Male Turkey = Quluq

Monkey = K'ooy

Mosquito = Us

Owl = Xkin

Quetzal [Bird] = K'uuk'

Rabbit = Umul

Rat = Ch'ooy

Scorpion = Sijna'y

Snake = Kumatz

Spider = Am

Toucan = Kucharoon [Kooch-uh-rohn]

Turkey = Xtu'x, Quluq

Turtle = Tortúuga

Worm = Juut

People / Winaq

Advisor = Ajtziij

Alcoholic = Q'ab'areel

Astrologer = Ajq'iij

Authorities = Q'atol Tziij

Authority = Q'atol Tziij

Baby = -yakii' (n-)

Boy [Little] = Talaa'

Boy [Little]= Ch'uuch'

Boy [Young] = Ak'aal

Boyfriend = Tziij (nuutziij – my boyfriend)

Brother [older] = -Nimaal

Brother [younger] = -Chaaq (Chaq'axeel) [nuuchaaq' – my brother]

Brother [younger] = Chaq'axeel (Chaq'ixeel) [nuuchaaq – my brother]

Brother of a woman = -Xiib'aal (n-)

Brother-in-law of a man = -B'aaluuk

Brother-in-law of a woman = -Ejchaam (w-)

Buyer; Purchaser = Ajlojq'om

Buyer; Purchaser = Ajloq'ol

Caretaker = Chajiineel

Children = -aala' (w-)

Citizen = Antinaamiit

Companion, Friend = -Aachb'iil (w-)

Counselor = Ajtziij

Couple = Ka'winaq

Cousin / Cousin of a woman = Ch'itii'aal (nch'itii'aal – my cousin)

Cousin = Ikaaq' (wikaaq' – my cousin)

Crazy person = Ch'u'jarinaq

Creator = Winaqirsaaneel

Criminal = Aj'iil

Dancer = Ajxajool

Debtor = Ajk'aas

Deer Hunter; Person that hunts Deer = Ajqatoon

Delincuent = Aj'iil

Devil = Itzel Winaq

Drunkard = Q'ab'areel

Egg seller; Egg Vendor = Ajk'ay sajmo'l

Elderly person = Tzab'u'q

Enemy = K'uleel

Family = Pamíilya

Father = -Tata' (nuu-)

Father; Papa = -Jool (nuu-)

Father-in-law of a man = -Jiinaam (njiinaam – my father-in-law)

Father-in-law of a woman = Aliinaam (waliinaam – my father-in-law)

Fortuneteller = Ajq'iij

Friend = Amíigo

Fugitive = Ajnoom

Girl [Little] = Ch'uuch'

Girl [Little] = Ti xtan (Ti xten)

Girl [Young] = Xtan / Xten

Girlfriend = Tziij (nuutziij – my girlfriend)

Granddaughter =-Iij mamaaj (wij nuumaam – my granddaughter)

Grandfather = -Mama' (n-)

Grandmother = -Ati't

Grandson = -Iij mamaaj (wij nuumaam – my grandson)

Guardian = Chajiineel

Habitant = Antinaamiit

Insane person = Ch'u'jarinaq

Leader = Ya'ool naa'ooj

Liar = Yaa'ool Tziij

Man = Aachi

Mother = -Taan (nuu-)

Mother = -Tee' (nuu-)

Mother-in-law of a man = -Jiitee' (n-)

Mother-in-law of a woman = Alitee' (w-)

Nutter = Ch'u'jarinaq

Old person = Tzab'u'q

People = Winaq

Person = Winaq

Person from Panajachel = Aj Panajche'eel

Person from Sololá = Aj Tzolola'

Professor = Ajtij mooso

Psychic = Ajq'iij

Questioner; Person that asks questions = Ak'axaaneel

Seller; Vendor = Ajk'aay

Sinner = Ajmajk

Sister of a man = -Aanaa'

Sister-in-law of a man = -Ixnaam (wixnaam – my sister-in-law)

Sister-in-law of a woman = Alb'atz

Sister-in-law of a woman = -Alii' (walii' – mi cuñada / my sister-in-law)

Someone that makes Tortillas = B'anol Waay

Soulmate = Yo'x raanmo

Speaker of Mam; Person that speaks Mam = Ajmam

Student = Tijoxeel

Teacher = Ajtij mooso

Teacher = Tijoneel

Translator = Q'axal Tziij

Twin = Yo'x (Yoxaa')

Woman = Ixoq

Woman = Q'aapooj

Woman that wears a Huipil = Ajkotoon

Woman that wears a Huipil = Ajpo't

Worker = Ajsamajeel

Writer = Ajtz'ijb'

Places / Xoraal

Bakery = B'anb'al kaxlanway

Bank = B'áanko

Bathroom = Mu'x, B'anb'al Mu'x, Mu'xb'al

Capital; The Capital (of Guatemala); Guatemala City = Armíita

Capital; The Capital (of Guatemala); Guatemala City = Waatemaala

Church = Roochooch Dyos

Church = Tyooxajaay

Dump (City Dump) = K'ojlib'al Mees

Dump (City Dump) = Tixb'al Mees

Forest = K'acheelaaj

Guatemala (Country) [Land of Corn] = Ixiimuleew

Home = Oochooch

House = Jaay

House = Oochooch

Jail; In jail = Pa' Chee'

Land = Uleep

Land = Uleew

Mountains = Juyu'

Panajachel (City) = Panajche'eel

Restroom = Mu'x, B'anb'al Mu'x, Mu'xb'al

Road = B'eey

San Jorge la Laguna = San Jóorje

San Juan la Laguna = San Jwáan

San Marcos la Laguna = San Máarkos

San Pablo la Laguna = San Páawlo

San Pedro la Laguna = San Péedro

Santa Clara la Laguna = Santa Kláara

Santiago Atitlán = Santyáago

School = Ajtijaal

School = Tijob'al rii'iil

Sololá (Department) = Tzolola'

Town = Tinamiit

Valley = Kojol juyu'

Village = Tinamiit

World = Rwach'uleep (Rwech'uleep)

Nature / Winaqiil

Cloud = Suutz'

Day = Q'iij

Flower = Kotz'i'j

Forest = K'acheelaaj

Lake = Chooy

Moon = Iik', Qati't

Mountains = Juyu'

Noche = Aq'a'

Plant = Tijko'm

Rain = Jab'

River = Raqan ya'

Rock = Aab'aj

Stone = Aab'aj

Sun = Q'iij

Tinta (type of plant used for dye) = Tíinta

The Sea = Maar

Tree = Chee'

Valley = Kojol juyu'

Wind = Xilaajuyu'

Other important words / Juutaaj q'iij tziij

Arrival = Ulub'al

Ball = Pelóota

Bed = Ch'ajt

Birth = Alaxb'al

Book = Wuuj

Bottle = Lame't

Breath = Uxlaa' (xlaa')

Car = Ch'ijch'

Car = Káaro

Chair = Ch'akat

Debt = K'aas

Desk = Tz'ijb'ab'al

Disease = Yaab'iil

Door = Pwéerta

Embarassment = K'ixb'al

English language = Ingles

Entrance = Okb'al

Excrement = Achaq, Chixaaj, Kis, O', Paamaaj

Exit = Elab'al

Favor = Utziil

Feces = Achaq, Chixaaj, Kis, O', Paamaaj

Fight = Ch'aa'ooj

Fire = Q'aaq'

Firewood = Sii'

Force = Chojq'ab'al (Chojq'ab'el)

Funeral = Mujqik

Gift = Sijp

Gift, Inheritance = Kooch

Hour = Óora

Inheritance, Gift = Kooch

Joke = Ojer tziij

Key = Laawe, Yáabe

Life = K'asleemaal

Light = Q'aaq'

Machete = Machat (Machet)

Marriage = K'ulub'ik

Medication = Aq'oom

Medicine = Aq'oom

Mirror = Spéeja

Money = Paq (Pwaq)

Mourning = Oq'iij

News = B'ixik

Paper = Wuuj

Peace = Kik'oteemaal

Power = Chojq'ab'al (Chojq'ab'el)

Problem = K'ayeewaal

Sadness (Great Sadness) = B'iis oq'iij

Sadness = B'iis

Sickness = Yaab'iil

Shame = K'ixb'al

Shit = Achaq, Chixaaj, Kis, O', Paamaaj

Sleep = Waraam

Spanish (language) = Kastiya

Strength = Chojq'ab'al (Chojq'ab'el)

Suffering = Poqonaal

Table = Meesa

Towel = Twáaya

Toy = Ajtz'ab'a'l (Ejtz'ab'a'l)

Tranquility = Utziil wachiil

Trash = Mees

Truck = Ch'ijch'

Week = Samáana

Window = Wanta'n

Work = Óobra

Common Adjectives / Tziij pa b'eyomarsaxik ja tziij

Alive = K'asli

Bad = Itzel

Beautiful = Jab'el

Big = Nim

Blind = Mooy

Clean = Ch'ajch'oj

Cloudy = Muqub', Muquli

Cold = Teep

Crazy = Ch'u'j

Cute = Ti Utz

Dangerous = Xib'ib'al rii'iil

Dark = Q'ejq'um

Difficult = K'aayeep

Dirty = Tz'iil

Edible = Ti'jik riij

Evil = Itzel

Fat = Chaq'

Fat = Choom

Fat = Jilaaj

Fat = Jub'olaaj

Fat = Xanaj

Good = Utz

Goofy = T'or

Hairy = B'uy

Handsome = Jab'el

Happy = Ki'iil

Hot = K'atan

Humble = Umíilde

Important = Q'iij

Indigenous = Naturaal

Innocent = Majun Ruumajk

Just = Jiik

Large = Nim

Little = Ko'li

Little = Ti No'y

Loveable = Ojb'een rii'iil

Loving = Ojb'een rii'iil

Married = K'ulaani

Miserable = Xu'y

New = K'aak'a

Obedient = Nimaaneel

Obscure = Q'ejqu'm

Pending = Jolaani

Silly = T'or

Skinny = B'aaq

Spicy = Poqon

Stupid = Rejcha' jaan

Stupid = T'or

Sweet = Kii'

Tall and Skinny = Yakayik

Useless = B'aqab'ik

The Body / ja B'aaqiil

Anus = Xuut' (Xuut'aaj)

Arm = Q'aab'aaj

Back = B'aqiil riij

Back = -iij (riij)

Beard = Smaachii' (simaachii')

Buttocks = Xuut' (Xuut'aaj)

Ear = Xkiinaaj

Eye = Wachaaj

Face = Palaj

Finger = Rwi' Q'ab'aaj

Fingernail = Xk'aq (ixk'aq)

Foot = Ruuxaaq aqanaaj

Hair = Smal wii'aaj

Hand = Q'aab'aaj

Head = Wii'aaj (rwi')

Heart = Aanimo (-Aanmo)

Leg = Aqaanaaj

Lip(s) = Tz'umal chii'aaj

Mouth = Chii'aaj

Nail (finger, toe) = Xk'aq (ixk'aq)

Nose = Tza'm (Tza'maaj)

Penis = Pun

Penis = Tz'ikin

Shoulder = Tale'k

Soul = Aanimo (-Aanmo)

Stomach = Paan (rpaan)

Toe = Rwi' Aqaanaaj

Tongue = -Aaq

Tooth; Teeth = Eeyaaj

Vagina = Chulub'al

Vagina = Tuuxaaj

Clothing / Tzyaaq

Baseball Cap = Pone't

Cap = Pone't

Cloth = Keem

Clothing = Tzyaaq

Fabric = Keem

Glasses; Bifocals = Antyóojo

Hat = Xampare'm

Hat = Xampareem

Huipil (Traditional dress for women) = Katoon

Huipil (Traditional dress for women) = Kotoon

Huipil (Traditional dress for women) = Po't

Pants = Karsoon

Pants = Pantaloon

Shirt = Kamíisa

Shoes = Xajajb'

Skirt = Ujq

T-shirt = Kamíisa

Weave = Keem

Colors / Rejtz'ab'a'liil

Black = Q'eq

Blue = Asuul

Brown = Q'aqq'oj (Q'eqq'oj)

Green = Rex (Rax)

Orange = Anaranjáado (Táanka)

Purple = Moráado

Red = Kaq

White = Saq

Yellow = Q'en (Q'an)

Tz'utujil Verbs:

Love = Ajo'xik (to Love), Ajo'oon (Loved), Xraajo' (He loved)

Alleviate = Utzirsaxik, Utzirsaan, Xrutzirsaaj

Alleviate = Utzursaxik, Utzursaan, Xrutzursaaj

Allow = Tzok'ob'a'xik, Tzok'ob'aan, Xtzok'ob'a'

Arrive = Uuleem, Ulnaq, Xuuli

Ask = Ak'axaaneem, Ak'axanaq, Xak'axaani

Bathe = Atineem, Atinaq, Xatiini

Be = K'e'naq, K'ooli (K'o), Xk'e'e (Xk'eje'e)

Be able to = Kowiineem, Kowiinaq, Xkowiini

Be born = Alaxeem, Alaxnaq, Xalaxi

Be hungry = Aq'anik paamaaj, Aq'aninaq rpaan, Xaq'an rpaan

Be quiet = Q'ilooj rii'iil, Q'iloon rii', Xuuq'il rii'

Be sleepy = K'o rwaaraam, K'enaq rwaaraam, Xk'eje'e rwaaraam

Be thirsty = Chaqi'jik chii'aaj, Chaqi'jnaq ruuchii', Xchaqi'j ruuchii'

Bear = Koch'ooj, Koch'oon, Xuukoch'

Bear well = Koch'och'oxik, Koch'och'oon, Xkoch'och'ooj

Beg; Pray for = Pwersa'ixik, Pwersa'iin, Xpwersa'iij

Bless = Tewuchixik, Tewuchiin, Xtewuchiij

Bloom = Kotz'iijaareem, Kotz'iijarnaq, Xkotz'iijaari

Bother = Naqooj, Naqoon, Xuunaq

Bother = Tzuruuj, Tzuruun, Xuutzuur

Break into little pieces = Bit'ooj, Bit'oon, Xuub'it

Break something = Raqooj, Raqoon, Xuuraq

Bring = K'amooj to, K'amoon to, Xuuk'am to

Buy = Loq'ooj, Loq'oon, Xuuloq'

Carry [something] = K'amooj, K'amoon, Xuuk'am

Carry [something] = -Meel

Carry [transport] = Uk'a'xik, Uk'aan, Xruk'aaj

Change = K'axooj, K'axoon, Xuuk'ax

Chew something = Kach'uxik, Kach'uun, Xkach'uuj

Choose = Cha'ooj, Cha'oon, Xuucha'

Close = Jub'ixik, Jub'iin, Xjuub'iij

Collect = Sik'ooj, Sik'oon, Xuusik'

Collect firewood = B'anooj sii', B'anoon sii', Xuub'an sii'

Come = Pejteem, Pejnaq / Pejtinaq, Xpeeti (Npi, Xpeeti, Xtipeet na)

Create = Winaqirsaxik, Winaqirsaan, Xwinaqirsaaj

Cross = Q'atooj, Q'atoon, Xuuq'at

Cry = Oq'neem, Oq'naq, Xooq'i

Cut = Ramixik, Ramiin, Xraamiij

Cut with a knife = Pusuuj, Pusuun, Xuupus

Cut with Machete or Axe = Choyooj, Choyoon, Xuuchoy

Dance = Xajoweem, Xxajowi (Xxajo)

Dance = Tijoj q'ojoom, Tijon q'ojoom, Xtijoj q'ojoom

Defecate = Pamaaneem, Pamaanaq, Xpamaani

Desire = Yaarixik, Yaariij, Xyaariij

Destroy = Turuuj, Turuun, Xuutur

Die = Kamik, Kamnaq, Xkami

Diminish = Xulub'axik, Xulub'aan, Xxulub'aaj

Do = B'aanooj, B'anoon, Xuub'an

Dream = Achik'eem, Achik'naq, Xachik'i

Dream of someone or something = Ach'kaxik, Ach'kaan, Xach'kaaj

Dress oneself = Tzyaaquxik, rii'iil, Tzyaaquun rii'iil, Xtzyaquuj rii'iil

Drink = Qumuuj, Qumuun, Xuuqum

Drive = Uk'a'xik, Uk'aan, Xruk'aaj

Earn = Ch'ekooj, Ch'ekoon, Xuuch'ek

Eat = Waa'iim, Xwa'i

Eat something = Tijooj, Tijoon, Xuutiij

Embarass = Yaa'ooj k'ix, Yaa'oon k'ix, Xuuya' k'ix

Embrace = Q'ejtexik, Q'ejteen, Xq'ejteej

End = K'i'sneem, K'i'snaq, Xk'i'si

Enrich = B'eyomarsaxik, B'eyomarsaan, Xb'eyomarsaaj

Enter = Okeem, Oknaq, Xooki

Exchange = K'axooj, K'axoon, Xuuk'ax

Explain = Cholooj, Choloon, Xuuchol

Fall = Pa'jeem, Pa'jnaq, Xpa'ji

Fall in love = B'ojchi'xik, B'ojchi'iin, Xb'ojchi'iij

Fall in love = Tijoj tziij, Tijon tziij, Xtijoj tziij

Feed = Tzuquuj, Tzuquun, Xuutzuq

Feel = Na'ooj, Na'oon, Xuuna'

Fight = Ch'a'ooj, Ch'a'oon, Xuuch'a'

Fight = Tijoj chojq'aaq, Tijon chojq'aaq, Xtijoj chojq'aaq

Find = K'uluuj, K'uluun, Xuuk'ul

Finish = K'i'sneem, K'i'snaq, Xk'i'si

Fix = Nuk'uuj, Nuk'uun, Xuunuk'

Flourish = Kotz'iijaareem, Kotz'iijarnaq, Xkotz'iijaari

Fly = Xik'aaneem, Xik'aanaq, Xxik'aani

Forget = Mestaxik / Mastaxik, Mestaan / Mastaan, Xmestaaj / Xmastaaj

Forgive = Kuyuuj, Kuyuun, Xuukuy

Gain = Ch'ekooj, Ch'ekoon, Xuuch'ek

Give = Yaa'ooj, Yaa'oon, Xuuya'

Give back = Meeloojeem, Meeloojnaq, Xmeelooji

Give birth to = Alaaneem, Alaanaq, Xalaani

Give shame = Yaa'ooj k'ix, Yaa'oon k'ix, Xuuya' k'ix

Give thanks = Maltyooxixik, Maltyoxiin, Xmaltyoxiij

Go = B'enaam, B'eenaq, Xb'e

Go across = Q'atooj, Q'atoon, Xuuq'at

Go to bed = Punuli, Xpune'e

Go with hunger = Aq'anya'jik paamaaj, Aq'anya'jnaq rpaan, Xaq'anya'j rpaan

Grow = K'iyareem, K'iyarnaq, Xk'iyari

Grow = Nimareem, Nimarnaq, Xnimari

Guide = Uk'a'xik, Uk'aan, Xruk'aaj

Happen = Ak'oweem, Ak'ownaq, Xak'owi (Xako') = Pasar / to Happen

Happen = Ok'oweem, Ok'ownaq, Xok'owi (Xok'o')

Hate = Etzelaaneem, Etzelaanaq, Xtzelaani

Have = K'e'naq, K'ooli (K'o), Xk'e'e (Xk'eje'e)

Hear = K'aaxaaxik, Xk'aaxaaj

Help = To'ooneem, To'oonaq, Xto'ooni

Help someone = To'ooj, To'oon, Xuuto'

Hide = Awaxik, Aawan, Xraawaaj

Hide out of sight = Awaxik, Aawan, Xraawaaj

Hit = Sokooj, Sokoon, Xuusok

Hug = Q'ejtexik, Q'ejteen, Xq'ejteej

Hurt = Ti'ooneem, Ti'onaq, Xti'ooni

Joke; Tell Jokes = K'oyineem, K'oyiinaq, Xk'oyiini

Joke; Tell Jokes = K'oyixik, K'oyiin, Xk'oyiij

Kill = Kamsaaxik, Xkamsaaj

Kiss = Tz'uub'axik, Xtz'uub'aaj

Know someone = Otaq / -Ojtaq

Know something = -Otaq / -Ojtaq

Laugh = Tzeb'eeneem, Tzeb'eenaq, Xtzeb'eeni

Laugh about / at = Tzeb'exik, Tzeb'een, Xtzeb'eej

Learn = Ojtaqixik, Ojtaqiin, Xrojtaqiij

Leave = -Eel

Leave = Eeleem, Xeeli

Leave = Tzok'ob'a'xik, Tzok'ob'aan, Xtzok'ob'a'

132

Let = Tzok'ob'a'xik, Tzok'ob'aan, Xtzok'ob'a'

Lie = Tz'aqoj tziij, Tz'aqoon tziij, Xuutz'aq tziij

Lie = Yaa'ooj tziij, Yaa'oon tziij, Xuuyaa' tziij

Lie down = Kotz'oli, Xkotz'e'e

Like something = Ojb'exik, Ojb'een, Xrojb'eej

Listen = K'aaxaaxik, Xk'aaxaaj

Live = K'asli, Xk'ase'e

Look for = Kanoneem, Kanonaq, Xkanooni

Lose = Tzaqooj, Tzaqoon, Xuutzaq

Love = Ajo'xik, Ajo'oon, Xraajo'

Love = Ojb'exik, Ojb'een, Xrojb'eej

Lower = Xulub'axik, Xulub'aan, Xxulub'aaj

Make = B'aanooj, B'anoon, Xuub'an

Make better = Utzirsaxik, Utzirsaan, Xrutzirsaaj

Make better = Utzursaxik, Utzursaan, Xrutzursaaj

Mend = Nuk'uuj, Nuk'uun, Xuunuk'

Miss someone = Mayooj, Mayoon, Xuumay

Mix = Xolooj, Xoloon, Xuuxol

Move = Silooj, Siloon, Xuusil

Move oneself = Silooj rii'iil, Siloon rii', Xuusil rii'

Move [to another location] = Jalk'ataxik, Jalk'ataan, Xjalk'ataaj

Need = K'atzineem, K'atzinaq, Xk'atziini

Nourish = Tzuquuj, Tzuquun, Xuutzuq

Obtain = Sik'ooj, Sik'oon, Xuusik'

Open = Jaqooj, Jaqoon, Xuujaq

Paint = Pinta'ixik, Pinta'iin, Xpinta'iij

Pardon = Kuyuuj, Kuyuun, Xuukuy

Park = Chakab'axik, Chakab'aan, Xchakab'aaj

Pay = Tojooj, Tojoon, Xuutoj

Piss = Chuluuneem, Chuluunaq, Xchuluuni

Place; Put = Kojooj, Kojoon, Xuukoj

Play = Ejtz'aaneem, Ejtz'aanaq, Xejtz'aani

Play = Tz'aaneem, Tz'aanaq, Xtz'aani

Pray = Tyoxixik, Tyoxiin, Xtyoxiij

Pray for = Tyoxixik, Tyoxiin, Xtyoxiij

Protect = Kolooj, Koloon, Xuukol

Punch = Sokooj, Sokoon, Xuusok

Punch = Sokooj, Sokoon, Xuusok

Put = Kojooj, Kojoon, Xuukoj

Put in storage = Yaakooj, Yaakoon, Xuuyak

Quit doing something = Kajb'a'xik, Kajb'aan, Xkajb'a'

Rain = Jab'iineem, Jab'iinaq, Xjab'iini

Relieve = Utzirsaxik, Utzirsaan, Xrutzirsaaj

Relieve = Utzursaxik, Utzursaan, Xrutzursaaj

Remain; Stay = K'e'naq Kaan, Xk'e'e Kaan / Xk'eje'e Kaan

Rest = Uxlaaneem, Uxlaanaq, Xuxlaani

Return = Meloojeem, Meloojnaq, Xmeloji

Return something= Meeloojeem, Meeloojnaq, Xmeelooji

Save = Kolooj, Koloon, Xuukol

Save well = K'ololooj, K'ololoon, Xk'ololooj

Say = B'iinaq, Xb'iini

Say something to someone = B'iixik, Xb'iij

Scratch = Matz'ooj, Matz'oon, Xuumatz'

Scratch = Matz'ooj, Matz'oon, Xuumatz'

Search = Kanoneem, Kanonaq, Xkanooni

See = Tz'atooj, Tz'atoon, Xuutz'at

See = Tz'etooj Tz'etoon, Xuutz'et

See = Tzu'uuj, Tzu'uun, Xuutzu'

Seek = Kanoneem, Kanonaq, Xkanooni

Sell = K'ayiineem, K'ayiinaq, Xk'ayiini

Send = Taqooj, Taqoon, Xuutaq

Send = Taqooj, Taqoon, Xuutaq

Shame = Yaa'ooj k'ix, Yaa'oon k'ix, Xuuya' k'ix

Shave oneself = Josooj chii'aaj, Josoon ruuchii', Xuujos ruuchii'

Shit = Pamaaneem, Pamaanaq, Xpamaani

Show = K'utuuj, K'utuun, Xuuk'ut

Shut (oneself) up = Q'ilooj rii'iil, Q'iloon rii', Xuuq'il rii'

Shut = Jub'ixik, Jub'iin, Xjuub'iij

Sing = B'ixaaneem, B'ixanaq, Xb'ixaani

Sit down = Tz'ub'uleem, Xtz'ub'e'e

Sleep = Waareem, Xwari

Smell = Saqooj, Saqoon, Xuusaq

Smile = Tzeb'eya'jeem, Tzeb'eya'jnaq, Xtzeb'eya'ji

Smoke a cigarrette or cigar = Siik'aan jun Siik', Xsiik'aaj jun Siik'

Smoke = Tijoj siik', Tijon siik', Xtijoj siik'

Speak = Tzijoneem, Tzijonaq, Xtzijoni

Speak to someone = Tzijob'ixik, Tzijob'een, Xtzijob'eej

Spend Time = Ak'oweem Tyeempo, Ak'ownaq Tyeempo, Xak'owi Tyeempo

Spit = Chub'aaneem, Chub'aanaq, Xchub'aani

Stay; Remain = Ka'najeem, Ka'najnaq (kaan), Xka'naji (kaan)

Stop doing something = Kajb'a'xik, Kajb'aan, Xkajb'a'

Store = Yaakooj, Yaakoon, Xuuyak

Strengthen = Jweerte'irsaxik, Jweerte'irsaan, Xjweerte'irsaaj

Study = Tijoj rii', Tijoon rii', Xtijoj rii'

Support = Tojq'axik, Tojq'aan, Xtojq'aaj

Take [food, medicine, water] = K'amooj, K'amoon, Xuuk'am

Take [out] = Alasaxik, Alasaan, Xlasaaj

Take [out] = Elasaxik, Elasaan, Xlasaaj

Take [out] = Lasaxik, Lasaan, Xlasaaj

Take a photo = Lasaxik jun rachb'al, Lasaan jun rachb'al, Xlasaaj jun rachb'al

Take care of = Chajixik, Chajiin, Xchajiij

Teach = K'utuuj, K'utuun, Xuuk'ut

Teach something = Tijooj, Tijoon, Xtijooj

Tell Jokes = K'oyineem, K'oyiinaq, Xk'oyiini

Tell Jokes = K'oyixik, K'oyiin, Xk'oyiij

There is / are... = K'e'naq, K'ooli (K'o), Xk'e'e (Xk'eje'e)

Think = Ch'ob'ooj, Ch'ob'oon, Xuuch'ob'

Throw = K'aqooj, K'aqoon, Xuuk'aq

Touch = Chopooj, Chopoon, Xuuchop

Translate = Q'axaxik Tziij, Q'axaan Tziij, Xq'axaaj Tziij

Travel = B'ya'jeem, B'ya'jnaq, Xb'ya'ji

Treat = B'aanooj tráata, B'aanoon tráata, Xuub'an tráata

Understand = Ch'ob'ooj, Ch'ob'oon, Xuuch'ob'

Unite = Tunuuj, Tunuun, Xuutun

Unite = Tunub'a'xik, Tunub'aan, Xtunub'a'

Urinate = Chuluuneem, Chuluunaq, Xchuluuni

Wait = Ayab'exik, Ayab'een, Xrayab'eej

Walk = B'ijneem, B'ejnaq, Xb'ijni

Want = Ojb'exik, Ojb'een, Xrojb'eej

Wash oneself = Ch'ajoneem, Ch'ajonaq, Xch'ajooni

Watch = Tz'atooj, Tz'atoon, Xuutz'at

Watch = Tz'etooj Tz'etoon, Xuutz'et

Watch = Tzu'uuj, Tzu'uun, Xuutzu'

Win = Ch'ekooj, Ch'ekoon, Xuuch'ek

Work = Samajeem, Samajnaq, Xsamaji

Wrap well = B'otzotzoxik, B'otzotzoon, Xb'otzotzooj

Write = Tz'ijb'aaneem, Tz'ijb'anaq, Xtz'ijb'aani

TZ'UTUJIL PHRASES:

*La guía de pronunciación en el fin de cada frase se intente por los hablantes de inglés por la gran distancia entre los idiomas del origen alemán…por los hablantes de español las pronunciaciones de las palabras son similares a la de español; y por supuesto hay un estrés muy enfatizado en los vocales (Mira la sección de gramática)

*El orden de las frases: español / inglés – tz'utujiil (pronunciación simplificada) / The order of the phrases are as follows: Spanish / English – Tz'utujiil (Simplified pronunciation)

*Remember that the 'j' is pronounced like in Spanish like a rough 'h' and in the grammar section '-iij' and '-eej' have the same sound value 'ehH'; in this section the rough throaty 'h' will be presented with 'H'

I)   Para Saludar y Despedir / Hello's and Goodbye's

¡Hola! / Hello! – ¡Saqara! (Sock-a-rah)

¡Buenos Días! / Good morning / afternoon! – ¡Saqara! (Sock-a-rah)

¡Buenas Noches! / Good night! - ¡Xoq aq'a'! (Shohk ah-ah)

¡Adiós! / Goodbye! – ¡Na'an! ... ¡Jat k'a! [a una persona / to one person] ¡Jix k'a! [a dos o más personas/ to two or more people] (Nah-uhn ... Hot kuh ... Heesh kuh)

¡Nos Vemos! / See you again soon! – ¡Xtiqatz'at chik na q'iij! (Shtee-qaw-dzawt cheek nah kehH)

¡Adiós! (coloquial) / Bye! – ¡B'e k'a! (Bay kuh)

¡Cuidate! ¡Cuidese! / Take care of yourself! – ¡Tab'ana kweenta awii'! (Tah-bahn-uh kwayn-tuh ah-wee)

¡Hasta Mañana! / See you in the morning! – ¡Chwaaq chik! (Chwaalk cheek)

¡Hablemos más tarde! / May we speak later! May we speak again soon! = ¡Toqtzijon chik! (Toke-dzee-hohn-cheek)

II)   Frases básicas de conversación / Basic phrases of conversation

Si / Yes – Jee' (Hay)

No / No – Mani', Ma kan ta (Mah-knee, Mah Kahn tah)

¿Qué onda? ¿Qué tal? / What's up? What's going on? – ¿Naq tb'iij? (Knocked-behH)

¿Cómo estás? ¿Cómo está Usted? / How are you? – ¿La utz awaach? ¿Utz awaach? ¿Utz rwach? (Lah oodz ah-watch, Oodz a-watch, Oodz er-watch)

Toy bien, Gracias! / I'm well, thank you. – Utz, maltyox / mitu'ex [col.] (Oodz, mawl-tyohsh / mee-too-ehsh)

¿Y tú? ¿Cómo estás? / And you? How are you? - ¿Atet? ¿La utz awach? (ah-teht … Lah oodz ah-watch)

Estoy bien también / I am well also - Utz chaqajaa'/ choqojaa' (col.) (Oodz chawk-uh-haw / Chohk-oh-haw)

¡Muchas Gracias! / Thank you very much. – Sib'alaaj maltyoox / mitu'ex [col.] (See-buh-law mawl-tyohsh / mee-too-ehsh)

De nada / You're Welcome – Ma' k'o ta xuub'an (Mah-koh tah shoe-bawn)

Éstá bien / All is well – Utz k'aari' (Oodz kaw-ree)

¿Cómo te llamas? / What's your name? – ¿Naq abii'? (knock ah-bee)

Me llamo… / My name is… - Inin / Anen [col.] nuub'ii'… (Een-een / ah-nehn new-bee…)

¿De dónde eres? / Where are you from? – ¿B'aakii' natpi wi'? (Bah-key not-pee wee)

Soy de los Estados Unidos / La Capital (Guat.) / I'm from the United States / Guatemala City – Pa' Estados Unidos / Armíita nink'ase'e (pah Eh-stad-ohs Oo-ni-dos neen-kahs-eh-eh)

¿Cuántos años tienes? / How old are you? – ¿Jaru' ajuunaa'?

(Jah-roo aw-hoo-naw)

*Tengo … años / I am … years old – K'o li … juunaa' (Koh-lee

… hoo-naw)

Juun – 1 [hoon]

Ka' – 2 [kuh]

Ox' – 3 [ohsh]

Keji' – 4 [keh-hee]

Jo' – 5 [hoh]

Waaq – 6 [wawk]

Wuq -7 [wook]

Wajxaq – 8 [waw-shahk]

B'elej – 9 [beh-lehH]

Lajuuj – 10 [lah-hooH]

Ju'lajuuj – 11 [hoo-lah-hooH]

Kab'lajuuj – 12 [kahb-lah-hooH]

Oxlajuuj – 13 [ohsh-lah-hooH]

Kajlajuuj – 14 [kawH-lahooH]

Jo'lajuuj – 15 [hoh-lahooH]

Waqlajuuj – 16 [wawk-lah-hooH]

Wuqlajuuj – 17 [wook-lah-hooH]

142

Wajxaqlajuuj – 18 [waw-shahk-lah-hooH]

B'eleejlajuuj – 19 [beh-lehH-lah-hooH]

Junwinaq – 20 [hoo-wee-knuck]

Junwinaq juun – 21

Junwinaq ka'i – 22

Junwinaq ox'i – 23

Junwinaq keji' – 24

Junwinaq jo'oo – 25

Junwinaq waaq – 26

Junwinaq wuq – 27

Junwinaq wajxaq – 28

Junwinaq b'elej – 29

Juwinaq lajuuj – 30

Ka'winaq – 40 [kuh-wee-knuck]

Ka'winaq lajuuj – 50

Oxk'ajl – 60 [ohsh-kawH-uhl]

Oxk'ajl lajuuj – 70

Jumch' – 80 [hoomch]

Jumuch' lajuuj – 90 [hoo-mooch...]

Por favor, Dime eso en español / Please, Tell me that in Spanish – Tatzijoona Kastiya (Tah-dzee-ho-nah Kah-stee-yah)

Yo hablo tz'utujiil / I speak Tz'utujiil – Inin nintzijooni Tzijob'al / Tz'utujiil tziij (Een-een neen-dzee-hohn-ee Dzee-hoh-bahl / Dzoo-too-heel dzehH)

No hablo tz'utujiil / I don't speak Tz'utujiil – Ma' tintzijooni ta Tzijob'al (Mah Teen-dzee-ho-knee tuh dzee-ho-bawl)

Por favor, Habla lento / Please Speak Slowly – Tatziijoona ejqaal (Tah-dzee-ho-nah eHkawl)

Por favor, Digáme eso otra vez / Please, Tell me that again – Kab'iij / Kab'ix chwe juutaj meej / muul (Kah-behH / Kah-beesh chway hoo-tahH mayH / mool)

¿Qué quieres que yo diga? / What do you want me to say? - ¿Naq nawajo' chi inin ninb'ix? (Knock nah-wah-ho chee een-een neen-beesh)

Tú hablas demasiado rápido / You talk to fast - Atet natzijoni juuch'aay ch'ajniim (ah-teht not-dzee-hoh-knee hoo-chay chaw-neem)

144

Lo siento / I'm sorry - Kinakuyu' (keen-ah-koo-you)

No entiendo / I don't understand – Ma' tinch'ob' ta (Mah teen-chohp ta)

¿Tú sabes? / Do you know? = ¿Awojtaq? (Ah-wohH-tuhk)

¿Tú no sabes? / ¿You don't know? = ¿Ma' awojtaq ta? (Mah Ah-wohH-tuhk tuh)

No, no se / No, I don't know = Mani', Ma' wojtaq (Mah-knee, Mah wohH-tuhk)

No quiero saber lo que pasó / I don't want to know what happened = Ma' tinwaajo' wojtaq chi xak'owi / xok'owi (Mah teen-wah-ho wohH-tuhk chee shah-koh-wee / Shoh-koh-wee)

No quiero saber / I don't want to know = Ma' tinwaajo' wojtaq (Mah teen-wah-ho wohH-tuhk)

¡Perdoname! / Excuse me! – ¡Chaa nuumaak! (chaw new-mawk)

¡Vete! ¡Vayase! ¡Vayanse! / Go! – ¡Jat! [a una persona / to one person] ¡Jix! [a dos o más gente/ to two or more people] (Hot … Heesh)

145

¡Ven acá! ¡Venga acá! ¡Vengan acá! / Come here! = ¡Katojo'

waawe'! [a una persona / to one person], ¡Kixojo' waawe'! [a

dos o más personas / to two or more people] (kaht-oh-hoh wah-

weh…Keesh-oh-hoh wah-weh)

¿Cuándo tu llegaste? / When did you arrive? = ¿Naq q'iij

xatujqaji'? (Knock kehH Shawt-ooH-kuh-hee wahw-eh)

Yo llegué ayer / I arrived yesterday = Iiwiir xinujqaji' (Ee-weer

sheen-ooH-kuh-hee wahw-eh)

¿En qué tu trabajas? / What kind of work do you do? = ¿Naq chi

Samaajiil naab'an? (Knock chee Sahm-ah-heel naw-bahn)

Soy un… / I work as a… = Inin / Anen (col.) … (Een-een / ah-

nehn)

B'anol kaxlanway = (Panadero / Baker) [bahn-ohl kah-shlahn-
way]

B'anol riikiil = (Cocinero / Cook) [bahn-ohl ree-keel]

B'anol sii' = (Leñador / Someone who collects firewood for the
purpose of selling it) [bahn-ohl see]

B'anol way = (Tortillera, Tamalera / Someone who makes
tortillas for a living) [bahn-ohl way]

B'anol xajajb' = (Zapatero / Shoemaker) [bahn-ohl xaw-hawb]

B'anol xampare'm = (Sombrerero / Hat maker) [bahn-ohl sham-pah-raym]

B'anol jaay = (Albañil, Constructor / Builder) [bahn-ohl hay]

¿Adónde vas? / Where are you going? = ¿B'aar natb'e wi? (Bar not-bay wee)

¿Adónde fuíste? / Where did you go? = ¿B'aar xatb'e wi? (Bar shot-bay wee)

¿Adónde van Ustedes? / Where are you all going? = ¿B'aar nixb'e wi? (Bar neesh-bay wee)

¿Adónde fueron Ustedes? / Where did you all go? = ¿B'aar xixb'e wi? (Bar sheesh-bay wee)

¿Con quién fuiste tú? / Who did you go with? = ¿Ch'oq k'iin xatb'e wi? (Choke keen shot-bay wee)

Tengo que ir / I have to go = Ninb'e na (neen-bay nuh)

Tengo que trabajar / I have to work = Ninsamaji na (neen-suh-mah-hee-nuh)

Tengo que salir / I have to leave = Nineeli na (neen-ayl-ee nuh)

Tengo que hacerlo / I have to do it = Ninb'an na (neen-bahn nuh)

Voy a regresar / I will return = Xkinmeloj na (Shkeen-meh-loh nuh)

Voy a regresar otra vez / I will return again = Xkinmeloj na chik (Shkeen-meh-loh nuh cheek)

Voy a regresar mañana / I will return tomorrow = Xkinmeloj na chwaaq (Shkeen-meh-loh nuh chwalk)

Voy a regresar en el próximo año / I will return next year = Xkinmeloj na pa juunaa' chik (Shkeen-meh-loh nuh pah hoonaw cheek)

Vamos a regresar en el próximo año / We will return next year = Xkojmeloj na paa juunaa' chik (ShkohH-meh-loh nuh pah hoonaw cheek)

¿Dónde está el banco? / Where is the bank? = ¿B'aar k'o wi ja B'áanko? (Bar koh wee hah Bawn-koh)

Llévame al banco / Take me to the bank = Kinawuk'aaj wi pa ja B'áanko (Keen-uh-woo-kawH wee pah hah Bawn-koh)

Necesito cambiar un poco dinero / I need to exchange a little money = Nk'atziin chwe nink'ax juun tz'iit pwaq (N-cot-dzeen chway neen-kahsh hoon dzeet pwahq)

Quiero cambiar [canjear] dinero / I want to exchange money = Nwaajo' nink'ax ja npaq (Nwah-hoe neen-kahsh hah n-pahk)

No tengo quetzales / I don't have Quetzales = Ma' k'o ta ja ketzaal (Mah koh tuh hah Keh-dzahl)

Quiero quetzales / I want Quetzales = Nwaajo' ja ketzaal (Nwah-hoe hah Keh-dzahl)

¿Dónde está el Mercado [Tienda]? / Where is the market [store]? = ¿B'aar k'o wi ja K'ayib'al? (Bar koh wee hah Kah-yee-bahl)

Llévame al Mercado / Take me to the market = Kinawuk'aaj wi pa ja K'ayib'al? (Keen-uh-woo-kawH wee pah hah Kah-yee-bahl)

Necesito comprar comida / I need to buy food = Nk'atziin chwe ninloq' ja riikiil? (N-cot-dzeen chway neen-lohk hah ree-keel)

Necesito comprar fruta / I need to buy fruit = Nk'atziin chwe ninloq' ja raxamuuniil? (N-cot-dzeen chway neen-lohk hah rah-shah-moo-neel)

¿Qué es eso? ¿Qué es esto? / What is that? What is this? What is it? = ¿Naq k'a? (Knock-ah)

¿Cuánto cuesta? / How much does it (that) cost? = ¿Jaru rajil? (Hah-roo rah-heel)

¿Cuánto te debo? / How much do I owe you? = ¿Jaru nuuk'aas? (Hah-roo noo-kaws)

No quiero comprar esto / I don't want to buy this = Ma' tinwaajo' ninloq' awari (Mah teen-wah-hoe neen-lohk uh-wah-ree)

Sí, lo quiero comprar / Yes, I want to buy it = Jee', Nwaajo ninloq awari (Hey, n-wah-hoe neen-lohk uh-wah-ree)

Lo siento, no lo puedo comprar / I'm sorry, I can't buy it =

Kinakuyu', Ma' kinkowiin ninloq' awari (Keen-uh-coo-you,

mah keen-koh-ween neen-lohk)

¿Hay algo más barato? / Is there something a lot cheaper? = ¿La

k'o li naquun maas b'aráato?

(Lah koh lee nah-coon mahs bah-rah-toh)

No tengo mucho dinero / I don't have much money = Ma' k'o ta

k'iy pwaq (Mah koh tuh kee pwahk)

Si yo tuviera dinero suficiente, Yo lo compraría / If I had

sufficient money, I would buy it = Wi taxa k'o k'iy pwaq,

ninloq' ta (Wee tah-shuh koh kee pwahk, neen-lohk tuh)

Me gusta / I like it = Nwojb'eej awari (NwohH-behH uh-wah-

ree)

No me gusta / I don't like it = Ma' tinwojb'eej awari (Mah teen-

wohH-behH)

¿Dónde está una tienda que vende…? / Where is there a store that sells…? = ¿B'aar k'o wi k'ayib'al chi nk'ayiini…? (Bar koh wee kah-yee-bahl chee n-kah-yee-nee…)

Ja Tzyaaq (Ropa / Clothing) [hah dzyahk]

Ja Kamíisa (Playera, Camisa, Camiseta / shirts, T-shirts) [hah Kah-mee-suh]

Ja Karsoon (Pantalones) [hah Kahr-sohn]

Ja Pantaloon (Pantalones) [hah Bahn-tah-lohn]

Ja Ujq (Faldas / Skirts) [hah ooHk]

Ja Xajajb' (Zapatos / Shoes) [hah Xaw-hawb]

Ja Riikiil (Comida / Food) [hah ree-keel]

Ja Ejtz'ab'a'l (Juguetes / Toys) [hah ehH-dzah-bahl]

Ja Keem (Tela; Tejido / Cloth, Fabric, Blankets, Weaved Fabric) [hah kaym]

Ja Xb'ajb'oj (Helado / Ice cream) [hah shbahH-bohH]

Ja Wuuj (Libros / Books) [hah voohH]

Ja Sijp (Regalos / Gifts) [hah sehHp]

Ja Xampare'm (Sombreros / Hats) [hah sham-pah-raym]

Ja Pone't (Gorras / Caps; Baseball Caps) [hah pohn-eht]

Quiero atravesar el lago / I want to cross the lake = Nwaajo'
ninq'at ja chooy (Nwah-hoe neen-kawt hah choy)

Queremos atravesar el lago / We want to cross the lake =
Nqaajo' nojq'at ja chooy (Nkah-hoe nohH-kawt hah choy)

Quiero ir a Santiago Atitlán / I want to go to Santiago Atitlán =
Nwaajo' ninb'e pa Santyáago (Nwah-hoe neen-bay pah Sahnt-
yah-goh)

Queremos ir a Santiago Atitlán / We want to go to Santiago
Atitlán = Nqaajo' noqb'e pa Santyáago (Nkah-hoe nohk-bay pah
Sahnt-yah-goh)

¿Cuanto cuesta? / How much does it cost? = ¿Jaru' rajiil? (Hah-
roo rah-heel)

Todos mis compañeros quieren ir al mercado para comprar / ver
las cosas allá / All of my friends want to go to the market to buy
/ see the things there = Konojelal waachb'iil nkaajo' neeb'e pa
k'ayib'al pa loq'ooj / tz'atooj naquun chila' (Koh-noh-hey-lahl
wahch-beel n-kaa-hoe ney-bay pah kah-yee-bahl pah lohk-ohH /
dzah-tohH nah-coon chee-lah)

Tengo hambre / I'm hungry = Naq'an npaan (Nahk-uh-ahn n-pahn)

Tengo sed / I'm thirsty = Nchaki'j nuuchii' (N-chah-kehH noo-chee)

Vamos a buscar comida / Let's look for food = Jo' pa kanoxik ja riikiil (Hoh pah kah-noh-sheek hah ree-keel)

Necesito usar el baño / I need to use the restroom = Nk'atziin che ninkoj ja mu'xb'al (N-cot-dzeen chway neen-kohH hah moosh-bahl)

¿Dónde está el baño? / Where is the bathroom? = ¿B'aar k'o wi juun mu'xb'al? (Bar koh wee hoon moosh-bahl)

Dáme un café, por favor / Give me coffee please = Taya'a juun kape (Tah-yuh-uh hoon kah-peh)

Tú ere muy hermoso [-a] / guapo [-a] / You are very beautiful / handsome = Atet qas jab'el (Ah-teht qaws haw-behl)

Tu tiene una cara muy linda / You have a very cute face = Atet qas ti utz apalaj (Ah-teht qaws tee oodz ah-pah-law)

¿Puedo sacar una foto? / I can take a photo? = ¿La ninkowiin ninlasaj jun rachb'al? (Lah neen-koh-ween neen-law-sawH hoon rahch-bahl)

¿Puedo tomar una foto aquí o no? / Can I take a photo here or no? = ¿La xkinkowiin na nlasaj jun rachb'al waawe o ma kan ta? (Lah shkeen-koh-ween nuh n-law-sawH hoon rahch-bahl wah-weh oh mah kahn tuh)

¿Hay un dormitorio o hotel aquí? / Is there a dormitory or hotel here? = ¿La k'o li juun warab'al oo óotel waawe'? (Lah koh hoon wah-rahb-ahl oh oh-tehl wah-weh)

Llévame al Dormitorio o Hotel / Take me to the Dormitory or Hotel = Kinawuk'aaj wi pa Warab'al oo Óotel (Keen-uh-woo-kahH wee pah wah-rahb-ahl oh oh-tehl)

¿Hay un cuarto disponible en cual puedo quedarme / dormir? / Is there a room available in which I can stay / sleep? = ¿La k'o juutaas waawe chi ninkowiin nk'eje' kaan / ninwar? (Lah koh hoo-taws wah-weh chee neen-koh-ween n-keh-heh kahn / neen-wahr)

¿Cuántas noches quieres quedarse? / How many nights do you want to stay? = ¿Jaru aq'a' nawaajo' nk'e' kaan waawe'? (Hah-roo ahk-uh-uh nah-wah-hoe n-keh kahn wah-weh)

Quiero quedarme aquí por uno / dos / tres noches / I want to stay here for one / two / three nights = Nwaajo nink'eje' kaan waawe juun / ka'i / ox'i aq'a' (Nwah-hoe neen-keh-heh kahn wah-weh hoon / kah-ee / oh-shee ahk-uh-uh)

¿Cuánto cuesta el cuarto? / How much does the room cost? = ¿Jaru rajiil juutaas? (Hah-roo rah-heel hoo-taws)

¿Puedo ver el cuarto? / Can I see the room? = ¿La ninkowiin nintz'et juutaas? (Lah neen-koh-ween neen-dzeht hoo-taws)

No me gusta / I don't like it = Ma tinwojb'eej (Mah teen-wohH-bayH)

Me gusta, quiero el cuarto / I like it, I'll take the room = Nwojb'eej, nwaajo ja wa taas (NwohH-bayH, nwah-hoe hah wah taws)

El cuarto es sucio, quiero otro / The room is dirty, I want a different one = Ja wa' taas tz'iil, nwaajo' juutaaj taas (Hah wah taws dzeel nwah-hoe hoo-tawhH taws)

Todas las sábanas son sucias / All of the sheets are dirty = Nojeel ja sawáana tz'iil

(Noh-Hayl hah sah-wah-nuh dzeel)

¿Durmieron Ustedes bien? / Did you all sleep well? = ¿Xixwari utz? (Sheesh-wah-ree oodz)

No dormí bien / I didn't sleep well = Ma' xinwar ta utz (Mah sheen-wahr tuh oodz)

¿Porqué? / Why? = ¿Naq chree...? (Knock chray...)

Había demasiado ruido / There was too much noise = K'o juuchay quulaaj waawe' (Koh hoo-chay koo-lawhH wah-weh)

Quiero salir / I want to leave = Nwaajo' nineel (Nwah-hoe neen-ayl)

¡Vamos a buscar otro dormitorio / hotel! / Let's look for another dormitory / hotel! = Jo' pa kanooxik juutaj Warab'al / Óotel (Hoh pah kah-noh-sheek hoo-tawhH wahr-ahb-ahl / Oh-tehl)

¿Quieres ir conmigo? / Do you want to go with me? = ¿La nawaaj natb'e wk'iin? (Lah nah-wahH knot-bay wuh-keen)

No, no puedo ir contigo / No, I can't go with you = Mani', Ma' kinkowiin ninb'e awk'iin (Mah-knee, Mah keen-koh-ween neen-bay ahw-keen)

No, no quiero ir contigo / No, I don't want to go with you = Mani', Ma' tinwaajo' ninb'e awk'iin (Mah-knee, Mah teen-wah-ho neem-bay ahw-keen)

¿Te puedo ayudar? / Can I help you? =¿ Ninkowiini natinto'? (neen-koh-wee-knee nah-teen-toh)

No te puedo ayudar / I can't help you = Ma' kinkowiini natinto' (Mah keen-koh-wee-knee nah-teen-toh)

Quiero que me ayudes / I want you to help me = Nwaajo' chi ninato' (Nwah-ho chee knee-nah-toh)

Si yo tuviera dinero, te ayudaría / If I had money, I would help you = Wi taxa k'o npaq, natinto' ta (Wee tah-shah koh m-pah-k, nah-teen-toh tuh)

Si yo tuviera dinero, me iría / If I had money, I would leave = Wi taxa k'o npaq, ninb'e ta (Wee tah-shah koh m-pak, neen-bay tuh)

¿Porqué me quieres ayudar? / Why do you want to help me? = ¿Naq chee nawaajo' ninato'? (knock chay nah-wah-ho neen-ah-toh)

¿Esto es tuyo? / Is this yours? = ¿La awxiin awari'? (Lah aw-sheen uh-wah-ree)

Esto no es tuyo / This is not yours = Ma awxiin ta awari' (Mah aw-sheen tuh uh-wah-ree)

No es mío / It's not mine = Ma wxiin ta awari' (Mah wuh-sheen tuh uh-wah-ree)

Sí, es mío / Yes, it's mine = Jee', wxiin awari' (Hey, wuh-sheen uh-wah-ree)

Ojalá tengas un buen día / I hope you have a good day = Taxa k'o li juun utz q'iij (Tah-shuh koh lee hoon oodz qehH)

Ojalá puedas venir / I hope you can come = Taxa natkowiin natpi (Tah-shuh knot-koh-ween not-pee)

Ojalá yo pueda encontrarlo / I hope I can find it = Taxa ninkowiin nink'ul (Tah-shuh neen-koh-ween neen-cool)

Ojalá no llueva hoy / Hopefully it doesn't rain today = Taxa ma' tijab'ini kamiik (Tah-shuh mah tee-hawb-ee-knee kah-meek)

¿Dónde está la iglesia? / Where is the church? = ¿B'aar k'o wi ja roochooch Dyos? (Bar koh wee hah roh-chohch Dyohs)

Llévame a la iglesia / Take me to the church = Kinawuk'aaj wi pa ja roochooch Dyos (Keen-uh-woo-kahH wee pah roh-chohch Dyohs)

¿Dónde está tu casa? / Where is your house? = ¿B'aar k'o wi awoochooch? (Bahr koh wee ah-woh-chohch)

Dios te bendiga / God bless you = Dyos natrtewuchiij (Dyohs nah-ter-teh-woo-chehH)

Dios los bendiga / God bless you all = Dyos nixrtewuchiij (Dyohs neesh-er-teh-woo-chehH)

Vamos a orar por la comida / Let's pray for this food = Qotyooxiij ja riikiil (Koh-tyoh-shehH hah ree-keel)

Vamos a orarle a Dios y darle gracias / Let's pray to God and give thanks = Qotyooxiij ja Dyos ii Qomaltyooxiij (Koh-tyoh-shehH ha Dyohs ee Koh-mahl-tyoh-shehH)

Vamos a orar por la comida / Let's pray for this food = Jo' pa tyooxixik ja riikiil (Hoh pah tyoh-shi-sheek hah ree-keel)

Dios es muy Bueno / God is good; God is great = Dyos qas utz (Dyohs qaws oodz)

Dios nos ha bendecido con otro día / God has blessed us with another day = Dyos tewuchiin chaqe k'iin juutaaj q'iij (Dyohs teh-woo-cheen chah-keh hoo-tawhH kehH keen)

Te amo / I love you = Natnwajob'eej (Not-nwah-hoe-behH)

¿Me amas? / Do you love me? = ¿La ninawajob'eej? (Lah neen-ah-wah-hoe-behH)

Te quiero besar / I want to kiss you = Nwaajo' natintz'uub'aaj (Nwah-hoe not-teen-dzoo-bawH)

Te quiero abrazar / I want to hug you = Nwaajo' natinq'ejteej (Nwah-hoe not-teen-keh-ihH-tehH)

Te quiero envolver bien en mis brazos / I want to wrap you in my arms = Nwaajo' natinb'otzotzooj pa taq nuuq'a' (Nwah-hoe not-teen-bohdz-ohdz-ohH pah tahk new-kahw)

Te extrañaré mucho / I will miss you very much = Xkatinmay na ma xa k'o (Shkah-teen-mai nuh mah shah koh)

Nunca te boy a olvidar / I will never forget you = Majalaal xkatinmestaaj na (Mah-hah-lahl Shkah-teen-meh-stawH nuh)

Solo quiero quedarme a tu lado / I only want to stay at your side = Xer nwaajo' nink'eje'e kaan pan axkiin (Shayr nwah-hoe neen-keh-heh-eh kahn pahn awsh-keen)

III) MANDATOS COMÚNES [Imperativos] / COMMON COMMANDS [Imperatives]:

¡Vete! ¡Vayase! ¡Vayanse! / Go! – ¡Jat! [a una persona / to one person] ¡Jix! [a dos o más gente/ to two or more people] (Hot … Heesh)

¡Ven acá! ¡Venga acá! ¡Vengan acá! / Come here! = ¡Katojo' waawe'! [a una persona / to one person], ¡Kixojo' waawe'! [a dos o más personas / to two or more people] (kaht-oh-hoh wah-weh…Keesh-oh-hoh wah-weh)

¡Ven conmigo! ¡Venga conmigo! ¡Vengan conmigo! / Come with me! = ¡Katojo' wk'iin [a una persona / to one person] ¡Kixojo' wk'iin [a dos o más personas / to two or more people] (Kaht-oh-hoh wuh-keen…Keesh-oh-hoh wuh-keen)

¡Vamos!!! ¡Vayamos!!! / Let's go!!! = ¡Jo'! (Hoh)

¡Vamos a comer!!! / Let's go eat!!! = ¡Jo' pa' waa'iim!!! (Hoh pah wah-eem)

¡Trabajemos!!! / Let's work!!! = ¡Qosamaji!!! (Koh-sahm-aah-hee)

¡Váyase a trabajar!!! / Go to work!!! = ¡Jasamaja!!! (Hah-sahm-aah-hee)

¡Hágamoslo!!! / Let's do it!!! = ¡Qob'ana!!! (Koh-bahn-uh)

¡Váyase a hacerlo!!! / Go do it!!! = ¡Jab'ana!!! (Hah-bahn-uh)

¡Hágalo!!! / Do it!!! = ¡Tab'ana!!! (Tah-bahn-uh)

¡No lo hagas! / Don't do it! = ¡Ma' kaab'an! (Mah kaw-bahn)

Hágame un favor / Do me a favor, Please = Tab'ana juun Utziil (Tah-bahn-uh hoon oodz-eel)

¡Vamos a hacerlo!!! / Let's do it!!! = ¡Jo' pa' b'aanooj!!! (Hoh pah bahn-ohH)

¡Vamos a hacer leña! / Let's collect firewood! = ¡Jo' pa' b'aanooj sii' (Hoh pah bahn-ohH see)

¡Vamos a bailar!!! / Let's dance!!! = ¡Jo' pa' xajoweem!!! (Hoh pah shah-hoh-waym)

¡Dámelo!!! / Give me it!!! = ¡Taya'a!!! (Tah-yah-uh)

164

Dame dos cervezas, Por favor / Give me two beers, Please = Taya'a ka'i k'uyaa' (Tah-yah-uh kah-ee coo-yaw)

Dame una botella de agua / una gaseosa / Give me a bottle of water / soda, Please = Taya'a juun lame't ya' / juun gasyóosa (Taya'a hoon lah-meht sheen yaw)

¡Beba! / Drink! = ¡Taquum! (Tah-koom)

¡Beba agua! / Drink water! = ¡Taquum ya'! (Tah-koom yaw)

¡No me toques! / Don't touch me! = ¡Ma' Kinachop! (Mah keen-uh-chohp)

¡Éntrate! / Enter! Come in! = ¡Katook! (kah-tohk)

¡Abra / Cierre la puerta / la ventana!, Open / Close the door / the window! = ¡Tajaq / Tajub'iij ja pwéerta / wanta'n! (Tah-Hahk / Tah-who-behH huh pwayr-tuh / wahn-than)

Bienvenidos a mi casa / Welcome to my home = Utz awuuliik pa woochooch (Oodz ah-woo-leek pah woh-chohch)

Aguárdame aquí / Wait for me here = Kinawayab'eej waawe' (keen-uh-wah-yah-behH wah-weh)

165

Llévame al mercado / Take me to the market = Kinawuuk'aaj wi

pa K'ayib'al (Keen-uh-woo-kaahH wee pah Kah-yee-bawl)

IV) *FRASES DE EMERGENCIA / EMERGENCY PHRASES:

¡Ayúdame! ¡Ayudenme! / Help me!!! – ¡Kinato'!!! [a una persona / to one person], ¡Kineto'!!! [a dos o más personas / to two or more people] (Keen-ah-toh … Keen-etoh)

¡Ten Cuidado!!! / Be Careful!!! = ¡Tachajiij awii'!!! (Tah-chah-hehH ah-wee)

¡No te caígas!!! / Don't Fall!!! = ¡Ma' katpa'ji!!! (Mah cot-pah-hee)

¡No me molestes!!! ¡No me chingues!!! / Don't mess with me!!! = ¡Ma' kinanaq!!! (Mah kee-nuh-knock)

¡Llama a la Policia!!! / Call the Police!!! – ¡Tasiik'iij ja Polisi'y!!! (Tah-seek-ehH hah Pohlee-see)

¡Hagálo!!! / Do it!!! = ¡Tab'ana!!! (Tah-bahn-uh)

Alguién me robó / Someone robbed me – K'o juun chi xinrelaq'aaj (Koh hoon chee shin-rehl-awq-aawH)

Alguien hurtó mis pertenecías / Someone stole my things – K'o juun chi xrelaq'aaj nnaquun (Koh hoon chee Shell-awk-aawH nah-coon)

¿Dónde está el hospital? / Where is the Hospital? – ¿B'aar k'o wi ja aq'omb'al rii'iil? (Bar koh wee hah Ah-comb-ahl ree-eel)

Una serpiente me mordió / A snake bit me = Juun Kumatz xinrk'oopiij / xinruutii' (Hoon coo-mahdz sheen-er-koh-pehH / sheen-roo-tee)

Un chucho me mordió / A dog bit me = Juun tz'e' xinrk'oopiij / xinruutii' (Hoon dzeh sheen-er-kohpehH / sheen-roo-tee)

Estoy sangrando mucho / I'm bleeding very bad – Nel nkik'eel maxko' (Nehl n-keek-ayl mahsh-koh)

Sangraba mucho / I was bleeding very bad – Xel nkik'eel maxko' (shayl n-keek-ayl mahsh-koh)

Necesito beber un poco agua / I need water = Nkatz'iin chwe ninqum juun tz'iit ya' (N-cot-dzeen chway neen-koom hoon dzeet yaw)

Estoy enfermo / I'm sick = Inin yaawaa' (Een-een yah-wah)

168

Tengo mucho dolor / I am in a lot of pain = Qas ninti'ooni (Kahs neen-tee-oh-knee)

(...) me duele / My ... hurts = Nti'oni [...] (N-tee-oh-knee)

-Aaq [awk] = Lengua / Tongue

Aqaanaaj [ah-kahn-naw] = Pierna / Leg

B'aqiil riij [bawk-eel rehH] = Espalda / Back

Chii'aaj [chee-aw] = Boca / Mouth

Chulub'al [choo-loo-bahl] = Vagina / Vagina

Eeyaaj [ay-yaw] = Diente / Tooth; Teeth

-iij (riij) [ehH; rehH] = Espalda / Back

Paan (rpaan) [pahn] = Estomago / Stomach

Palaj [pah-law] = Cara; Rostro / Face

Pun [poon] = Pene / Penis

Q'aab'aaj [kuh-awb-awH] = Brazo; Mano / Arm; Hand

Ruuxaaq aqanaaj [roo-shawk uh-kahn-naw] = Pie / Foot

Rwi' Aqaanaaj [er-wee uh-kahn-naw] = Dedo de pie / Toe

Rwi' Q'ab'aaj [er-wee kuh-awb-awH] = Dedo de mano / Finger

Tale'k [Tahl-ek] = Hombros / Shoulders

Tuuxaaj [toosh-aw] = Vagina / Vagina

Tz'ikin [dzee-keen] = Pene / Penis

Tz'umal chii'aaj [dzoo-mahl chee-aw] = Labio / Lip(s)

Tza'm (Tza'maaj) [dzuh-ahm; dzuh-mawH] = Nariz / Nose

Wachaaj [wuh-chaw] = Ojo / Eye

Wii'aaj (rwi') [wee-aw] = Cabeza / Head

Xkiinaaj [shkeen-awH] = Oreja / Ear

Xuut' (Xuut'aaj) [shoot; shoot-awH] = Trasero / Buttocks

Tengo diarrea / I have diarrea = K'o li ja chooy (Koh lee hah chohy)

Tengo diarrea y vomitos = K'o li chooy xa'aab' (Koh lee chohy shuh'aawb)

Tengo miedo / I'm afraid = Ninxib'ej wii' (Neen-shee-behH wee)

Tenía miedo, Tuve miedo / I was afraid = Xinxib'ej wii' (Sheen-shee-behH wee)

No tengas miedo / Don't be afraid = Ma' katxib'ej awii' (Mah cot-shee-behH ah-wee)

Llévame al hospital / Take me to the Hospital – Kinawuuk'aaj wi pa Aq'omb'al rii'iil (Keen-uh-woo-k'aahH wee pah ah-comb-awl ree-eel)

B) K'ICHE' (QUICHÉ)

Language name:

QATZIJOB'AL, K'ICHE' TZIJ, TZIJOB'AL K'ICHE'

Region / Country: VARIOUS REGIONS OF GUATEMALA; MOMOSTENANGO, PÉTEN, TOTONICAPÁN, ETC. & REGIONS IN SOUTHERN MÉXICO

Quantity of native speakers: 2,000,000+

K'ICHE' VOCABULARY:

Food / Riki'l

Apple = MANSA'N

Avocado = OOJ

Banana = ANKANE'Y

Banana = SAQ'UUL

Beans = KINAQ'

Bread = KAXLAAN WA

Cabbage = QULIX

Cacao / Cocoa = KAKAW

Cacao / Cocoa = KAKOW

Cactus (Fruit) = NACHTI'

Cactus (Fruit) = NOXTI'

Cheese = KEXO'

Cheese = KEXU'

Cherry = K'UXUMK'EL

Chicken = EK' / AK'

Chile = IIK

Chocolate = CHAQIIYA'

Chorizo = CHORIISO

Cinnamon = KANELA

Coconut = KOKA

Coconut = KOKO

Coffee = KAPE

Corn = IXIIM

Egg = SAQMOL

Fruit = PRUTA

Garlic = AXUX

Ginger = XINXIPRE

Guava = KAQ'

Güicoy Squash = MUKUN

Güisquil (Regional Vegetable in Guatemala) = CH'IMA

Honey = JUYUB'AL KAB

Honey = RAAX KAAB

Icecream = XB'AJB'OJ

Jocote (Regional fruit in Guatemala) = Q'INOM

Lime = LIMA'

Liquor = KUXA

Mango = MAANKO

Meat = TI'J

Milk = LEECHE

Mustard = MARTANSA

Orange = ALANXAAX

Papaya = PAPAAY

Peach = TURA'S

Peanut butter = MANII'Y

Pineapple = CH'OP

Plantain = NAX

Pomegranate = NABIAL

Potato = NUX

Repollo (very similar to coleslaw) = REPO'L (REPO'Y)

Rice = ARROZ

Salt = ATZ'AM

Squash = K'UUM

Sugar = ASUKAL

Sweet Potato / Yam = IIS

Sweet Potato = IXQ'ANAJOY

Sweet Potato = KAMOT

Tamale with meat = KATAMAL

Tobacco = ME'T

Tomato = PIX

Tortilla = LEEJ

Tortilla = WA

Water = JA'

Watermelon = SANDII'Y

Animals / Chikop

Armadillo = IBOY

Bat = SOTZ'

Beast = AWAJ

Bird = AWAJ AJ UWO KAJ

Bird = TZ'IKIN

Bull; Ox = WAKAAX

Butterfly = PEMPEN

Cat = ME'S

Centipede = IXTZOL

Cow = WAKAAX

Coyote = UTIW

Crab = TAP

Crab = TOP

Crab = XTOP

Deer = MASAAT

Dog = TZ'I'

Dove = IXPUMUY

Eagle = KOT

Fish = CH'U'

Fish = KAAR

Flea = K'YAQ

Fly = AMOLO

Frog = IXTUTZ'

Grasshopper = KAACHO'PINIK

Grasshopper = LOK

Horse = KEJ

Iguana = IWAN

Jaguar = BALAAM

Lizard = AYIN

Macaw = KYAQ K'IX

Maggot = RACHAQ AMOLO

Monkey = BATZ'

Mosquito = US

Mouse = CH'O

Owl = K'URUPUP

Owl = TUKUR

Ox; Bull = WAKAAX

Pig = AQ

Quetzal [Bird] = K'UK'

Rabbit = UMUL

Rat = BAJI'S

Rat = BAYI'S

Rat = CH'O

Rooster = AMA' AK'

Salamander = I'X

Scorpion = IXKAB

Shrimp = CHO'M

Snail = LOJOJ AWAJ

Snake = KUMATZ

Spider = AM

Spider Monkey = K'OY

Toad = IXPAAQ

Toad = IXPEQ

Toad = IXPUTZ

Tortoise = K'O'X AWAJ

Turkey = NO'S

Turtle = TORTUGA

Vulture = K'UCH

Wasp = AQAJ

Whale = AYIN KAAR

Worm = IXJUT

Worm = JUXJUT

People / Winaq

Advisor = AJTZIJ

Alcoholic = Q'AB'AREEL

Astrologer = AJKAJBALACH

Aunt = CH'UTIN NAN

Authorities = Q'ATOL TZIJ

Authority = Q'ATOL TZIJ

Baby = NUCH'

Baby Boy = NUCH' ALA

Baby Boy = NUCH' ALI

Blacksmith = AJCH'AYAL CH'ICH'

Bow Hunter; Person that hunts with Bow = AJJUB

Boy [Little] = ALA

Boy [Young] = AK'AAL

Brother [older] = ACHALAL

Brother [younger] = CHAQ'AXEL (CHAQ')

Brother [younger] = CHAQ'IXEL (CHAQ')

Brother of a woman = -XIB'AL

Brother-in-law of a man = -B'AALUUK

Buyer; Purchaser = LOQ'OMANEL

Buyer; Purchaser = LOQ'OMINEL

Caretaker = CHAJINEL

Child = ALK'WALAXEL

Clown = CHAQAB

Companion, Friend = ACHI'L

Counselor = PIXABINEL

Couple = K'ULAJ

Cousin = RAL UCH'UTIN NAN

Coward = AJXIB

Crazy person = MOX

Creator = WINAQIRISANEEL

Criminal = B'ANAL ETZELAL

Dancer = AJXOJOJ

Dead Person = KAAMINAQ

Delincuent = B'ANAL ETZELAL

Demon = QOXTOK

Devil = ITZEL WINAQ

Doctor = KUNANEL

Drunkard = Q'AB'AREEL

Egg vendor = AJK'AY SAQMOL

Enemy = K'ULEL

Family = ACHALAXIK

Family = CHINAMIT

Family = JA WINAQ

Father = -TAT

Fool = NAKANIK

Foreigner = AJBE'IL

Fortuneteller = AJKAJBALACH

Founder = WINAQIRISANEEL

Friend = ACHI'L

Friend = LOQ' ACHI

Girl [Little] = CH'UCH'

Girl [Young] = ALI

Granddaughter = -I'MAM

Grandfather = MAM

Grandmother = ATI'T

Grandmother = NOY

Grandson = -I'MAM

Guardian = CHAJINEL

Guide = K'AMOL BE

Horseman = AJKIEJ

Hunter = K'YAAQANEL

Husband = ACHAJILOM

Idiot = NAKANIK

Insane person = MOX

Killer = KAAMISANEL

King = AJAWINEL

Lawyer = KOJOL TZIJ

Lazy Person = K'EYO

Leader = K'AMAL BE

Leader = NIMAL

Liar = B'ANAL TZIIJ

Man = ACHI

Mother = CHUCH

Murderer = KAAMISANEL

Neighbor = K'UL JA

Neighbors = K'UL TAQ JA

New Born Baby = NE'

Nutter = MOX

Old Person = RI'J WINAQ

Owner = AJCHAQ'E

Owner = AJCHOQ'E

People = WINAQ

Person = WINAQ

Police = PATANIL KE

Prisoner = AJ PA CHE'

Psychic = AJKAJBALACH

Queen = CHICHU' AJAWINEL

Quiché people = AJK'ICHE' WINAQ

Seller = AJK'AY

Singer = BIXONEL

Sinner = AJMAK

Small child = NOYA

Soldier = AJCH'O'J

Someone that makes Tortillas = B'ANOL WA

Soulmate = YOX RANIMA'

Stranger = AJCH'AKAP

Student = TIJOXEL

Stupid Person = JOLOM CHIJ

Stupid Person = JOLOM KEJ

Teacher = TIJONEL

Thief = AJXIK

Thief = ELAQ'OM

Traitor = JACHANEL

Translator = K'EXEL TZIJ

Translator = Q'AXAL TZIJ

Traveler = AJBE

Twin = YOX

Uncle = CH'UTIN TAT

Vendor = AJK'AY

Witch = AJITZ

Woman = CHICHU'

Woman = IXOQ

Woman = Q'APOJ

Worker = AJCHAK

Worker = CHAKUNEL

Writer = AJTZ'IB

Places / K'olib'al

Bakery = B'ANB'AL KAXLANWA

Bank = B'AANKO

Bathroom = CHULUB'AAL

Capital; The Capital (of Guatemala); Guatemala City = ARMIITA

Capital; The Capital (of Guatemala); Guatemala City = WAATEMALA

Church = RACHOCH DIOS

Church = ROCHOCH RE' DIOS

Forest = K'ACHELAAJ

Guatemala (Country) [Land of Corn] = IXIIMULEW

Hill = MUMUS

Home = OCHOCH

Hotel = OQXA'NIB'AL

House = JA

House = OCHOCH

Jail; In jail = PA CHE'

Land = ULEW

Mountains = JUYUB

Restroom = CHULUB'AAL

Road = BE

School = AJTIJAL

School = TIJOB'AL RIIB'

Town = TINIMIT

Town = TINAMIT

Valley = BEYA'

Village = TINIMIT

Village = TINAMIT

Nature / Winaqiil

Cloud = SUUTZ'

Day = Q'IIJ

Flower = KOTZ'I'J

Forest = K'ACHELAAJ

Forest = KECHELAAJ

Jungle = ITZEL K'ACHELAAJ

Lake = CHO

Lunar Eclipse = KAAM IK'

Mildew = RACHAQ IXPEQ

Moon = IIK'

Mountains = JUYUB

Noche = AQ'AB

Plant = TIJKO'M; CHE'

Rain = JAB

Rainbow = CH'UPIKAQ

River = NIM JA'

Rock = ABAAJ

Snow = ABAAJ TEW

Solar Eclipse = KAAM Q'IJ

Stone = ABAAJ

Sun = Q'IIJ

The Sea = MAAR

Thunder = EJINAMIK

Tinta (type of plant used for dye) = TIINTA

Tree = CHEE'

Valley = BEYA'

Valley = LYA'NIK

Waterfall = CHIYUL

Wind = IQ'

Wind = KAAQ'IQ'

Other important words

Ability = KOWINEM

Arrival = ULUB'AL

Ball = SURSIK

Beauty = JE'LAL

Bed = CH'AT

Bible = LOQ'ALAJ WUJ

Birth = ALAXIBAL

Book = WUUJ

Bottle = LIMET

Bottle = LIMITA

Box = KAXOON

Breath = UXLABAJ (UXLAB)

Burial = MUQNAJIK

Car = CH'IICH'

Car = KARROK

Chair = XILA'

Childhood = AK'ALIL

Cup = SEL

Death = KAAMIKAL

Dictionary = MULULIK TZIJ

Disease = YAB'IL

Door = UCHI' JA

Dream = ACHIK'

Dream = ICHIK'

English language = INGLES

Entrance = OKB'AL

Example = K'AMB'AL BE

Excrement = ACHAQ

Excrement = KIS

Exit = ELABAL

Favor = UTZIIL

Feces = ACHAQ

Fight = CH'O'J

Fight = CH'O'JIB'AL

Fire = Q'AAQ'

Firewood = SII'

Forgiveness = KUYUB'AL MAK

Funeral = MUJQIK

Funeral = MUQNAJIK

Gift = SIPAB'AL

Gift = SIPANIK

Gift, Inheritance = ECHB'AL

Glass [drinking] = SEL

God = QAJAW; DIOS

Hope = KU'LB'AL K'UX

Hour = CH'AQAP Q'IIJ

Hour = OORA

Idea = NA'OJ

Inheritance, Gift = ECHB'AL

Jar [Glass] = BUK'UL

Joke = ETZ'ANEM TZIJ

Joke = PUK

Key = LAAWE, YAABE

Knowledge = NA'OJ

Language = CH'AWIB'AL

Language = TZIJOB'AL

Life = K'ASLEMAL

Light = Q'AAQ'

Machete = MACHAT

Marriage = K'ULANEM

Medication = KUNAB'ALIL

Medicine = KUNAB'ALIL

Mirror = ILB'AL IB

Money = PWAQ

Myth = AQ'BAL

Pain = Q'OXOM

Paper = WUUJ

Peace = KIK'OTEMAL

Pillow = CH'AKAT

Power = KOWINEM

Power = KWINEM

Sadness = B'IIS

Shit = ACHAQ

Sickness = YAAB'IL

Sleep = WARAAM

Song = B'IX

Spanish (language) = KASTIYA

Spanish (language) = KAXLAN TZIJ

Suffering = POQONAL

Table = MEESA

Tool = CHAKB'AL

Towel = TWAAYA

Toy = ETZ'AB'AL

Tranquility = JAMARIL

Trap = LAJAB

Trash = MEES

Truck = CH'IICH'

War = LABAL

Week = WUQUBIIX

Window = WANTA'N

Witchcraft = ITZB'AL

Work [Job] = CHAK

Work [academic] = OOBRA

Year = JUNAB'

Common Adjectives

Alive = K'ASLIK

Ancient = NAJTIR

Bad = ITZEL

Beautiful = JE'LIK

Beautiful = JEBEL

Beautiful = JELELAJ

Beautiful = MU'S

Big = NIM

Blind = MOY

Clean = CH'AJCH'OJ

Cold = JORON

Crazy = CH'U'J

Deaf = T'OR

Dirty = TZ'IL

Edible = KAATIJIK

Evil = ITZEL

Fat = CHOM

Fat = JILIJIK

Fat = JUSANAJ

Good = UTZ

Hairy = PATZ' -WI'

Handsome = JEBEL

Happy = KI'IIL

Hot = K'ATAN

Humble = KEM

Important = Q'IIJ Q'IIJ

Indigenous = NATURAL

Large = NIM

Little = ALAJ

Little = LA'J

Little = XIL

Married = K'ULANIK

New = K'AAK'

Obedient = NIMANEL

Skinny = BAQ

Spicy = POQON

Sticky = NAK'AK'IK

Stupid = BA'X

Sweet = KI'

Wet [very] = CH'AQACH'OJ

Wet = CH'AQALIK

The Body / Baqil

Anus = XUT'

Arm = Q'ABAJ (Q'AB)

Back = WORACHAL

Back = IJAJ, -IJ

Beard = -ISMAL CHII'

Buttocks = CH'ENCH'KIL

Eye = BAQ'WAACH

Eye = WACHAJ (-WACH)

Face = PALAJ; PALAJAAJ

Finger (Index) = NABE ALK'WALAXEL

Fingernail = IXK'YAQ

Foot = AQANAJ (AQAN)

Hand = Q'ABAJ (Q'AB)

Head = JOLOMAAJ (JOLOM)

Heart = ANIMA'

Intestines = IXKO'LAJ (IXKO'L)

Leg = AQANAJ (AQAN)

Lip(s) = TZ'UMAL CHII'

Lung = PATZPOY

Mouth = CHII'AJ (CHII')

Nail (finger, toe) = IXK'YAQ

Nose = TZA'M

Shoulder = TALE'K

Skull = UBAQIL JOLOMAJ

Soul = ANIMA'

Stomach = PAAM

Toe = -WI' AQANAAJ

Tongue = AQ; AQAAJ

Tooth; Teeth = E'AJ (-E)

Clothing / Atzyaaq

Baseball Cap = PUNE'T

Cap = PUNE'T

Cloth = CHEKUB'AL

Clothing = ATZYAAQ

Clothing = TZYAAQ

Fabric = CHEKUB'AL

Glasses; Bifocals = ANTYOJO

Hat = PWI'

Huipil (Traditional dress for women) = KATOON

Huipil (Traditional dress for women) = KOTOON

Huipil (Traditional dress for women) = PO'T

Jacket = KOTOON

Pants = KASOON

Sandals = LEH XAJAAB

Shirt = KAMIXA

Shoes = XAJAAB

Skirt = UJQ

T-shirt = KAMIXA

Weave = CHEKUB'AL

Weaving = KYEM

Colors / Rejtz'ab'alil

Black = Q'EQ

Blue = JE KAAKA'Y KAJ

Brown = KAQOJ

Green = RAX

Orange = ANARANJADO

Purple = MORA'T

Red = KAQ

White = SAQ

Yellow = Q'AN

K'ICHE' (QUICHÉ) VERBS:

Alleviate = UTZIRIK

Arrive = -UUL, XUUL

Ask = TAYIK, XTAYIK

Ask = TAYO, XUTAYO

Bathe = ATINIK, XRATINIK

Be = K'OLIK, XK'E'IK

Be able to = KOWIN, XKOWIN

Be born = ALAXIK, XRALAXIK

Be thirsty = CHAQI'J -CHII', XCHAQI'J -CHII'

Bear = KOCH', XUKOCH'

Bless = TEWICHIJ, XTEWICHIJ

Bloom = KOTZ'IJARIK, XKOTZ'IJARIK

Bother = NAQO, XUNAQO

Bother = TZURUJ, XTZURUJ

Break into little pieces = BIT', XUBIT'

Bring = K'AM ULOQ, XUK'AM ULOQ

Buy = LOQ'O, XULOQ'O

Carry [something] = K'AMO, XUK'AMO

Change = K'EXO, XUK'EXO

Chew something = KACH'UJ, XKACH'UJ

Choose = CHA'NIK, XCHA'NIK

Close [lock] = JU', XUJU'

Close = TZ'AAPIJ, XTZ'AAPIJ

Collect firewood = B'ANO SII', XUB'ANO SII'

Come = -PEETIK, XPEETIK

Create = WINAQIRISAJ, XWINAQIRISAJ

Cross = Q'AXIK, XQ'AXIK

Cry = OQ'IK, XOQ'IK

Cut = RAMIJ, XRAMIJ

Cut with a knife = PUSU, XUPUSU

Cut with Machete or Axe = CHOYO, XUCHOYO

Dance = XOJOWIK, XXOJOWIK

Defecate = CHULUNIK, XCHULUNIK

Destroy = WULIJ, XWULIJ

Die = KAMIK, XKAMIK

Do = B'AN, XUB'ANO

Dream = ACHIK'IK, XRACHIK'IK

Dream of someone or something = ACHIK'AJ, XRACHIK'AJ

Dress oneself = ATZYAAQUJ -IB', XRATZYAAQUJ
-IB'

Drink = UK'YAJ, XUK'YAJ

Earn = CH'EK'IK, XCH'EK'IK

Eat = WA'IK, XWA'IK

Eat something = TIJO, XUTIJO

Embrace = MATZ'EJ, XMATZ'EJ

End = K'ISIK, XK'ISIK

Enrich = Q'INOMARSAJ, XQ'INOMARSAJ

Enter = OKIK, XOKIK

Exchange = K'EXO, XUK'EXO

Fall = WOLQ'OTILA' -IIB', XWOLQ'OTILA' RIIB'

Fall in love = BOCH'IJ, XBOCH'IJ

Feed = TZUQ, XUTZUQ

Feel = NA', XUNA'

Fight = CH'O'JIJ, XCH'O'JIJ

Find = RIQ, XURIQ

Finish = K'ISIK, XK'ISIK

Fix = K'IJIJ, XK'IJIJ

Flourish = KOTZ'IJARIK, XKOTZ'IJARIK

Fly = XIK'IK'IK, XXIK'IK'IK

Forget = SACH PA -JOLOM, XUSACH PA UJOLOM

Forgive = KUYU, XUKUYU

Gain = CH'EK'IK, XCH'EK'IK

Gather together = MULI'K, XMULI'K

Give = YAA', XUYAA'

Give birth to = ALANIK, XRALANIK

Give thanks = MALTYOXIJ, XMALTYOXIJ

Go = -B'E, XB'E

Go across = Q'AXIK, XQ'AXIK

Go down = XULI'K, XXULI'K

Go up = PAKI'K, XPAKI'K

Grow = NIMARIK, XNIMARIK

Guide = K'AMO BE, XK'AMO BE

Happen = OK'OWIK, XOK'OWIK

Hate = ETZELAJ, XRETZELAJ

Have = K'OLIK

Hear = TATAB'EJ, XTATAB'EJ

Hear = TA, XUTA

Help = TO'IK, XTO'IK

Help someone = TO'O, XUTO'O

Hide = K'U', XUK'U'

Hug = MATZ'EJ, XMATZ'EJ

Hurt = QOXOWIK, XQOXOWIK

Kill = KAMISAJ, XKAMISAJ

Kiss = TZ'UMAJO, XTZ'UMAJO

Know = -ETA'M

Know someone = -ETA'M -WACH

Laugh = TZE'NIK, XTZE'NIK

Laugh about / at = TZE'J, XTZE'J

Learn = ETA'MAJ, XRETA'MAJ

Leave = -EEL, XEEL

Lie down = Q'OYI'K, XQ'OYI'K

Listen = TATAB'EJ

Listen = TA'NIK, XTA'NIK

Live = K'ASI'K, XK'ASI'K

Look = KA'YIK, XKA'YIK

Look = KA'YEJ, XKA'YEJ

Look for = TZUKUJ, XTZUKUJ

Lose = TZAQO, XUTZAQO

Love = -AAJ, XARAAJ

Make = B'ANO, XUB'ANO

Make better = UTZIRIK, XUTZIRIK

Marry = K'ULI'K, XK'ULI'K

Mend = NUK'U, XUNUK'U

Miss someone = MAYO, XUMAYO

Mix = XOLO, XUXOLO

Move [to another location] = JALK'ATIJ, XJALK'ATIJ

Nourish = TZUQ, XUTZUQ

Obtain = K'AMOWIK, XK'AMOWIK

Open = JAQO, XUJAQO

Paint = TZ'AJO, XUTZ'AJO

Pardon = KUYU, XUKUYU

Pay = TOJONIK, XTOJONIK

Piss = CHULUNIK, XCHULUNIK

Place; Put = KOJO, XUKOJO

Play = ETZ'ANIK, XRETZ'ANIK

Play = TZ'ANIK, XTZ'ANIK

Pray = TYOXIJ, XTYOXIJ

Pray = TYOXINIK, XTYOXINIK

Protect = KOLO, XUKOLO

Put = KOJO, XUKOJO

Rain = JAB'INIK, XJAB'INIK

Relieve = UTZIRIK, XUTZIRIK

Remain; Stay = KANAJIK, XKANAJIK

Rest = UXLANIK, XUXLANIK

Return = TZALIJ, XTZALIJ

Save = KOLO, XUKOLO

Say = -B'IJ, XUB'IJ

Search = TZUKUJ, XTZUKUJ

Search = TZUKUJ, XTZUKUJ

See = -IL, XARILO

See = TZU', XUTZU'

Seek = TZUKUJ, XTZUKUJ

Sell = K'AYIK, XK'AYIK

Send = TAQO, XUTAQO

Shave oneself = JOS -IB', XUJOS -IB'

Show = K'UTU, XUK'UTU

Shut = JU', XUJU'

Sin = MAKUJ, XMAKUJ

Sing = BIXIK, XBIXIK

Sit = KU'I'K, XKU'I'K

Sit down = T'UYI'K, XT'UYI'K

Sleep = WARIK, XWARIK

Smile = TZE'NIK, XTZE'NIK

Smoke a cigarrette or cigar = SIK'AJ JUN SIIK', XSIK'AJ JUN SIIK'

Speak = TZIJONIK, XTZIJONIK

Speak to someone [counsel] = TZIJOB'EJ, XTZIJOB'EJ

Spit = CHUB'ANIK, XCHUB'ANIK

Stand = TAK'I'K, XTAK'I'K

Stay; Remain = KANAJIK, XKANAJIK

Study = TIJOJ -IIB', XTIJOJ -IIB'

Support = CHAKUYIK, XCHAKUYIK

Take [food, medicine, water] = K'AMO, XUK'AMO

Take [out] = ELESAJ, XRELESAJ

Take [out] = ESAJ, XRESAJ

Take care of = CHAJIJ, XCHAJIJ

Talk = TZIJONIK, XTZIJONIK

Teach = K'UTU, XUK'UTU

Teach something = TIJOJ, XTIJOJ

There is / are… = K'OLIK, XK'E'IK

Think = CH'OMANIK, XCH'OMANIK

Touch = CHAPO, XUCHAPO

Translate = Q'AXAJ TZIJ, XQ'AXAJ TZIJ

Travel = B'INIK, XB'INIK

Treat = B'ANO TRAATA, XUB'ANO TRAATA

Understand = CH'OMANIK, XCH'OMANIK

Urinate = CHULUNIK, XCHULUNIK

Wait = IYE'NIK, XRIYE'NIK

Wait = IYE'BIK, XRIYE'BIK

Wait = IYE'J, XRIYE'J

Walk = B'INIK, XB'INIK

Want = -AAJ, XARAAJ

Wash oneself = CH'AJO, XUCH'AJO

Watch = -IL, XARILO

Watch = TZU', XUTZU'

Win = CH'EK'IK, XCH'EK'IK

Work = CHAKUNIK, XCHAKUNIK

Wrap = BOTZ', XUBOTZ'

Write = TZ'IBANIK, XTZ'IBANIK

K'ICHE' (QUICHÉ) PHRASES:

*El orden de las frases: Español / Inglés – K'iche' / The order of the phrases are as follows: Spanish / English – K'iche'

*Remember that the 'j' is pronounced like in Spanish with a rough 'h' sound and in the grammar section '-iij' and '-eej' have the same sound value 'ehH'

III)   Para Saludar y Despedir / Hello's and Goodbye's

¡Hola! / Hello!

= ¡SAQARIK!

¡Buenos Días! / Good morning / afternoon!

= ¡SAQARIK!

¡Buenos Días! ¡Buenas Tardes! / Good afternoon! Good evening!

= ¡XEQ'IJ!

¡Buenas Noches! / Good night!

= ¡XOK AQ'AB!

¡Adiós! / Goodbye!

= ¡JAT K'A! [a una persona / to one person] ¡JIX K'A! [a dos o más personas/ to two or more people]

¡Adiós! / Goodbye!

= ¡CH'AB'EJ CHIK!

¡Cuidate! ¡Cuidese! / Take care of yourself!

= ¡NO'JIM KATB'E WI!

¡Cuidate! ¡Cuidese! / Take care of yourself!

= ¡NO'JIM KATB'EK!

¡Hasta Mañana! / See you in the morning!

= ¡CHWE'Q CHIK!

¡Nos vemos! / We shall see each soon!

= ¡KATINWILO CHIK MATA'M APANOQ!

¡Hablemos más tarde! / May we speak later! May we speak again soon!

= ¡KUJCH'AWIK CHIK MATA'M APANOQ!

¡Ten prisa! / Hurry up! = ¡WANE'J!

IV) Frases básicas de conversación / Basic phrases of conversation

Si / Yes – JEE'

No / No – JA'II

¿Qué onda? ¿Qué tal? / What's up? What's going on?

= ¿JAS KUB'IJ?

¿Cómo estás? ¿Cómo está Usted? / How are you?

= ¿LA UTZ AWACH? ¿LA UTZ UWACH?

Toy bien, Gracias! / I'm well, thank you.

= UTZ, MALTYOX

¿Y tú? ¿Cómo estás? / And you? How are you?

= ¿AT? ¿LA UTZ AWACH?

Estoy bien también / I am well also

= UTZ CHUKE'

¡Muchas Gracias! / Thank you very much.

= SIB'ALAJ MALTYOX

De nada / You're Welcome

= MAN K'O TA XUB'AN

¿Cómo te llamas? / What's your name?

= ¿JAS ABII'?

Me llamo… / My name is…

 = NUBII'…

¿De dónde eres? / Where are you from?

= ¿JAWICHI' KATPEET WI?

Soy de los Estados Unidos / La Capital (Guat.) / I'm from the
United States / Guatemala City

= PA ESTADOS UNIDOS / ERMITA KINK'AS'IK

¿Cuántos años tienes? / How old are you?

= ¿JANIPA' AJUNAB'?

*Tengo … años / I am … years old

= K'O LIK … JUNAB'

Juun – 1 [hoon]

Keb' – 2 [kehb]

Oxib' – 3 [ohsh-eeb]

Kajib' – 4 [kah-heeb]

Jo'ob – 5 [hoh-ohb]

Waakib' – 6 [wawk-ahb]

Wuqub -7 [wook-oob]

Wajxaqib'– 8 [waw-shahk-eeb]

B'elejeb' – 9 [beh-lehH-ehb]

Lajuuj – 10 [lah-hooH]

Ju'lajuuj – 11 [hoo-lah-hooH]

Keb'lajuuj – 12 [kehb-lah-hooH]

Oxlajuuj – 13 [ohsh-lah-hooH]

Kajlajuuj – 14 [kawH-lahooH]

Jo'lajuuj – 15 [hoh-lahooH]

Waqlajuuj – 16 [wawk-lah-hooH]

Wuqlajuuj – 17 [wook-lah-hooH]

Wajxaqlajuuj – 18 [waw-shahk-lah-hooH]

B'eleejlajuuj – 19 [beh-lehH-lah-hooH]

Junwinaq – 20 [hoon-wee-knuck]

Junwinaq juun – 21

Junwinaq keb' – 22

Junwinaq oxiib' – 23

Junwinaq kajib' – 24

Junwinaq jo'oob' – 25

Junwinaq waaqiib' – 26

Junwinaq wuqub' – 27

Junwinaq wajxaqiib' – 28

Junwinaq b'elejeb' – 29

Juwinaq lajuuj – 30

Ka'winaq – 40 [kuh-wee-knuck]

Ka'winaq lajuuj – 50

Oxk'ajl – 60 [ohsh-kawH-uhl]

Oxk'ajl lajuuj – 70

Jumuch' – 80 [hoomch]

Jumuch' lajuuj – 90 [hoo-mooch…]

Por favor, Dime eso en español / Please, Tell me that in Spanish

= CHATZIJONA' KASTIYA / KAXLAN TZIJ

¿Hablas K'iche'? / Do you speak K'iche'?

= ¿LA KATTZIJONIK QATZIJOB'AL / K'ICHE'?

Yo hablo K'iche' / I speak K'iche'

= IN KINTZIJONIK QATZIJOB'AL / K'ICHE'

No hablo K'iche' / I don't speak K'iche'

= MAN KINTZIJONIK TA QATZIJOB'AL / K'ICHE'

Por favor, Habla lento / Please Speak Slowly

= CHATTZIJONA' NO'JIIM

Por favor, Digáme eso otra vez / Please, Tell me that again = ¡CHAB'IJ CHIK!

¿Qué quieres que yo diga? / What do you want me to say? = ¿JAS KAAWAAJ CHI KINCHA'?

Tú hablas demasiado rápido / You talk to fast

= AT KATTZIJONIK CHANIIM

Lo siento / I'm sorry

= CHINAKUYU'

No entiendo / I don't understand

= MAN KINCH'OMANIK TA / MAN KINTA TA

¿Tú sabes? / Do you know?

= ¿AWETA'M?

¿Tú no sabes? / ¿You don't know?

= ¿MAN AWETA'M TA?

No, no se / No, I don't know

= JA'II, MAN WETA'M TA

No se / I don't know

= JANIK' / NIK' (coll.)

No quiero saber lo que pasó / I don't want to know what happened

= MAN KWAAJ WETA'M CHI XOK'OWIK

No quiero saber / I don't want to know

= MAN KWAAJ WETA'M

¡Vete! ¡Vayase! ¡Vayanse! / Go!

= ¡JAT! [a una persona / to one person] ¡JIX! [a dos o más gente/ to two or more people]

¡Ven acá! ¡Venga acá! ¡Vengan acá! / Come here!

= ¡KATOJO' WARAAL! [a una persona / to one person], ¡KIXOJO' WARAAL! [a dos o más personas / to two or more people]

¿Cuándo tu llegaste? / When did you arrive?

= ¿JAS Q'IIJ XATUUL AT?

Yo llegué ayer / I arrived yesterday

= IWIIR IN XINUL

¿En qué tu trabajas? / What kind of work do you do?

= ¿JAS UWACH CHAK KAB'AN AT?

Soy un… / I work as a…

= IN …

B'ANOL KAXLANWA = (Panadero / Baker)

B'ANOL RIIKI'L = (Cocinero / Cook)

B'ANOL SII' = (Leñador / Someone who collects firewood for the purpose of selling it)

B'ANOL WA = (Tortillera, Tamalera / Someone who makes tortillas for a living)

B'ANOL XAJAB' = (Zapatero / Shoemaker)

B'ANOL PWI' = (Sombrerero / Hat maker)

B'ANOL JA = (Albañil, Constructor / Builder)

Q'AXAL TZIJ = (Traductor / Translator)

¿Adónde vas? / Where are you going?

= ¿JAWI' KATB'E WI?

¿Adónde fuíste? / Where did you go?

= ¿JAWI' XATB'E WI?

¿Adónde van Ustedes? / Where are you all going?

= ¿JAWI' KIXB'E WI?

¿Adónde fueron Ustedes? / Where did you all go?

= ¿JAWI' XIXB'E WI?

¿Con quién fuiste tú? / Who did you go with?

 = ¿JACHINAQ UK' XATB'E WI?

Tengo que ir / I have to go

= RAJAWAXIK KINB'E

Tengo que trabajar / I have to work

= RAJAWAXIK KINCHAKUNIK

Tengo que salir / I have to leave

= RAJAWAXIK KINEEL

Tengo que hacerlo / I have to do it

= RAJAWAXIK KINB'ANO

Voy a regresar / I will return

= KINTZALIJ

Voy a regresar otra vez / I will return again

= KINTZALIJ CHIK

Voy a regresar mañana / I will return tomorrow

= KINTZALIJ CHIK CHWE'Q

Voy a regresar en el próximo año / I will return next year

= KINTZALIJ PA JUNAB' CHIK

Vamos a regresar en el próximo año / We will return next year

= KUJTZALIJ PA JUNAB' CHIK

¿Dónde está el banco? / Where is the bank?

= ¿JAWI' K'O WI B'AANKO?

Llévame al banco / Take me to the bank

= CHINAWUK'AJ WI PA B'AANKO

Necesito cambiar un poco dinero / I need to exchange a little money

= RAJAWAXIK KINK'EXO WE' PWAAQ

Quiero cambiar [canjear] dinero / I want to exchange money

= KWAAJ KINK'EXO WE' PWAAQ

No tengo quetzales / I don't have Quetzales

= MAN K'O TA KETZAL

Quiero quetzales / I want Quetzales

= KWAAJ KETZAAL

¿Dónde está el Mercado [Tienda]? / Where is the market [store]?

= ¿JAWI' K'O WI K'AYIB'AL?

Llévame al Mercado / Take me to the market

= CHINAWUK'AJ WI PA K'AYIB'AL

Necesito comprar comida / I need to buy food

= RAJAWAXIK KINLOQ'O RIIKI'L

Necesito comprar fruta / I need to buy fruit

= RAJAWAXIK KINLOQ'O PRUTA

¿Cuánto cuesta? / How much does it (that) cost?

= ¿JACHINAQ RAJIL?

¿Cuánto te debo? / How much do I owe you?

= ¿JACHINAQ NUK'AS?

No quiero comprar esto / I don't want to buy this

= MAN KWAAJ KINLOQ'O WA'

Sí, lo quiero comprar / Yes, I want to buy it

= JEE', KWAAJ KINLOQ'O WA'

Lo siento, no lo puedo comprar / I'm sorry, I can't buy it

= CHINAKUYU', MAN KWAAJ KINLOQ'O WA'

¿Hay algo más barato? / Is there something a lot cheaper?

= ¿LA K'O LIK JASACH MAS B'ARATO?

No tengo mucho dinero / I don't have much money

= MAN K'O TA K'I PWAAQ

Si yo tuviera dinero suficiente, Yo lo compraría / If I had sufficient money, I would buy it

= WE K'OLIK K'I PWAAQ, KINLOQ'O TA

Me gusta / I like it

= KWAAJ

No me gusta / I don't like it

= MAN KWAAJ

¿Dónde está una tienda que vende…? / Where is there a store that sells…?

= ¿JAWI' K'O WI K'AYIB'AL CHI KAK'AYI…?

ATZYAAQ (Ropa / Clothing)

KAMIXA (Playera, Camisa, Camiseta / shirts, T-shirts)

KASON (Pantalones)

UJQ (Faldas / Skirts)

XAJAB' (Zapatos / Shoes)

RIKI'L (Comida / Food)

ETZ'AB'AL (Juguetes / Toys)

KYEM (Tela; Tejido / Cloth, Fabric, Blankets, Weaved Fabric)

XB'AJB'OJ (Helado / Ice cream)

WUUJ (Libros / Books)

SIPAB'AL / SIPANIK (Regalos / Gifts)

PWI' (Sombreros / Hats)

PUNE'T (Gorras / Caps; Baseball Caps)

Quiero atravesar el lago / I want to cross the lake

= KWAAJ KINQ'AXIK WE' CHO

Queremos atravesar el lago / We want to cross the lake

= KAQAAJ KUJQ'AXIK WE' CHO

Quiero ir a Santiago Atitlán / I want to go to Santiago Atitlán

= KWAAJ KINB'E WI PA SANTYAKO

Queremos ir a Santiago Atitlán / We want to go to Santiago Atitlán

= KAQAAJ KUJB'E WI PA SANTYAKO

¿Cuanto cuesta? / How much does it cost?

= ¿JACHINAQ RAJIL?

Todos mis compañeros quieren ir al mercado para comprar / ver las cosas allá / All of my friends want to go to the market to buy / see the things there

= KONOJEL TAQ WACHI'L KAKAAJ KEB'E PA K'AYIB'AL PA LOQ'OJ / TZU'UJ TAQ JASAACH CHILA'

Tengo hambre / I'm hungry

= KINNUMIK

Tengo sed / I'm thirsty

 = KACHAQI'J NUCHII'

Vamos a buscar comida / Let's look for food

= KUJTZUKUJ RI' RIKI'L

Necesito usar el baño / I need to use the restroom

= RAJAWAXIK KINB'E WI PA CHULUB'AAL

¿Dónde está el baño? / Where is the bathroom?

= ¿JAWI' K'O WI JUN CHULUB'AAL?

Dáme un café, por favor / Give me coffee please

= CHAYA'A' JUN SEL KAPE

Tú ere muy hermoso [-a] / guapo [-a] / You are very beautiful / handsome

= AT QAS JEBEL / AT QAS JE'L

Tu tiene una cara muy linda / You have a very cute face

= AT QAS JEBEL APALAJ

¿Puedo sacar una foto? / I can take a photo?

= ¿LA KINKOWIN KINWELESAJ JUN RACHB'AL?

¿Puedo tomar una foto aquí? / Can I take a photo here?

= ¿LA KINKOWIN KINWELESAJ JUN RACHB'AL WARAAL?

¿Hay un hotel aquí? / Is there a hotel here?

= ¿LA K'O LIK JUN OQXA'NIB'AL PA WA' TINAMIT?

Llévame al Hotel / Take me to the Hotel

= CHINAWUK'AJ WI PA RI' OQXA'NIB'AL

¿Hay un cuarto disponible en cual puedo quedarme / dormir? / Is there a room available in which I can stay / sleep?

= ¿LA K'O WARAB'AL CHI KINKOWIN KINKANAJ / KINWARIK?

¿Cuántas noches quieres quedarse? / How many nights do you want to stay?

= ¿JACHINAQ AQ'AB KAAWAAJ KATKANAJ?

Quiero quedarme aquí por uno / dos / tres noches / I want to stay here for one / two / three nights

= KWAAJ KINKANA JUN / KEB' / OXIB' AQ'AB'

¿Cuánto cuesta el cuarto? / How much does the room cost? = ¿JACHINAQ RAJIL RI' WARAB'AL?

¿Puedo ver el cuarto? / Can I see the room?

= ¿LA KINKOWIN KINWILO RI' WARAB'AL?

No me gusta / I don't like it

= MAN KWAAJ

Me gusta, quiero el cuarto / I like it, I'll take the room

= IN KWAAJ, KWAAJ WA' WARAB'AL

El cuarto es sucio, quiero otro / The room is dirty, I want a different one

= WA' WARAB'AL QAS TZ'IL, KWAAJ MAN JUNAM TAJ WARAB'AL

Todas las sábanas son sucias / All of the sheets are dirty

= KONOJELAL SAWAANA QAS TZ'IL

¿Durmieron Ustedes bien? / Did you all sleep well?

= ¿XIXWARIK UTZ?

No dormí bien / I didn't sleep well

= MAN XINWARIK TA UTZ

¿Porqué? / Why?

= ¿JASCHE…?

Había demasiado ruido / There was too much noise

= K'O QAS JUMUJ PA LE' WARAB'AAL

Quiero salir / I want to leave

= KWAAJ KINEL

¡Vamos a buscar otro dormitorio / hotel! / Let's look for another dormitory / hotel!

= QATZUKUJ NIK'AJ CHIK OQXA'NIB'AL

¿Quieres ir conmigo? / Do you want to go with me?

= ¿LA KAAWAAJ KATB'EK WUK'?

No, no puedo ir contigo / No, I can't go with you

= JA'II, MAN KINKOWIN KINB'E AWUK'

No, no quiero ir contigo / No, I don't want to go with you

= JA'II, MAN KWAAJ KINB'E AWUK'

¿Te puedo ayudar? / Can I help you?

= ¿LA KINKOWIN KATINTO'O?

No te puedo ayudar / I can't help you

= MAN KINKOWIN NATINTO'O

Quiero que me ayudes / I want you to help me

= KWAAJ CHI KINATO'O

Si yo tuviera dinero, te ayudaría / If I had money, I would help
you

= WE K'O PWAAQ, KATINTO'O TA

Si yo tuviera dinero, me iría / If I had money, I would leave =

WE K'O PWAAQ, KINB'E TA

¿Porqué me quieres ayudar? / Why do you want to help me?

= ¿JASCHE KAAWAAJ KINATO'O?

¿Esto es tuyo? / Is this yours?

= ¿LA AWEECH WA'?

Esto no es tuyo / This is not yours

= MAN AWEECH TA WA'

No es mío / It's not mine

= MAN WEECH TA WA'

Sí, es mío / Yes, it's mine

= JEE', WEECH WA'

¿Dónde está la iglesia? / Where is the church?

= ¿JAWI' K'O WI ROCHOCH DIOS?

Llévame a la iglesia / Take me to the church

= CHINAWUK'AJ WI PA ROCHOCH DIOS)

¿Dónde está tu casa? / Where is your house?

= ¿JAWI' K'O WI AWOCHOCH?

Dios te bendiga / God bless you

= DIOS KATRUTEWICHIJ

Dios los bendiga / God bless you all

= DIOS KIXRUTEWICHIJ

Vamos a orar por la comida / Let's pray for this food =
QATYOXIJ WE' RIKI'L

Vamos a orarle a Dios y darle gracias / Let's pray to God and
give thanks

= QATYOXIJ DIOS II QAMALTYOXIJ

Vamos a orar por la comida / Let's pray for this food =
QATYOXIJ PA WE' RIKI'L

Dios es muy Bueno / God is good; God is great

= DIOS QAS UTZ

Dios nos ha bendecido con otro día / God has blessed us with another day

= DIOS TEWICHIM CHAQE RUK' NIK'AJ CHIK Q'IIJ

Te amo / I love you

= KATWAJ

¿Me amas? / Do you love me?

= ¿LA KINAWAJ?

Te quiero besar / I want to kiss you

= KWAAJ KATINTZ'UMAJ

Te quiero abrazar / I want to hug you

= KWAAJ KATINMATZ'EJ

Te quiero envolver bien en mis brazos / I want to wrap you in my arms

= KWAAJ KATINBOTZ'OTZ'OJ PA TAQ NUQ'AB'

Te extrañaré / I will miss you

= KATB'AAN EXTRAÑAR NUMAL

Nunca te voy a olvidar / I will never forget you

= MAJUN MUL KATINSACH PA NUJOLOM

Solo quiero quedarme contigo / I only want to stay with you

= XA KWAAJ KINK'E' AWUK'

V) MANDATOS COMÚNES [Imperativos] / COMMON COMMANDS [Imperatives]:

¡Vete! ¡Vayase! ¡Vayanse! / Go!

= ¡JAT! [a una persona / to one person] ¡JIX! [a dos o más gente/ to two or more people]

¡Ven acá! ¡Venga acá! ¡Vengan acá! / Come here!

= ¡KATOJO' WARAAL! [a una persona / to one person], ¡KIXOJO' WARAAL! [a dos o más personas / to two or more people]

233

¡Ven conmigo! ¡Venga conmigo! ¡Vengan conmigo! / Come with me!

= ¡KATOJO' WUK' [a una persona / to one person] ¡KIXOJO' WUK' [a dos o más personas / to two or more people]

¡Vente! / Come! [coll.]

= ¡TASAJ!

¡Vamos!!! ¡Vayamos!!! / Let's go!!!

= ¡JO'!

¡Vamos a comer!!! / Let's go eat!!!

= ¡KUJWA'OQ!

¡Trabajemos!!! / Let's work!!!

= ¡KUJCHAKUNOQ!

¡Váyase a trabajar!!! / Go to work!!!

= ¡JACHAKUNOQ!!!

¡Hágamoslo!!! / Let's do it!!!

= ¡QAB'ANA!

¡Váyase a hacerlo!!! / Go do it!!!

= ¡JAB'ANA!

¡Hágalo!!! / Do it!!!

= ¡CHAB'ANA'!

¡No lo hagas! / Don't do it!

= ¡ MAN KAB'AN TA!

Hágame un favor / Do me a favor, Please

= CHAB'ANA' JUN UTZIIL

¡Vamos a hacer leña! / Let's collect firewood!

= ¡QAB'ANA' SII'!

¡Vamos a bailar!!! / Let's dance!!!

= ¡QAXOJOWOQ!

¡Dámelo!!! / Give me it!!!

= ¡CHAYA'A'!

Dame dos cafés, Por favor / Give me two coffees, Please

= CHAYA'A' KEB' SEL KAPE

Dame una botella de agua / una gaseosa / Give me a bottle of

water / soda, Please

= CHAYA'A' JUN LIMET JA' / JUN LIMET GASYOSA

¡Beba! / Drink! = ¡CHAWUK'YAJ!

¡Beba agua! / Drink water!

= ¡CHAWUK'YAJ JA'!

¡No me toques! / Don't touch me!

= ¡ MAN KINACHAP TA!

¡Éntrate! / Enter! Come in! = ¡CHAWOKOQ!

¡Abra / Cierre la puerta / la ventana! Open / Close the door / the

window!

= ¡CHAJAQA' / CHATZ'AAPIJ LE' UCHI' JA / LE'

WANTA'N!

Bienvenidos a mi casa / Welcome to my home

= KATINK'ULAJ PA WOCHOCH

Aguárdame aquí / Wait for me here

= CHINAWIYE'J WARAAL

¡Siéntate! / Sit down!

= ¡KAT'UY'ULOQ!

¡Siéntense! / Sit down! [all of you]

= KIXT'UY'ULOQ

Llévame al mercado / Take me to the market

= CHINAWUK'AJ WI PA K'AYIB'AL

VI)   *FRASES DE EMERGENCIA /
EMERGENCY PHRASES:

¡Ayúdame! ¡Ayudenme! / Help me!!!

= ¡CHINATO'O! [a una persona / to one person],

¡CHINITO'O!!! [a dos o más personas / to two or more people]

¡Ten Cuidado!!! / Be Careful!!!

= ¡CHACHAJIJ AWIIB'!

¡No te caígas!!! / Don't Fall!!!

= ¡ MAN KAWOLQ'OLTILA' AWIIB' TA!

¡No me molestes!!! ¡No me chingues!!! / Don't mess with me!!!

= ¡ MAN KINATZUR TA! / ¡ MAN KINANAQ TA!

¡Llama a la Policia!!! / Call the Police!!!

= ¡CHASIK'IJ PATANIL KE / POLISI'Y!

¡Hagálo!!! / Do it!!!

= ¡CHAB'ANA!

Alguién me robó / Someone robbed me

= K'O JUN CHI XINRELEQ'AJ

Alguien hurtó mis pertenecías / Someone stole my things

= K'O JUN CHI XRELEQ'AJ TAQ NUJASACH

¿Dónde está el hospital? / Where is the Hospital?

= ¿JAWI' K'O WI KUNAB'AL RIIB'?

Una serpiente me mordió / A snake bit me

= JUN KUMATZ XINRUTII'O

Un chucho me mordió / A dog bit me

= JUN TZ'I' XINRUTII'O

Estoy sangrando mucho / I'm bleeding very bad

= KEL NUKIK'EL

Sangraba mucho / I was bleeding very bad

= XEL NUKIK'EL

Necesito beber un poco agua / I need water

= RAJAWAXIK KINWUK'YAJ JA'

Estoy enfermo / I'm sick

= IN QAS YAB'

Tengo mucho dolor / I am in a lot of pain

= QAS KINQOXOWIK

(...) me duele / My … hurts

= KAQOXOWIK CHWE […]

AQ; AQAAJ = Lengua / Tongue

AQANAJ (AQAN) = Pierna / Leg

CH'ENCH'KIL = Trasero / Buttocks

CHII'AJ (CHII') = Boca / Mouth

E'AJ (-E) = Diente / Tooth; Teeth

JOLOMAJ (JOLOM) = Cabeza / Head

PAAM = Estomago / Stomach

PALAJ = Cara; Rostro / Face

Q'ABAJ (Q'AB') = Brazo; Mano / Arm; Hand

T'OOT' = Vagina / Vagina

TALE'K = Hombros / Shoulders

TZ'IKIN = Pene / Penis

TZA'M = Nariz / Nose

TZU'M CHII'AJ = Labio / Lip(s)

UWI' AQANAJ = Dedo de pie / Toe

UWI'Q'AB'AJ = Dedo de mano / Finger

WACHAJ [WACH] = Ojo / Eye

WORACHAL = Espalda / Back

-XAAQ AQANAJ = Pie / Foot

XIKINAJ (XIKIN) = Oreja / Ear

Tengo diarrea / I have diarrea

= K'O JA' CHNUPAAM

Tengo diarrea, nausea y vomitos / I have diarrhea, nausea and vomiting

= K'O XA'WEM

Tengo miedo / I'm afraid

= KINXIB'IJ WIIB'

Tenía miedo, Tuve miedo / I was afraid

= XINXIB'IJ WIIB'

No tengas miedo / Don't be afraid

= MAN KAXIB'IJ AWIIB' TA

Llévame al hospital / Take me to the Hospital

= CHINAWUK'AJ WI PA KUNAB'AL RIIB'

Necesito que tu vayas conmigo / I need you to go with me

= RAJAWAXIK KATB'EK WUK'

No puedo caminar / I can't walk

= MAN KINKOWIN KINB'INIK

C) CH'OL

Language name: LAK T'AN / LAK TY'AÑ

Region / Country: TUMBALÁ, CHIAPAS, MÉXICO

Quantity of native speakers: 100,000+

CH'OL VOCABULARY:

Food - Waj

Achiote [Regional Spice] = Jo'ox

Aguardiente [Regional Alcoholic Beverage] = Chicha

Aguardiente [Regional Alcoholic Beverage] = Lembal

Aguardiente [Regional Alcoholic Beverage] = Ts'a'an

Aguardiente [Regional Alcoholic Beverage] = Ya'lel

Atol [Regional non-alcoholic Beverage] = Ul

Banana = Ja'as

Beans = Bu'ul

Black Corn = Chäkchab

Black Corn = Xchäk chab ixim

Black Corn = Yaxum

Bread = Kaxlanwaj

Butter = Lew

Cacao / Cocoa = Käkäw

Caldo [Soup, Broth, Stew] = Ya'lel

Carp = Xk'änchäy

Chayote (Regional Vegetable) = Ch'ijch'um

Chayote (Regional Vegetable) = Ni'uk'

Chayote root [Cueza; Edible Root] = Xko'sin

Chicken = Bi'ti mut

Chicken = Ch'iton mut

Chile = Ich

Cilantro = Kulanta

Cilantro = Xkulante

Coffee = Kajpe'

Coffee = Kajwe'

Coffee = Kape

Corn = Ixim

Corn-on-the-Cob [Elote] = Wajtan

Cow = Wakax

Crab = Mep'

Deer; Venison = Me'

Egg = Tumut

Egg Yolk = K'äñel

Elote [Corn Cob] = Wajtan

Fish [For food or in general] = Chäy

Fruit = Wut

Fruit = Yäk'bal

Garlic = Axux

Garlic = X'axux

Grape = Ts'usub

Honey = Chab

Icecream = Ña'al tsäñal

Juice = Ya'lel

Lobster = Meba' jijch

Mango = Manko

Meat = We'el

Meat = We'eläl

Mushroom [Edible] = K'o'loch

Mustard = Xkulix

Orange = Alaxax

Papaya = Uch'unte'

Peanut = Mañax bu'ul

Pepita [Edible Seed from Squash] = Bäkch'ujm

Peppermint [*Hierbabuena*; Plant] = Araweno

Peppermint [*Hierbabuena*; Plant] = X'araweno

Pig = Chitam

Pineapple = Pajch'

Pork = Chitam

Repollo [Regional Cabbage dish; Coleslaw] = Xuxuk' pimel

Rice = Arus

Salt = Ats'am

Sardine [Fish] = Stsats

Shrimp = Xex

Shrimp = Xun

Sour sop [Guanábana] = K'ätsats

Squash = Ch'ujm

Sugar = Asukal

Sweet Potato / Yam = Ajkum

Taco = K'omoch

Tamale with beans = Pats'

Tomato = Koya'

Tortilla = Waj

Tortilla with beans = Bu'le waj

Tripe = Soyta'

Turkey [Female Domesticated] = Kox, Ña' ak'ache

Turkey [Male Domesticated] = Ajtso', Xpajlek

Venison; Deer = Me'

Water = Ja'

White Corn = Säk waj

Yellow Corn = K'añal

Yellow Tortilla = K'änwaj

Yucca root = Ts'ijn

Zapote [Regional Fruit] = Way ja'as

Zapote Amarillo [Yellow variety] = Pij

Zapote Prieto [Black variety] = I'ik' bä way ja'as

Animals – Bälmate'el

Agutí [Regional Rodent] = Ujchib, Xuchijp

Ant = Xinich'

Armadillo = Ib, Wech, Xwech

Bat = Suts'

Bird = Tsunkay

Boa [Snake] = Uchchan

Butterfly = Pejpem

Cat = Mis

Cockroach = Mako', Pewal

Common Deer = Chijmay, Säkme'

Cow = Wakax

Coyote = Mate'el ts'i'

Crow = I'ik' mut

Crab = Mep'

Deer = Me'

Dog = Ts'i'

Duck = Pech

Eagle = Kolem bä xiye'

Fish = Chäy, Chänil ja'

Fly = Jaj, Us

Fox [in general] = Pajäy

Fox, Grey = Wax

Frog = Chänil ja', Tujts', Xtujte'

Grasshopper = Sajk'

Head lice = Uch', Sakat

Hen [Chicken] = Mut, Ña' mut

Iguana = Kolem p'ok, Juj, Jujl p'ok, Mäch

Insect = Chänil pañimil

Jaguar = Bajlum

Jaguar = Bo'lay

Jaguar = K'än bo'lay

Jaguar = Xik' sajp

Jaguarundi [A black specie of Jaguar] = Stsuk bajlum

Larva [Butterfly] = Xyäx chup

Larva [Mosquito] = Xmänäksi

Larva = Chup

Leopard = Xik' sajp

Lice = Uch', Sakat

Lizard, Female = Xyäx p'ok, Xmanchajk

Lizard, Male = P'ok

Mammal = Bäte'el

Monkey = Bats'

Mosquito = Us

Ocelot [Small Jungle Cat] = Ik'sajp, Tsuk bajlum, Ik'bo'lay

Opossum = Uch

Owl = Pujyu'

Panther = Bajlum

Pig = Chitam

Porcupine = Ch'ix uch

Puma [Mountain Lion] = Chäk bajlum

Quail = Ñakob, Ñakol, Xwak che'e'

Quail, Common = Tojk'ay

Quetzal [Bird] = Xmank'uk', Xkenzal

Rabbit = T'ul

Raccoon = Ejmech

Rat = Tsuk

Red Deer = Xwajch' me'

Roadrunner [Bird] = Ajkunts'u'

Rooster [Chicken] = Kayu, Mut

Salamander [Poisonous] = Ajluk'

Salamander = Ses p'ok

Sardine [Fish] = Stsats

Scorpion = Siñan

Snake = Lukum

Spider = Am

Spider Monkey = Ijk'al max

Squirrel = Chuch, Chäkjocho chuch

Tiger = Bajlum

Toad = Xpekejk, Pokok, Popok, Xpokok

Toucan = Kolem päm

Toucan = Päm

Turkey [in general] = Ak'ach

Turkey, Female = Kox, Ña' ak'ache

Turkey, Male = Ajtso', Xpajlek'

Turkey, Wild = Yäxak'ach

Turtle = Chänil ja'

Tuza [Regional Rodent] = Baj, Ajbaj

Wasp = Xux

Woodpecker [Bird] = Xjuk'te'

Worm = Motso'

People – Winikob

Alcoholic = Xlemoñel

Animal Caretaker = Xkäñä aläl

Assistant = Xkoltaya

Authority = Am bä i yet'el

Authority, Not Indigenous = Yumäl

Blind Person = Xpots'

Boss = Yumäl

Brother [in general] = Yaj

Brother = Eran

Brother = Ermanu

Brother of my Father = Yumijel

Brother, Little = Ijts'in

Brother, Older = Askun

Brother, Older = Äskun

Brother, Step = Majan äskun

Brother, Step = Majan ijti'an

Brother, Younger = Xut

Brother-in-law = Ja'an [of the man]

Caller = Xpäyoñel

Caretaker = Xkäñan

Caretaker = Xkäntaya

Child [of a woman] = Ajt'al

Child, Boy = Alob

Child, Female = Xch'ok

Children = Alpeñelob

Confused Person = Xkajka

Dad = Tata

Daughter, First = Yäx'aläl

Daughter, Oldest = Yäx'aläl

Demon = Ajal

Demon = Ajaw

Demon = Xiba

Devil = Xiba

Disciple = Ajkänt'an

Disciple = Xk'änt'an

Disobedient Person = Xñusat'an

Disorderly Person = Xñusat'an

Elderly Person = Xñox

Employee = Xk'äjnibäyel

Enemy = Kontra

European Woman = Xiñolaj

Evil Spirit = Ajal

Evil Spirit = Ajaw

Evil Spirit = Xiba

Father = Tat

Father = Tatäl

Father, Religious [Priest] = Pale

Girl = Xch'ok

God = Ch'ujutat

Godfather = Jalatat

Godmother = Jalaña'

Government Employee = Xk'äjnibäyel

Grandfather, Paternal = Tatuch

Grandmother = Chuchu'

Grandmother = Ko'äl

Grandmother = Kolaj

Guard = Xk'elojel

Guardian = Xkäñan

Guardian = Xkäntaya

Guest = Jula'

Guide = Xpäsbij

Habitant = Ajchumtäl

Habitant = Xchumtäl

Helper = Xkoltaya

Husband = Ñoxi'al

Husband = Pi'äl

Injured Person with broken bone = Xk'äskujel

Laborer = X'et'el

Lady of the Night = Xmoja

Liar = Xlot

Mama, Mom = Nana

Man = Winik

Man, of the house = Chumte'

Mayor [of town] = Ajkal

Medicine Man = Xwujt

Men = Winikob

Messenger = Ak'jun

Messenger = X'ak'jun

Mom, Mama = Nana

Mother = Ña'

Mother and Father-in-law = Ä'lib (of the woman)

Mother and Father-in-law = Nij'al (of the man)

Mother, Step = Majan Ña'

Mother-in-law = Nij'an ña'

Needy Person = Xk'ajtiya

Neighbor = Pi'äl

Neighbor = Pi'äl tyi chumtäl

Nephew = Bik'ti ijts'in

Nomad = Xchumchumniyel

Obedient Person = Xjak'oñel

Old Person = Xñox

One that always accuses others = Xk'änt'an

One that saves = Ajkoltaya

One who always asks for help = Xk'ajtiya

One who always drinks liquor = Xlemoñel

One who always seeks a wife = Xk'ajtiya

One who calls = Xpäyoñel

One who carries a message = Ak'jun

One who carries money [to pay a debt] = X'ak'bet

One who comes with a message = X'ak'jun

One who cures = Xwujt

One who cuts fruit = Xtuk'oñel

One who delivers messages = X'ak'jun

One who dwells in a certain place = Xchumtäl

One who frequents parties = Ajk'inijel

One who frequents parties = Xk'inijel

One who guards = Xk'elojel

One who guides = Xpäsbij

One who is blind = Xpots'

One who is obedient = Xjak'oñel

One who is of the ethnicity Tzeltal = Amiku

One who is prisoner = Ajkächol

One who is sick = Xk'amäjel

One who lies = Xlot

One who prays = X'alt'an

One who runs = X'ajñel

One who searches for something = Xsäklaya

One who seeks = Xsäklaya

One who sins = Ajmulil

One who sins = Xmulil

One who speaks = X'alt'an

One who spies = Xyojch'oya

One who spies on others = Xchijt

One who steals = Ajxujch'

One who steals = Xujch'

One who takes care of animals = Xkäñä aläl

One who wanders = Xchumchumniyel

One who works on a Finca = Xk'äjnibäyel

One who works or labors = X'et'el

One who writes = Ajts'ijb

One whose bone is broken = Xk'äskujel

Orphan = Meba'

Orphan = Meba' aläl

Outsider, Female = Xiñolaj

Owner of a Finca = Yumäl

Papa = Tata

Party-goer = Ajk'inijel

Party-goer = Xk'inijel

Pastor = Ajsubt'an

People = Winikob

Person = Winik

Person = Kixtañu

Person that cuts fruit = Xtuk'oñel

Preacher = Ajsubt'an

Prisoner = Ajkächol

Prostitute = Xmoja

Robber = Xujch'

Runner = X'ajñel

Sales Clerk = Xchoñoñel

Salesman = Xchoñoñel

Savior = Ajkoltaya

Scribe = Ajts'ijb

Searcher = Xsäklaya

Seeker = Xsäklaya

Shaman = Xwujt

Sick Person = Xk'amäjel

Sinner = Ajmulil

Sinner = Xmulil

Sister = Chich

Sister = Chichäl

Sister, Older = Ñoj chich

Sister, Step = Majan chich

Sister, Step = Majan ijti'an

Sister-in-law = Jawän (of the woman)

Sister-in-law = Mu' (of the man)

Soldier = Soraru

Son, First = Yäx'al

Son, Last = Xutäl

Son, Oldest = Yäx'al

Soothesayer = Xwujt

Speaker = X'alt'an

Spirit of the Forest = Ajal

Spirit of the Forest = Ajaw

Spy = Xchijt

Spy = Xyojch'oya

Teacher = Xkäñtesa

Thief = Ajxujch'

Thief = Xujch'

Tzeltal Person = Amiku

Uncle = Yumijel

Vendor = Xchoñoñel

Warrior = Soraru

Wife = Ijñam

Wife = Pi'äl

Witch = Xwujt

Woman = X'ixik

Woman with long hair = Xtamijol

Woman, Not Indigenous = Xiñolaj

Women = X'ixikob

Worker = X'et'el

Writer = Ajts'ijb

Young girl = Xch'ok

Young Person = Alo'

Younger Brother = Xut

Youngest Son = Xutäl

Places – Ajnibäl tak

Alleyway [in City] = Kayajon

Bathroom = Ts'ämel

Cafetal [Coffee Plantation] = Kajpe'lel

Cafetal [Coffee Plantation] = Kapejol

Cerro Alto [Mountain Range in Tumbalá] = K'uk'wits

Cave = Ch'en

Church = Lesia

Forest (Small) = Te'el

Forest (Large) = Ñojte'el

Home = Otot

House = Otot

Jail= Mäjkibäl

Jail = Ñujpi'bäl

Prison = Mäjkibäl

Prison = Ñujp'ibäl

Land (property) = Lumal

Land (Hot; Arid) = K'ixnilel

Land (Hot; Arid) = Tikwälel

Land (Cold; Barren) = Tsäwan pañimil

Land (Black; Fertil) = Yik'el lum

Mountains = Wits tak

Mountain = Wits

Restroom = Ts'ämel

Road = Bij

Road (Large) = Kolem Bij

Street Corner = Xo'täl

Town = Tejklum

Town = Lum

Valley = Joktäl

Village = Tejklum

Village = Lum

World = Mulawil

World = Pañimil

Nature – Pañimil jini Lak Selol

Ceiba (Tree) = Yäxte'

Cloud = Tokal

Day = K'in

Dew = Tijil

Flint (Stone) = K'äntok'

Flint (Stone) = Tok'

Flower = Bob

Flower = Nichim

Forest (Large) = Ñojte'el

Forest (Small) = Te'el

Laguna = Aban

Laguna = Arayojil

Laguna = Petem

Moon = Uw

Moon, Full = Pomol uw

Mountain = Wits

Mountains = Wits tak

Noche = Ak'älel

Planet = Ñoj ek'

Plant = Tsuy me'

Rain = Ja'al

River (Large) = Kolem ja'

River = Ja'

River = Ñoja'

River = Ñojpa'

Rock = Tun

Rock = Xajlel

Sea = Kolem abal

Sea = Kolem ja'

Sea = Ñajb

Stone = Tun

Stone = Xajlel

Sun = Ch'ujutat

Tree = Te'

Valley = Joktäl

Other Important Words

Abundance = K'amel

Abundance = K'amlel

Abundance = P'ejwlel

Adultery = Ts'i'lel

Agreement = Trato

Ash = Täñäl k'ajk

Basket = Chikib

Bed, Fixed = Ch'ak

Bed, Moveable = Wäyib

Bed, Moveable = Wäyibäl

Book = Jun

Bottle = Limete

Broom = Misujib

Change (Money) = Sujtib

Constipation = Mäkta'

Cry = Uk'el

Dance = Son

Debt = Bet

Destiny = K'otib

Difficulty = Wokol

Disease = Chämel

Disease = K'amäjel

Disease = Wokol

Door (of the house) = Werta

Door = Ñujp'il

Drawing (On Paper) = Ts'ijbal

Embarassment = Kisin

Embarassment = Kisnil

Embarassment = Yäjil

Enclosure [of a house] = Ñejt'il

Excrement = Ta'

Feces = Ta'

Fire = K'ajk

Firewood = Si'

Flavor = Sumuklel

Force = Wersa

Funeral (Place) = Mujkibäl

Funeral (Place) = Mukonibäl

Gift = Majtañäl

Health = K'ok'lel

Hour = Tiempojlel

Joke = Alas t'an

Key = Yabejlel

Knife = Kuchilu

Labor = Yäk'bal

Laughter = Tse'ñal

Letter = Jun

Lie = Lot

Life = Kuxtälel

Light = K'ajk

Light = Säklel

Machete = Machit

Medication = Ts'ak

Medication = Ts'äkal

Medicine = Ts'ak

Medicine = Ts'äkal

Meteorite = Ta'ek'

Money = Tak'in

Mourning (of a child) = Ch'e'lel

Mourning = Uk'el

Noise [from animal or human] = Uk'el

Opening = Kawtilel

Orifice = Kawtilel

Paper = Jun

Peace = Ñäch'chocoya

Peace = Ñäch'tilel

Peace = Yajwälel

Pillow = K'änjoläl

Poison = Chämib

Poison = Chämibäl

Rash = Sal

Rifle = Julonib

Ring = Mätk'äb

Sadness = Ch'ijikniyel

Sadness = Pensar

Sadness = Xäp'äkñäyel

Salvation = Koltäntel

Scissors = Texelex

Scream = Uk'el

Seat = Buchlib

Shame = Kisin

Shame = Kisnil

Shame = Yäjil

Shit = Ta'

Sickness = Chämel

Sickness = K'amäjel

Sickness = Wokol

Sin = Malojlel

Skeleton = Bäkel joläl

Slavery = Mosojil

Sleep = Ñajal

Spanish (Language) = Kastiya

Strength = Wersa

Stupidity = Tontojlel

Table (To eat on) = Yeklib i bäl ñäk'äl

Table, Small (To eat on) = We'te'

Teaching (the act of) = Käntesa

Teaching (the act of) = Käntesäbal

Teaching (the act of) = Käntesaya

Teaching (the act of) = Päsbal

Teaching (the act of) = Toj'ijib

Time = Tiempojlel

Toy = Älas

Toy = Alasäl

Trash = Misujeläl

Vapor = Yowix

Week, Middle of = Uxp'ejk'in

Window = K'elonib

Work = E'tel

Yell = Uk'el

Common Adjectives

Abundant = Sejel

Active = Bäx

Alive = Kuxul

All = Laj

All = Pejtel

All = Pejtelel

All = Petol

Aromatic = Xojokña

Awake = Kañal lak wut

Awake = P'ixil

Bad = Jontol

Bad = Simaron

Beautiful (Sound) = Tsäntsäña

Beautiful = K'ota

Beautiful = T'ojol

Big (Animal, Cargo) = Pittäl

Big = Kolem

Big = Ñoj

Big = Ñuk

Bitter = Ch'aj

Bland (Food) = K'un

Blind = Pots'

Borrowed = Majan

Brave = Ch'ejl

Brave = Ch'ejl i pusik'al

Chosen = Yajkäbil

Clean (House, Room) = Säkpoyan

Clean (Road or Path) = Chäk

Clean (Shirt; Clothing) = Säkpochan

Clean (Vegetation) = Ak'äl

Clean (Water) = Yäx

Clean = Säk

Clear (Luz) = Chäkleman

Clear (Night) = K'inlaw

Clear (Water) = Yäx

Clear = Chäkkolan

Cold = Tsäñä

Cold = Tsäñal

Collective = Tem cha'an

Complete = Ts'äkäl

Content = K'ajakña

Content = Tijikña

Crazy = An a jol

Crunchy = Woch'okña

Cute (Sound) = Tsäntsäña

Cute = K'ota

Cute = T'ojol

Dangerous = Simaron

Dark (Cave) = Ik't'ojñal

Dark (House, Cave) = Ich'ch'ipan

Dark (House, Cave) = Ik'yoch'an

Dark = Ik'jowan

Dark = Mäkäl

Dark = Sämlaw i yik'an

Dead = Chämen

Dead = Sajtem

Deaf = Kojk

Dear = K'uxbibil

Different = Jelchojk

Difficult = Wokol

Dirty (Clothes) = Ik'sowan

Dirty (Face) = Mistuntik

Dirty (Face) = Ta'ta'

Dirty (Liquid) = Tit

Dirty = Bibesäbil

Dirty = Bibi'

Disgusting (Odor) = Xijin

Disgusting = Bi'ijtik

Disobedient = Ñunt'an

Disobedient = Xñusat'an

Disoriented = Ch'älch'älña

Disoriented = Sojkem

Distinct = Jelchojk

Dry (Beans) = Tsäk'ojm

Dry (Beans) = Tsäk'om

Dry (Land) = Chäkbulan

Dry (Road, Wood, Coffee) = Tikin

Dry = Täkin

Durable (Shirt) = Ch'äjy

Easy (very) = Ñuk ñumejach

Easy = Mach wokolik

Edible = K'uxbälel

Edible = K'uxbil

Elected = Yajkäbil

Enough (Men, Animals, Clouds) = Wets'ekña

Enough (Work) = Yilal

Enough (Work) = Yokä

Enough = On

Enough = Ts'iwil

Evil = Jontol

Evil = Simaron

Expensive = Letsem

Extracted = Jots'bil

Faithful = Jump'ejl i pusik'al

Faithful = Xuk'ul

False = Payxo

Fat (very) = Bayakña

Fat = Bontilel

Fat = Jujp'em

Fine = Ts'ubukña

Full = But'ul

Good = Uts

Goofy = Tonto

Ground up = Ts'ubukña

Growing = But'ja'

Guilty = Bäjäch

Handsome = T'ojol

Happy = Tijikña i pusik'al

Healthy = K'ok'

Heavy = Al

Holy = Ch'ujul

Hot (a little) = K'ixin

Hot (atmosphere) = Chäpäkña

Hot (very) = Tikäw

Humble = Umilde

Important = Ñuk

Impossible = Mach mejlik

Imprisioned = Kächäl

Incarcerated = Kächäl

Incredible = Jemachtika

Indigenous = Indigena

Infinite = Läbäkña

Just = Toj

Large = Kolem

Large = Ñoj

Large = Ñuk

Last = Kojix

Last = Wi'ilix

Little (Child, Animal) = Alä to

Loaned = Majan

Loveable = K'uxbibil

Loveable = Uts i pusik'al

Loved = K'uxbibil

Loving = K'uxbibil

Mature = K'än

Mature = K'äñel

Mountainous (Region) = Witsilel

Naked (Chicken) = Bulux

Naked (Child) = Tañal

Naked (in general) = Chakal

Naked (Person, Banana, Corn) = Pits'il

Negative = Kasä

Negative = Käxti

Negative = Kixtä

New = Tsijib

Next = Läk'äl

Obedient = Xjak'oñel

Obscure (Cave) = Ik't'ojñal

Obscure (House, Cave) = Ich'ch'ipan

Obscure (House, Cave) = Ik'yoch'an

Obscure = Mäkäl

Obscure = Sämlaw i yik'an

Old (Object) = Tsukul

Old (Person) = Ñox

Old = Kolib

Only (One of a kind) = Kojon

Only = Bajan

Only = Bajñel

Open (Door of house) = Jajmen

Open (Door of house) = Tokol

Open (Mouth) = Kawakña

Open (Mouth) = Kawal

Other = Yambä

Over-cooked = Echem

Painful = Täk'äkña

Palid (Cold, Clammy) = K'än

Palid (Cold, Clammy) = Säkliban

Passive = K'un

Peaceful (Liquid) = Sämäl

Peaceful (Water, River) = Ts'ämäl

Peaceful = Ch'inch'iña

Peaceful = Ñäjch'em

Pending (Work or Labor) = Kepel

Poor = Obol

Poor = P'ump'un

Poor = Täwäl

Pregnant = Käntäbil

Pretty (Sound) = Tsäntsäña

Pretty = K'ota

Pretty = T'ojol

Quiet (Liquid) = Sämäl

Quiet (Water, River) = Ts'ämäl

Quiet = Ch'inch'iña

Quiet = Ñäjch'em

Rainy = Weswesña

Rebel = Ch'aplom

Reduced = Tsätsä ñu't'ul

Rich = Chumul

Ripe = K'än

Ripe = K'äñel

Round = Selel

Sacred = Ch'ujul

Sad = Ch'ijiyem

Sad = K'uxtayem

Salted (with Salt) = I Yäts'mil

Separated (Feet, Paws) = Xat wa'al

Separated (Feet, Paws) = Xatal

Short (very) = Komatax

Short = Kom

Short = P'ots

Short = Tutsul

Sick = K'am

Silly = Tonto

Skinny (Person) = Yajyaj

Skinny = Jay

Smelly = Chäbäkña

Soft (Wood) = K'unluk'an

Spicy = Ts'a'an

Squared = Joyxujk

Stained = Ta'ta'

Sticky = Ch'äyäkña

Sticky = Läp'

Sticky = Täk'

Sticky = Tsäyäkña

Strong = Wersa

Strong [sound] = Ch'e'

Stupid = Tonto

Sufficient (Men, Animals, Clouds) = Wets'ekña

Sufficient (Work) = Yilal

Sufficient (Work) = Yokä

Sufficient = On

Sufficient = Ts'iwil

Sweet = Chäb

Sweet = Tsaj

Sympathetic = Kuxu i t'ojol

Tall and Skinny = Bilil

Tasty = Sumuk

Tired (Feet, Legs) = Sop'

Tired (Person, Animal) = Lujb

Tired (Person, Animal) = Lujben

Toasted (Tortilla, Wood) = Woch'

Too = Käläx

Tranquil (Liquid) = Sämäl

Tranquil (Water, River) = Ts'ämäl

Tranquil = Ch'inch'iña

Tranquil = Ñäjch'em

True = Isujm

Turbulent (Water) = Wamlaw

Turbulent (Water) = Watlaw

Urgent = Yomojax

Useless (Wood, Land) = Wojts

Violent = Simaron

Weak (Body, Large stick) = K'un

Weak (Body, Large stick) = K'unlitsan

Wet (very; from the morning dew) = Chijlaw

Wet = Ach'

Wet = Ach'esäbil

Very [Emphatic; Emphasis] = Wen

- **Wen** ch'e' i yuk'el jini bats' = The monkey's cry was very strong.

The Body – Bäk'taläl / Pächälel

Ankle = Bik' la kok

Ankle = Wut la kok

Anus = Ch'uyit

Arm = K'äbäl (I k'äb = his arm)

Back = Pat

Beard = Tsukti'

Beard = Tsutsel lak choj

Belly button = Mujk

Blood = Ch'ich'

Body = Bäk'taläl

Body = Pächälel

Bone = Bak'

Breast = Chu'

Breast = Jol chu'

Buttocks = Choj'it

Buttocks = Kolo'it

Buttocks = Ñuchil

Cheek = Choj

Chest = Chu'

Chest = Chu'äl

Dandruff = Xixjol

Ear = Chikin

Eye = Wut

Eyebrow = Mätsab

Face = Wut

Finger (Index) = Tuch'onib

Finger (Middle) = xink'äb

Finger (Pinkie) = Xut laj k'äb

Fingernail = Ejk'ach

Foot = Ok

Hair (On Head) = Tsutsel la kol

Hand = K'äbäl (I k'äb = his hand)

Head = Jol

Heart = Pusik'al

Kidney = Kuchi'tun

Knee = Pix

Leg = Ya'

Lip(s) = Pächälel la kej

Liver = Olmal

Liver = Sot'ot'

Lung = Potsots

Mouth = Ejäl

Mouth = Yej

Muscle = Tomel

Muscle = Ya'

Nail (finger, toe) = Ejk'ach

Nose = Ni'

Saliva = Sits'

Saliva = Tujb

Saliva = Ya'lel la kej

Shoulder = Kejlab

Shoulder = Kejlo

Skin = Pächälel

Stomach = Chuyib

Stomach = Chuyo'

Stomach = Jo'ñal

Stomach = Ñäk'

Tail (Animals) = Ñej

Testicles = Bäk' i yat

Testicles = Tun'at

Testicles = Yat

Thumb = Ña'al laj k'äb

Toe = Yal la kok

Tongue = Ak'

Tooth; Teeth (Front) = Pamäk ej

Tooth; Teeth = Bäkel ejäl

Wing (Bird) = Wich'

Clothing – Pisil, Pislel

Cloth = Pisil

Clothing = Pisil

Dress = P'o'

Earing = Uya'

Fabric = Pisil

Hat = Pixoläl

Pants = -Wex, Wexäl

Sandal(s) = Warach

Shirt = Bujkäl

Shoes = Pats'

Shoes = Xäñäbäl

Skirt = Majtsäl

Weave = Pisil

Colors – Bojnil / Ts'ijbal

Black = I'ik'

Blue = Yäjyäx

Blue, Dark = Yäxmulan

Brown = Moreno

Green - Yäxmulan

Green = Yäjyäx

Green = Yäxel

Brown = Moreno

Orange = Anaranjado

Purple = Yäxmojan

Red = Chäkwa'an

White = Säkchaxan

White = Säkwa'an

White = Säsäk

Yellow = K'änk'än

Yellow = K'äntijan

CH'OL VERBS:

Love = K'uxbin (to Love), K'uxbibil (Loved), Mi K'uxbin (He loves), Tsi' K'uxbi (He loved)

Alleviate = T'ojläwel, T'ojläwem, Mi T'ojläwel, Tsi' T'ojläwi

Arrive here = Julel, Julem, Mi Julel, Tsi' Juli

Arrive there = K'otel, K'otem, Mi K'otel, Tsi' K'oti

Ask = K'ajtin, K'ajtibil, Mi K'ajtin, Tsi' K'ajti

Ask for = K'ajtin, K'ajtibil, Mi K'ajtin, Tsi' K'ajti

Ask for = K'ajtiben, K'ajtibebil, Mi K'ajtiben, Tsi' K'ajtibe

Bathe = Ts'änsan, Ts'änsäbil, Mi Ts'änsan, Tsi' Ts'änsa

Be = An (Añon, Añet, An, etc.) [There is / are…]

Be (Future Tense); Will be = Batika

Be able to = Mejlel, Mejlem, Mi Mejlel, Tsi' Mejli

Be afraid = Bäk'en (Bäk'eñon, Bäk'eñet, Bäk'en, etc.)

Be born = Ilan pañimil, Mi yilan pañimil, Tsi' yila pañimil

Become angry = Mich'an, Mich'äbil, Mi Mich'an, Tsi' Mich'a

Be hungry = Wi'ñal (Wi'ñalon, Wi'ñalet, Wi'ñal, etc.)

Bear (Task or Pain) = Lät', Lät'bil, Mi Lät', Tsi' Lät'ä

Bear (Day of Labor) = Mäl, Mälbil, Mi Mäl, Tsi' Mälä

Boil [food, water] = Ch'äx, Ch'äxbil, Mi Ch'äx, Tsi' Ch'äxä

Bother = Tik'lan, Tik'läbil, Mi Tik'lan, Tsi' Tik'la

Bother (with Words) = Wolts'in, Wolts'ibil, Mi Wolts'in, Tsi' Wolts'i

Bother = Tsil, Mi Tsil, Tsi' Tsili

Bring = Ch'äm Tilel, Mi Ch'äm Tilel, Tsi' Ch'ämä Tilel

Bring = Päy Tilel, Mi Päy Tilel, Tsi' Päyä Tilel

Bring (Person, Animal) = Wets', Wets'bil, Mi Wets', Tsi' Wets'e

Buy = Män, Mämbil, Mi Män, Tsi' Mänä

Carry [something] = Päy Majlel, Mi Päy Majlel, Tsi' Päyä Majlel

Carry [something] (Various Trips) = Bejlan, Mi Bejlan, Tsi' Bejla

Carry [something] (Take) = Ch'äm, Mi Ch'äm, Tsi' Ch'ämä

Carry [something] (In Hand) = Ye', Mi Ye', Tsi' Ye'e

Carry [something] (In Hand) = Ch'äm Majlel, Mi Ch'äm Majlel, Tsi' Ch'ämä Majlel

Change = K'axel, K'axem, Mi K'axel, Tsi' K'axi

Change = K'ex, K'exbil, Mi K'ex, Tsi' K'exe

Change (Money) = Jaw, Jawbil, Mi Jaw, Tsi' Jawä

Change (Place, Color) = Yän, Yämbil, Mi Yän, Tsi' Yänä

Chew something = Jach', Jach'bil, Mi Jach', Tsi' Jach'ä

Choose = Yajkan, Yajkäbil, Mi Yajkan, Tsi' Yajka

Close (House) = Ñup', Ñup'bil, Mi Ñup', Tsi' Ñup'u

Close (Eyes) = Muts', Muts'bil, Mi Muts', Tsi' Muts'u

Close with Key; Lock = Ts'ot, Ts'otbil, Mi Ts'ot, Tsi' Ts'oto

Collect firewood = Cha'len Si', Mi Cha'len Si', Tsi' Cha'le Si'

Come = Tilel, Tilem, Mi Tilel, Tsi' Tili

Come = Tälel, Tälem, Mi Tälel, Tsi' Täli

Come = Tal (Talon, Talet, Tal, etc.)

- ¡La'! = Come!

Cross (vi.) = K'axel, K'axem, Mi K'axel, Tsi' K'axi

Cross something (vt.) = K'axtan, K'axtäbil, Mi K'axtan, Tsi' K'axta

Cry = Uk'el, Mi Yuk'el, Tsi' Yuk'ele

Cry = Mi Cha'len Uk'el, Mi Cha'len Uk'el, Tsi' Cha'le Uk'el

Curse [vi] = Ch'äkojel, Ch'äkojem, Mi Ch'äkojel, Tsi' Ch'äkoji

Curse someone [vt] = Ch'äk, Ch'äkbil, Mi Ch'äk, Tsi' Ch'äkä

Cut (Paper, Cloth, Hair) = Set', Set'bil, Mi Set', Tsi' Set'e

Cut (Round object) = K'ok, K'okbil, Mi K'ok, Tsi' K'oko

Cut (Round object) = Tuk', Tuk'bil, Mi Tuk', Tsi' Tuk'u

Cut into Chunks = P'asun, P'asubil, Mi P'asun, Tsi' P'asu

Cut with Machete or Axe = Jot, Mi Jot, Tsi' Joto

Dance = Cha'len Son, Mi Cha'len Son, Tsi' Cha'le Son

Destroy = Jem, Jembil, Mi Jem, Tsi' Jeme

Destroy = Jisan, Jisäbil, Mi Jisan, Tsi' Jisa

Die = Chämel, Chämen, Mi Chämel, Tsi' Chämi

Diminish = Jubel, Jubem, Mi Jubel, Tsi' Jubi

Disappear = Säk Jilel, Mi Säk Jilel, Tsi' Säkä Jilel

Discover = Tsiktiyel, Tsiktiyem, Mi Tsiktiyel, Tsi' Tsiktiyi

Do = Cha'len, Mi Cha'len, Tsi' Cha'le

Do = Mel, Mi Mel, Tsi' Mele

Do = Tumben, Tumbebil, Mi Tumben, Tsi' Tumbe

Dream = Ñajlen, Ñajlebil, Mi Ñajlen, Tsi' Ñajle

289

Dream = Cha'len ñajal, Mi Cha'len ñajal, Tsi' Cha'le ñajal

Dress oneself = Xoj, Xojbil, Mi Xoj, Tsi' Xojo

Drink = Jap, Mi Jap, Tsi' Japä

Dwell; Live = Chumtäl, Mi Chumtäl, Tsi' Chumle

Grope (with Hand) = Pik'xun, Pik'xubil, Mi Pik'xun, Tsi' Pik'xu

Earn = Chobejtan, Chobejtäbil, Mi Chobejtan, Tsi' Chobejta

Eat = K'ux, Mi K'ux, Tsi' K'uxu

Embarass = Kisnin, Kisnibil, Mi Kisnin, Tsi' Kisni

Embrace = Mek', Mek'bil, Mi Mek', Tsi' Mek'e

End = Ujtesan, Ujtesäbil, Mi Ujtesan, Tsi' Ujtesa

Enter = Ochel, Ochem, Mi Ochel, Tsi' Ochi

Exchange (Money) = Jaw, Jawbil, Mi Jaw, Tsi' Jawä

Exploit = Tojmel, Tojmem, Mi Tojmel, Tsi' Tojmi

Extend = Tsuy, Mi Tsuy, Tsi' Tsuyu

Fall = Yajlel, Yajlem, Mi Yajlel, Tsi' Yajli

Fall in love = Pejkan, Pejkäbil, Mi Pejkan, Tsi' Pejka

Fear = Bäk'ñan, Bäk'ñäbil, Mi Bäk'ñan, Tsi' Bäk'ña

Feed (Animals) = Buk'san, Buk'säbil, Mi Buk'san, Tsi' Buk'sa

Feel = Ubin, Mi Ubin, Tsi' Ubi

Find = Taj, Mi Taj, Tsi' Taja

Finish =Jojmel, Jojmem, Mi Jojmel, Tsi' Jojmi

Fly = Wejlel, Wejlem, Mi Wejlel, Tsi' Wejli

Forget = Ñajätesan, Ñajätesäbil, Mi Ñajätesan, Tsi' Ñajätesa

Gain = Chobejtan, Chobejtäbil, Mi Chobejtan, Tsi' Chobejta

Get Better; Recuperate = Uts'atiyel, Uts'atiyem, Mi Uts'atiyel, Tsi' Uts'atiyi

Get on something = Letsel, Letsem, Mi Letsel, Tsi' Letsi

Give = Äk', Mi Yäk', Tsi' Yäk'ä

Give back = Sutk'in, Sutk'ibil, Mi Sutk'in, Tsi' Sutk'i

Go = Sami (Samiyon, Samiyet, Sami, etc.)

Go = Majlel (Majliyon, Majliyet, Majli, etc.)

- ¡Kuku! = Go!

Go across = K'axtan, K'axtäbil, Mi K'axtan, Tsi' K'axta

Go to bed = Ñolchokon, Ñolchokobil, Mi Ñolchokon, Tsi' Ñolchoko

Go to bed = Tots'chokon, Tots'chokobil, Mi Tots'chokon, Tsi' Tots'choko

Grow = Ñuk'an, Ñuk'äbil, Mi Ñuk'an, Tsi' Ñuk'a

Grow = Kolel, Kolem, Mi Kolel, Tsi' Koli

Guide = Toj'esan, Toj'esäbil, Mi Toj'esan, Tsi' Toj'esa

Happen = Ñusan, Ñusäbil, Mi Ñusan, Tsi' Ñusa

Hate = K'uxkel, K'uxkem, Mi K'uxkel, Tsi' K'uxki

Have = An (Añon, Añet, An, etc.)

Hear = Ubintel, Mi Ubintel, Tsi' Ubinti

- ¡Abi! = Hear!
- ¡Jeyaj! = Hear, Listen!

Help = Koltan, Koltäbil, Mi Koltan, Tsi' Kolta

Help someone = Koltan, Koltäbil, Mi Koltan, Tsi' Kolta

Hide = Muk, Mukbil, Mi Muk, Tsi' Muku

Hide out of sight = Puts'tan, Puts'täbil, Mi Puts'tan, Tsi' Puts'ta

Hit (Person or animal) = Jats', Jats'bil, Mi Jats', Tsi' Jats'ä

Hold [in hand] = Chuk, Chukbil, Mi Chuk, Tsi' Chuku

Hug = Mek', Mek'bil, Mi Mek', Mi Mek'e

Hug = Tul Mek', Tulbil Mek', Mi Tul Mek', Tsi' Tulu Mek'

Hurry = P'ulben, P'ulbebil, Mi P'ulben, Tsi' P'ulbe

Hurry = Sebun, Sebubil, Mi Sebun, Tsi' Sebu

- ¡La'ñun! ¡Se'ñun! = Hurry up! Hurry! Be quick!

Hurt = (K'ux + [Possesional Pronoun + Part of body]) – K'ux k
Pusik'al = My heart hurts

Joke; Tell Jokes = Mi Cha'len Alas T'an, Tsi' Cha'len Alas Tán

Kill = Jisan, Jisäbil, Mi Jisan, Tsi' Jisa

Kill = Tsänsan, Tsänsäbil, Mi Tsänsan, Tsi' Tsänsa

Kiss = Ts'ujts'un, Ts'ujts'ubil, Mi Ts'ujts'un, Tsi' Ts'ujts'u

Kneel = Ñokchokon, Ñokchokobil, Mi Ñokchokon, Tsi'
Ñokchoko

Kneel down (oneself) = Ñoktäl, Mi Ñoktäl, Tsi' Ñokle

Know someone = -Ujil (Kujil, Awujil, Yujil, etc.)

Know something = -Ujil (Kujil, Awujil, Yujil, etc.)

Laugh = Tse'tan, Tse'täbil, Mi Tse'tan, Tsi' Tse'ta

Learn = Kän, Känbil, Mi Kän, Tsi' Känä

Learn = Ñop, Ñopbil, Mi Ñop, Tsi' Ñopo

Learn = Sojlel, Sojlem, Mi Sojlel, Tsi' Sojli

Leave = Lok'el, Lok'em, Mi Lok'el, Tsi' Lok'i

Lie = Äk' Lot, Äk'bil Lot, Mi Yäk' Lot, Tsi' Yäk'ä Lot

Lie = Mi Cha'len Lot, Tsi' Cha'len Lot

Like something = Mulan, Muläbil, Mi Mulan, Tsi' Mula

Listen = Nich'tan, Nich'täbil, Mi Nich'tan, Tsi' Nich'ta

Listen = Ubin, Mi Ubin, Tsi' Ubi

Live = Kuxtiyel, Mi Kuxtiyel, Tsi' Kuxtiyi

Live; Dwell = Chumtäl, Mi Chumtäl, Tsi' Chumle

Look for = Sajkan, Sajkäbil, Mi Sajkan, Tsi' Sajka

Look for = Säklan, Säkläbil, Mi Säklan, Tsi' Säkla

Lose = Bujlel, Bujlem, Mi Bujlel, Tsi' Bujli

Lose = Sajtel, Sajtem, Mi Sajtel, Tsi' Sajti

Love = K'uxbin, K'uxbibil, Mi K'uxbin, Tsi' K'uxbi

Lower = Jubel, Jubem, Mi Jubel, Tsi' Jubi

Make = Cha'len, Cha'lenbil, Mi Cha'len, Tsi' Cha'le

Make = Mel, Mi Mel, Tsi' Mele

Make = Tumben, Tumbebil, Mi Tumben, Tsi' Tumbe

Make s.o. angry = Mich'esan, Mich'esäbil, Mi Mich'esan, Tsi' Mich'esa

Mix = Xäb, Mi Xäb, Tsi' Xäbä

Move (Hand, Machete, Stick) = Pänts'un, Pänts'ubil, Mi Pänts'un, Tsi' Pänts'u

Move oneself = Nijkan, Nijkäbil, Mi Nijkan, Tsi' Nijka

Move oneself = Nijkel, Nijkem, Mi Nijkel, Tsi' Nijki

Need…

- (It is) Necessary = Wersa

Nourish (Animals) = Buk'san, Buk'säbil, Mi Buk'san, Tsi' Buk'sa

Open = Jam, Mi Jam, Tsi' Jamä

Open (Mouth) = Kaw, Mi Kaw, Tsi' Kawä

Open (Eyes) = Kan, Mi Kan, Tsi' Kanä

Paint = Bon, Bombil, Mi Bon, Tsi' Bono

Pay = Toj, Tojbil, Mi Toj, Tsi' Tojo

Pay = Tojolan, Tojoläbil, Mi Tojolan, Tsi' Tojola

Piss = Mi Cha'len Pich, Tsi' Cha'len Pich

Place; Put = K'äkchokon, Mi K'äkchokon, Tsi' K'äkchoko

Play = Mi Cha'len Alas, Tsi' Cha'len Alas

Pray = Ch'ujiyel, Ch'ujiyem, Mi Ch'ujiyel, Tsi' Ch'ujiyi

Pray for = Ch'ujiyel, Ch'ujiyem, Mi Ch'ujiyel, Tsi' Ch'ujiyi

Protect = Lot, Lotbil, Mi Lot, Tsi' Loto

Punch = Bajben, Bajbenbil, Mi Bajben, Tsi' Bajbe

Punch (Person or animal) = Jats', Jats'bil, Mi Jats', Tsi' Jats'ä

Put = K'äkchokon, Mi K'äkchokon, Tsi' K'äkchoko

Rain = Mi Cha'len Ja'al, Tsi' Cha'le Ja'al

Recuperate; Get better = Uts'atiyel, Uts'atiyem, Mi Uts'atiyel,
Tsi' Uts'atiyi

Relieve = T'ojläwel, T'ojläwem, Mi T'ojläwel, Tsi' T'ojläwi

Remain; Stay = Kälel, Kälem, Mi Kälel, Tsi' Käli

Remain; Stay = Yajñel, Yajñem, Mi Yajñel, Tsi' Yajñi

Rest = K'aj la ko, K'ajbil la ko, Mi K'aj la ko, Tsi' K'ajä la ko

Rest (through the night) = Jijlel, Jijlem, Mi Jijlel, Tsi' Jijli

Return = Sujtel, Sujtem, Mi Sujtel, Tsi' Sujti

Return something = Sutk'in, Sutk'ibil, Mi Sutk'in, Tsi' Sutk'i

Save = Koltan, Koltäbil, Mi Koltan, Tsi' Kolta

Say = Al, Älbil, Mi Yäl, Tsi' Yälä

Scratch (Skin) = Lajchin, Lajchibil, Mi Lajchin, Tsi' Lajchi

Scratch (Skin) = Läch, Lächbil, Mi Läch, Tsi' Lächä

Scratch (Head) = Jot', Jot'bil, Mi Jot', Tsi' Jot'o

Search = Sajkan, Sajkäbil, Mi Sajkan, Tsi' Sajka

Search = Säklan, Säkläbil, Mi Säklan, Tsi' Säkla

See = K'el, Mi K'el, Tsi' K'ele

Seek = Sajkan, Sajkäbil, Mi Sajkan, Tsi' Sajka

Seek = Säklan, Säkläbil, Mi Säklan, Tsi' Säkla

Sell = Chon, Chombil, Mi Chon, Tsi' Chono

Send Here = Chok Tilel, Chokbil Tilel, Mi Chok Tilel, Tsi' Choko Tilel

Send There = Chok Majlel, Chokbil Majlel, Mi Chok Tilel, Tsi' Choko Majlel

Send = Wets', Wets'bil, Mi Wets', Tsi' Wets'e

Shame = Low, Lowbil, Mi Low, Tsi' Lowo

Shame oneself = Lojwel, Lojwem, Mi Lojwel, Tsi' Lojwe

Shave oneself = Jujchin, Jujchibil, Mi Jujchin, Tsi' Jujchi

Show = Päs, Päsbil, Mi Päs, Tsi' Päsä

Shut oneself up...

- ¡Ch'äbix! (Imperative)

Shut (House) = Ñup', Ñup'bil, Mi Ñup', Tsi' Ñup'u

Sing = K'äyin, K'äyibil, Mi K'äyin, Tsi' K'äyi

Sing = Mi Cha'len K'ay, Tsi' Cha'le K'ay

295

Sit down = Buchtal, Mi Buchtal, Tsi' Buchle

Sleep = Wäyel, Wäyem, Mi Wäyel, Tsi' Wäyi

Sleep = Mi Cha'len Wäyel, Tsi' Cha'le Wäyel

Smell = Sik', Sik'bil, Mi Sik', Tsi' Sik'i

Smile = Mi Cha'len Tse'ñal, Tsi' Cha'len Tse'ñal

Smoke a cigarrette or cigar = K'ujtsijel, K'ujtsijem, Mi K'ujtsijel, Tsi' K'ujtsiji

Speak = Pejkan, Pejkäbil, Mi Pejkan, Tsi' Pejka

Speak = Mi Cha'len T'an, Tsi' Cha'le T'an

Spend Time = Ñusan Tiempojlel, Mi Ñusan Tiempojlel, Tsi' Ñusa Tiempojlel

Spit = Tujban, Tujbäbil, Mi Tujban, Tsi' Tujba

Stay; Remain = Kälel, Kälem, Mi Kälel, Tsi' Käli

Stay; Remain = Yajñel, Yajñem, Mi Yajñel, Tsi' Yajñi

Stop oneself (Person) = Wa'täl, Mi Wa'täl, Tsi' Wa'le

Stop oneself (Bird) = T'uchtäl, Mi T'uchtäl, Tsi' T'uchle

Swim = Ñuxijel, Ñuxijem, Mi Ñuxijel, Tsi' Ñuxiji

Take [medicine, water] = Uch'en, Mi Uch'en, Tsi' Uch'e

Take [away; something or someone] = Chil, Chilbil, Mi Chil, Tsi' Chili

Take [grab; drag; in hand in order to carry away] = Chuk, Chukbil, Mi Chuk, Tsi' Chuku

Take [out] = Lok', Lok'bil, Mi Lok', Tsi' Lok'o

Take [out] = Lok'san, Lok'säbil, Mi Lok'san, Tsi' Lok'sa

Take [out] = Wets', Wets'bil, Mi Wets', Tsi' Wets'e

Take [out] (Tooth) = Jots', Jots'bil, Mi Jots', Tsi' Jots'o

Take [out] (Water) = Wejk'an, Wejk'äbil, Mi Wejk'an, Tsi' Wejk'a

Take a Foto = Lok' Ejtaläl, Lok'bil Ejtaläl, Mi Lok' Ejtaläl, Tsi' Lok'o Ejtaläl

Take a Foto = Lok' Yejtal, Lok'bil Yejtal, Mi Lok' Yejtal, Tsi' Lok'o Yejtal

Take care of = Käntan, Käntäbil, Mi Käntan, Tsi' Känta

Take care of oneself = Tsajin, Tsajibil, Mi Tsajin, Tsi' Tsaji

Teach = Käntesan, Käntesäbil, Mi Käntesan, Tsi' Käntesa

Teach = Päs, Mi Päs, Tsi' Päsä

Tell Jokes = Mi Cha'len Alas T'an, Tsi' Cha'len Alas T'an

There is / are… = An (Añon, Añet, An, etc.)

Think (vt) = Ña'tan, Ña'täbil, Mi Ña'tan, Tsi' Ña'ta

Think (vi) = Ña'täntel, Ña'täntem, Mi Ña'täntel, Tsi' Ña'tänti

Throw = Chok, Mi Chok, Tsi' Choko

Touch = Täl, Mi Täl, Tsi' Tälä

Touch (Shell, Trompet) = Wus, Mi Wus, Tsi' Wusu

Treat = Jop, Mi Jop, Tsi' Jopo

Turn off = Yäp, Yäpbil, Mi Yäp, Tsi' Yäpä

Understand = Ch'ämben Isujm, Ch'ämbebil Isujm, Mi Ch'ämben Isujm, Tsi' Ch'ämbe Isujm

Understand = Ña'tan, Ña'täbil, Mi Ña'tan, Tsi' Ña'ta

Unite = Ñuts, Ñutsbil, Mi Ñuts, Tsi' Ñutsu

Urinate = Cha'len Pich, Mi Cha'len Pich, Tsi' Cha'le Pich

Wait = Pijtan, Pijtäbil, Mi Pijtan, Tsi' Pijta

Wait (as a prisoner) = Chijtan, Chijtäbil, Mi Chijtan, Tsi' Chijta

Walk = Xäntesan, Xäntesäbil, Mi Xäntesan, Tsi' Xäntesa

Want = -Om (Kom, A wom, Yom, etc.)

Wash (Head) = Jo', Mi Jo', Tsi' Jo'o

Wash (Hands, Face, Dishes) = Pok, Mi Pok, Tsi' Poko

Wash (Clothing) = Wuts', Mi Wuts', Tsi' Wuts'u

Watch = Chäntan, Chäntäbil, Mi Chäntan, Tsi' Chänta

- Look! = ¡Un Tsa'!

Win = Chobejtan, Chobejtäbil, Mi Chobejtan, Tsi' Chobejta

Work = Mi Cha'len E'tel, Tsi' Cha'le E'tel

Wrap = Pix, Mi Pix, Tsi' Pixi

Wrap = Tep, Mi Tep, Tsi' Tepe

Wrap (Creature) = Bäk', Mi Bäk', Tsi' Bäk'ä

Write = Ts'ijban, Ts'ijbäbil, Mi Ts'ijban, Tsi' Ts'ijba

Write = Ts'ijbujel, Ts'ijbujem, Mi Ts'ijbujel, Tsi' Ts'ijbuji

Write = Ts'ijbun, Ts'ijbubil, Mi Ts'ijbun, Tsi' Ts'ijbu

CH'OL PHRASES:

* The order of the phrases are as follows: Spanish / English – Ch'ol Maya (Simplified pronunciation)

*Remember that the 'j' is pronounced like in Spanish like a rough 'h' and in this section the rough throaty 'h' will be presented with 'H'

V)   Hello's and Goodbye's

¡Hola! / Hello! = ¡Kotañet! (Coat-ahn-yet)

¿Qué onda? ¿Qué tal? / What's up? What's going on? = ¿Kojko? (KohH-koh)

¿Como se va? ¿Qué tal? / What's up? What's going on? How are things? = ¿Chuki ma' wäl? [*literally: What do you say?*] (Chew-key mah-wuhl)

¿Estás bien? ¿Cómo estás? / Are you well? How are you? = ¿Añet ba uts'at / wen? (An-yeht buh oodz-uht / wehn)

¡Nos Vemos! / See you again soon! = ¡Mi bä kaj lak k'el! (Mee buh kahH lahk kayl)

¡Adiós! / Goodbye! Bye! = ¡Koto! (Koh-toh)

¡Cuidate! ¡Cuidese! ¡Cuidense! / Take care of yourself! = ¡Tsajin! [singular] ¡Tsajinla! [plural] (Dzah-heen, Dzah-heen-lah)

¡Hasta Mañana! / See you in the morning! = ¡Jinto ti tsijib k'in! (Heen-toh tyee dzee-Heeb keen)

Platicaremos otra vez más tarde / We will chat again later = Mi kaj lojon k pejkan cha' [between two people] / Mi kaj

299

lak pejkan cha' [between 2 or more people] (Mee kahH lohH-ohn kuh pehH-kahn chuh, Mee kahH lahk pehH-kahn chuh)

VI)   Basic phrases of conversation

Si / Yes [affirmative] – Yomäch, Jinkuyi, Jinkwäyi (Yoh-much, Heen-koo-yee, Heenk-wuh-yee)

No / No – Ma', Mach'an, Ma'an (Mah, Mahch-uhn, Mah-uhn)

¡Por Favor! / Please! = ¡A wokolik! (Ah wohk-oh-leek)

¡Por Favor! / Please! = ¡Wokol T'an! (Wohk-kohl tahn)

¡Por Favor! / Please! = ¡Poj! [for limited time] (PohH)

¿Cómo estás? ¿Cómo está Usted? / How are you? – ¿Bajche' a wilal? [informal] ¿Bajche' yilal? [formal] (BawH-cheh ah wee-lahl, BawH-cheh yee-lahl)

¡ 'Toy bien, Gracias! / I'm well, thank you. – ¡Añon wen / uts'at, wokol a wälä! (Ahn-yohn when / oodz-aht, woh-kohl ah wuh-luh)

¿Y tú? ¿Cómo estás? / And you? How are you? - ¿A wik'ot? ¿Bajche' a wilal? (Ah wee-koht…BahH-cheh ah wee-lahl)

Estoy bien también / I am well also – Añon wen ja'el (Anyohn wehn Hah-ehl)

¡Muchas Gracias! / Thank you very much. – ¡Wokolix a wälä! ¡Wokol a wälä! (Wohk-oh-leesh uh wuh-luh, Woh-kohl uh wuh-luh)

De nada / You're Welcome – K'ebto (Kehb-toh)

Éstá bien / All is well – An wen (Ahn when)

¿Cómo te llamas? / What's your name? – ¿Chuki a k'aba'? ¿Bajche' a k'aba'? (Chew-kee ah kah-buh, BahH-cheh ah kah-buh)

Me llamo… / My name is… - J k'aba'… (Juhk-ahb-uh)

No te conozco / I don't know you – Ma'anix mij käñet (Mah-uh-neesh mihH Kuhn-yet)

Tú no me conoces / You don't know me – Ma'anix ma' käñon (Mah-uh-neesh mah kuhn-yohn)

¿De dónde eres? / Where are you from? – ¿Baki talet? ¿Bak talet? (Bah-key tah-leht, Bahk tah-leht)

Soy de los Estados Unidos / Tumbalá (Chiapas) / I'm from the United States / Tumbalá (Chiapas, Mex.) – Cha'an Estados Unidos / Tumbala talon (Chah-uhn…/…tah-lohn)

¿Cuántos años tienes? / How old are you? – ¿Jayp'ejl jabil añet jatet? (High-pehH-uhl hah-beel uh-nyet hah-teht)

*Tengo … años / I am … years old – Añon … jabil (Ah-nyohn … hah-beel)

Jump'ejl – 1 [Hoom-pehH-uhl]

Cha'p'ejl – 2 [Chah-pehH-uhl]

Uxp'ejl – 3 [Oosh-pehH-uhl]

Chämp'ejl – 4 [Chum-pehH-uhl]

Jo'p'ejl – 5 [Hoh-pehH-uhl]

Wäkp'ejl– 6 [Wuhk-pehH-uhl]

Wukp'ejl-7 [Wook-pehH-uhl]

Waxäkp'ejl– 8 [Wah-shuck-pehH-uhl]

301

Bolomp'ejl– 9 [Boh-lohm-pehH-uhl]

Lujump'ejl / Lämp'ejl – 10 [Loo-hoom-pehH-uhl / Luhm-pehH-uhl]

Buluch / Junlujump'ejl – 11 [Boo-looch / Hoon-loo-hoomp-ehH-uhl]

Lajchämp'ejl – 12 [LahH-chump-ehH-uhl]

Uxlujump'ejl – 13 [Oosh-loo-hoomp-ehH-uhl]

Chänlujump'ejl – 14 [Chuhn-loo-hoom-pehH-uhl]

Jo'lujump'ejl – 15 [hoh-loo-hoom-pehH-uhl]

Wäklujump'ejl – 16 [wawk-loo-hoom-pehH-uhl]

Wuklujump'ejl – 17 [wook-loo-hoom-pehH-uhl]

Waxäklujump'ejl – 18 [waw-shahk-loo-hoom-pehH-uhl]

Bolonlujump'ejl – 19 [boh-lohn-loo-hoom-pehH-uhl]

Junk'al – 20 [hoon-kuhl]

Jump'ejl i cha'k'al – 21

Cha'p'ejl i cha'k'al – 22

Uxp'ejl i cha'k'al – 23

Chämp'ejl i cha'k'al – 24

Jo'p'ejl i cha'k'al – 25

Wäkp'ejl i cha'k'al – 26

Wukp'ejl i cha'k'al – 27

Waxäkp'ejl i cha'k'al – 28

Bolomp'ejl i cha'k'al – 29

Lujump'ejl i ch'ak'al – 30

Junlujump'ejl i ch'ak'al – 31

Lajchämp'ejl i cha'k'al – 32

Uxlujump'ejl i cha'k'al – 33

Chänlujump'ejl i cha'k'al – 34

Jo'lujump'ejl i cha'k'al – 35

Wäklujump'ejl i cha'k'al – 36

Wuklujump'ejl i cha'k'al – 37

Waxäklujump'ejl i cha'k'al – 38

Bolomlujump'ejl i cha'k'al – 39

Cha'k'ajl – 40

Jump'ejl yuxk'al – 41

Cha'p'ejl yuxk'al – 42

Uxp'ejl yuxk'al – 43

Chämp'ejl yuxk'al – 44

Jo'p'ejl yuxk'al – 45

Wäkp'ejl yuxk'al – 46

Wukp'ejl yuxk'al – 47

Waxäkp'ejl yuxk'al – 48

Bolomp'ejl yuxk'al – 49

Lujump'ejl yuxk'al – 50

Junlujump'ejl yuxk'al – 51

Lajchämp'ejl yuxk'al – 52

Uxlujump'ejl yuxk'al – 53

Chänlujump'ejl yuxk'al – 54

Jo'lujump'ejl yuxk'al – 55

Wäklujump'ejl yuxk'al – 56

Wuklujump'ejl yuxk'al – 57

Waxäklujump'ejl yuxk'al – 58

Bolomlujump'ejl yuxk'al – 59

Uxk'al – 60

Jump'ejl chänk'al – 61

Cha'p'ejl chänk'al – 62

Uxp'ejl chänk'al – 63

Chämp'ejl chänk'al – 64

Jo'p'ejl chänk'al – 65

Wäkp'ejl chänk'al – 66

Wukp'ejl chänk'al – 67

Waxäkp'ejl chänk'al – 68

Bolomp'ejl chänk'al – 69

Lujump'ejl chänk'al – 70

Junlujump'ejl chänk'al – 71

Lajchämp'ejl chänk'al – 72

Uxlujump'ejl chänk'al – 73

Chänlujump'ejl chänk'al – 74

Jo'lujump'ejl chänk'al – 75

Wäklujump'ejl chänk'al – 76

Wuklujump'ejl chänk'al – 77

Waxäklujump'ejl chänk'al – 78

Bolomlujump'ejl chänk'al – 79

Chänk'al – 80

Jump'ejl jo'k'al – 81

Cha'p'ejl jo'k'al – 82

Uxp'ejl jo'k'al – 83

Chämp'ejl jo'k'al – 84

Jo'p'ejl jo'k'al – 85

Wakp'ejl jo'k'al – 86

Wukp'ejl jo'k'al – 87

Waxäkp'ejl jo'k'al – 88

Bolomp'ejl jo'k'al – 89

Lujump'ejl jo'k'al – 90

Junjump'ejl jo'k'al – 91

Lajchämp'ejl jo'k'al – 92

Uxlujump'ejl jo'k'al – 93

Chänlujump'ejl jo'k'al – 94

Jo'lujump'ejl jo'k'al – 95

Waklujump'ejl jo'k'al – 96

Wuklujump'ejl jo'k'al – 97

Waxäklujump'ejl jo'k'al – 98

Bolomlujump'ejl jo'k'al – 99

Por favor, Dime eso en español / Please, Tell me that in Spanish – Pejkan Kaxlan T'an (PehH-kahn kahsh-lahn tahn)

Yo hablo Ch'ol / I speak Ch'ol – Joñon mik pejkan lak t'an ch'ol (Hoh-nyon meek pehH-kahn lahk tahn chohl)

No hablo Ch'ol / I don't speak Ch'ol – Ma'anix mik pejkan lak t'an ch'ol (Mah-uh-neesh meek pehH-kahn lahk tahn chohl)

Por favor, Habla lento / Please Speak Slowly – Ch'alen t'an ch'ujukña (Chah-lehn tahn chuh-Hoohk-nyah)

Por favor, Digáme eso otra vez / Please, Tell me that again – Alä jini cha' (Ah-luh hee-nee chuh)

¿Qué quieres que yo diga? / What do you want me to say? - ¿Chuki a wom jini mi käl? (Chew-key ah wohm hee-nee mee kuhl)

Tú hablas demasiado rápido / You talk to fast – Jatet ma' ch'alen t'an käläx seb (hah-teht mah chah-lehn tahn kuh-luhsh sehb)

Lo siento, perdoname / I'm sorry, forgive me – Tsak ch'ale malojlel, chili lojwem pusik'al (Dsahk chah-leh mah-lohH-layl, chee-lee lohH-wehm poos-eek-uhl)

No entiendo / I don't understand – Ma'anix mik ch'ämben isujm / Ma'anix mik ña'tan (Mah-uh-neesh meek chumb-ehn ees-oohHm / Mah-uh-neesh meek nyah-tahn)

¿Tú sabes? / Do you know? = ¿A wujil ba? (Ah woo-heel buh)

¿Tú no sabes? / ¿You don't know? = ¿Mach awujilik ba? (Mahch ah-woo-heel-eek buh)

No, no se / No, I don't know = Ma', mach kujilik (Mah, mahch koo-heel-eek)

No quiero saber lo que pasó / I don't want to know what happened = Mach komik kujil jini tsi' ñusa (Mahch kohm-eek koo-heel hee-nee dzee nyoo-suh)

No quiero saber / I don't want to know = Mach komik kujil (Mahch kohm-eek koo-heel)

¡Perdoname! / Excuse me! – ¡Chili lojwem pusik'al! (Chee-lee lohH-wehm poos-ee-kuhl)

¡Ten prisa! ¡Tenga prisa! ¡Apúrate! / Hurry! Be quick! = ¡La'ñun! ¡Se'ñun! (Lah-nyoon, Seh-nyoon)

¡Vete! ¡Vayase! ¡Vayanse! / Go! – ¡Kuku! [a una persona / to one person] ¡Kukula! [a dos o más gente/ to two or more people] (koo-koo … koo-koo-luh)

¡Ven acá! ¡Venga acá! ¡Vengan acá! / Come here! = ¡La' wä'i! [a una persona / to one person], ¡La'la wä'i! [a dos o más personas / to two or more people] (Lah-wuh-ee … Lah-lah-wuh-ee)

¿Cuándo tu llegaste aquí? / When did you arrive here? = ¿Jalaj tsa' k'oti? [arrive there] ¿Jalaj tsa' juli? [arrive here] (Hah-lahH dzah-koh-tee, Hah-lahH dzah hoo-lee)

Yo llegué aquí ayer / I arrived here yesterday = Tsaj k'oti ak'bi [arrive there] Tsak juli ak'bi [arrive here] (DsahH koh-tee ahk-bee, DsahH hoo-lee ahk-bee)

¿En qué tu trabajas? / What kind of work do you do? = ¿Chuki e'tel ma' cha'len jatet? (Chew-key eh-tehl mah-chah-layn hah-teht)

Soy un… / I work as a… = Joñon… (Hoh-nyohn)

Ajcha'len Kaxlanwaj = (Panadero / Baker) [AhH-chah-layn kahsh-lahn-wahH]

Ajtik'an waj = (Cocinero / Cook) [AhH-tee-kahn wahH]

307

Ajcha'len si' = (Leñador / Someone who collects firewood for the purpose of selling it) [AhH-chah-layn see]

Ajcha'len waj = (Tortillera, Tamalera / Someone who makes tortillas for a living) [AhH-chah-layn wahH]

Ajcha'len pats' / xäñäbäl = (Zapatero / Shoemaker) [AhH-chah-layn pahdz / shuhn-yuh-buhl]

Ajcha'len pixoläl = (Sombrerero / Hat maker) [AhH-chah-layn pee-shoh-luhl]

Ajcha'len otoch = (Albañil, Constructor / Builder) [AhH-chah-layn otoch]

¿Adónde vas? / Where are you going? = ¿Bak majliyet? ¿Bak samiyet? (Bahk mahH-lee-yeht, Bahk Sah-mee-yeht)

¿Adónde fuíste? / Where did you go? = ¿Bak tsajniyet? (Bahk dzahH-nee-yeht)

¿Adónde van Ustedes? / Where are you all going? = ¿Bak majliyetla / samiyetla? (Bahk mahH-lee-yeht-luh / sah-mee-yeht-luh)

¿Adónde fueron Ustedes? / Where did you all go? = ¿Bak tsajniyetla? (Bahk dzahH-nee-yeht-luh)

¿Con quién fuiste tú? / Who did you go with? = ¿Majki yik'ot tsajniyet? (MahH-key yee-coat dzahH-nee-yeht)

Tengo que ir / I have to go = Wersa mik majlel, Wersa samiyon, Wersa majliyon (Wayr-suh meek mahH-layl, Wayr-suh sah-mee-yohn, Wayr-suh mahH-lee-yohn)

Tengo que trabajar / I have to work = Wersa mik cha'len e'tel (Wayr-suh meek chah-layn eh-tehl)

Tengo que salir / I have to leave = Wersa mik lok'el (Wayr-suh meek lohk-ayl)

308

Tengo que hacerlo / I have to do it = Wersa mik cha'len (Wayr-suh meek chah-layn)

Voy a regresar / I will return = Mi kaj k sujtel (Mee kahH k-soo-tayl)

Voy a regresar otra vez / I will return again = Mi kaj k sujtel cha' (Mee kahH k-soo-tayl chuh)

Voy a regresar mañana / I will return tomorrow = Mi kaj k sujtel läk'äl k'iin (Mee kahH k-soo-tayl luck-uhl keen)

Voy a regresar en el próximo año / I will return next year = Mi kaj k sujtel tyi läk'äl jabil (Mee kahH k-soo-tayl tyee luck-uhl jah-beel)

Vamos a regresar en el próximo año / We will return next year = Mi kaj k sujtel lojon tyi läk'äl jabil (Mee kahH k-soo-tayl loh-hohn tyee luck-uhl hah-beel)

¿Dónde está el banco? / Where is the bank? = ¿Baki jump'ejl Banko? (Bah-key hoom-pehH-uhl Bahn-koh)

Llévame al banco / Take me to the bank = Päyon majlel tyi jump'ejl Banko (Puh-yohn mahH-layl tyee hoom-pehH-uhl Bahn-koh)

Necesito cambiar un poco dinero / I need to exchange a little money = Yom mik jaw tak'iin (Yohm meek how tahk-een)

Quiero cambiar [canjear] dinero / I want to exchange money = Kom k jaw tak'iin (Kohm kuh-how tahk-een)

No tengo Pesos / I don't have Pesos = Mach'an Pesos (Mahch-ahn Pay-sohs)

Quiero Pesos / I want Pesos = Kom Pesos (Kohm Pay-sohs)

¿Dónde está el Mercado [Tienda]? / Where is the market [store]? = ¿Bak an jump'ejl choñonibäl? (Bahk ahn hoom-pehH-uhl choh-nyohn-ee-buhl)

Llévame al Mercado / Take me to the market = Päyon majlel tyi jump'ejl choñonibäl (Puh-yohn mahH-layl tyee hoom-pehH-uhl choh-nyohn-ee-buhl)

Necesito comprar comida / I need to buy food = Yom mik män waj (Yohm meek muhn wahH)

Necesito comprar fruta / I need to buy fruit = Yom mik män wut / yäk'bal (Yohm meek muhn woot / yuck-bahl)

¿Qué es eso? ¿Qué es esto? / What is that? What is this? What is it? = ¿Chuki an? (Chew-key ahn)

¿Cuánto cuesta? / How much does it (that) cost? = ¿Bajche' i tojol? (BahH-cheh ee toh-hole)

¿Cuánto te debo? / How much do I owe you? = ¿Bajche' k bet? (BahH-cheh kuh-beht)

No quiero comprar esto / I don't want to buy this = Mach komik män jini (Mahch kohm-eek muhn hee-knee)

Sí, lo quiero comprar / Yes, I want to buy it = Yomäch, kom män (Yoh-much, kohm muhn)

Lo siento, no lo puedo comprar / I'm sorry, I can't buy it = Chili lojwem pusik'al, mach mejlik män jini (Chee-lee lohH-waym poos-ee-kahl, mahch mehH-leek muhn)

¿Hay algo más barato? / Is there something a lot cheaper? = ¿Am ba jump'ejl bej barato? (Ahm buh hoom-pehH-uhl behH buh-rah-toh)

No tengo mucho dinero / I don't have much money = Mach'an bajk'äl tak'iin (Mahch-ahn bahH-kuhl tah-keen)

Si yo tuviera dinero suficiente, Yo lo compraría / If I had sufficient money, I would buy it = An ku bajk'äl tak'iin, jini mik män (Ahn koo bahH-kuhl tah-keen, hee-nee meek muhn)

Me gusta / I like it = Kom (Kohm)

No me gusta / I don't like it = Mach komik (Mahch-kohm-eek)

¿Dónde está una tienda que vende…? / Where is there a store that sells…? = ¿Bak an jump'ejl choñonibäl jini mi chon…? (Bahk ahn hoom-pehH-uhl choh-nyohn-ee-buhl hee-knee mee chohn…)

Pisil, Pislel (Ropa / Clothing) [pee-seel, pees-layl]

Bujkäl (Playera, Camisa, Camiseta / shirts, T-shirts) [BoohH-kuhl]

Wexäl (Pantalones / Pants) [Weh-shuhl]

Majtsäl (Faldas / Skirts) [MahH-dzuhl]

Pats' (Zapatos / Shoes) [Pahdz]

Xäñäbäl (Zapatos / Shoes) [Shuhn-yuhn-ee-buhl]

Waj (Comida / Food) [WahH]

Alasäl (Juguetes / Toys) [Ah-luh-suhl]

Pisil, Pislel (Tela; Tejido / Cloth, Fabric, Blankets, Weaved Fabric) [Pee-seel, Pees-layl]

Ña'al tsäñal (Helado / Ice cream) [Nya-uhl dzuh-nyuhl]

Jun tak (Libros / Books) [Hoon tahk]

Majtañäl tak (Regalos / Gifts) [MahH-tahn-yuhl tahk]

Pixoläl tak (Sombreros / Hats) [Peesh-oh-luhl tahk]

Quiero atravesar el río / I want to cross the river = Kom k'ätel jini ñoja' (Kohm cut-ayl hee-knee nyohH-huh)

Queremos atravesar el río / We want to cross the lake = Kom lojon k'ätel jini ñoja' (Kohm loh-hohn cut-ayl hee-knee nyohH-huh)

¿Cuanto cuesta? / How much does it cost? = ¿Bajche' i tojol? (BahH-cheh ee toh-hole)

Todos mis compañeros quieren ir al mercado para comprar / ver las cosas allá / All of my friends want to go to the market to buy / see the things there = Pejtel k pi'älob yomob majlel tyi jump'ejl choñonibäl yik'ot mi mänob / mi k'elob bäl ya' (PehH-tehl kuh-pee-uhl-ohb yoh-mohb mahH-layl tyee hoom-pehH-uhl choh-nyohn-ee-buhl yee-koht mee muhn-ohb / mee kayl-ohb buhl yah)

Tengo hambre / I'm hungry = An wi'ñal (Ahn wee-nyahl)

Tengo sed / I'm thirsty = Yom mik jap (Yohm meek hahp)

Vamos a buscar comida / Let's look for food = Mi kaj lak sajkan waj (Mee kahH lahk sahH-kahn wahH)

Necesito usar el baño / I need to use the restroom = Yom mik majlel tyi ts'ämel (Yohm meek mahH-layl tyee dzuhm-ehl)

¿Dónde está el baño? / Where is the bathroom? = ¿Baki an jump'ejl ts'ämel? (Bah-key ahn hoom-pehH-uhl dzuhm-ehl)

Dáme un café, por favor / Give me coffee please = Äk'äyon junwejt kajpe', awokolik (Uh-kuh-yohn hoon-wehHt kaw-peh, uh-woh-kohl-eek)

Dános dos cafés, por favor / Give us two coffees, please = Äk'äyon lojon cha'wejt kajpe', awokolik (Uh-kuh-yohn loh-hohn chah-wehHt kaw-peh, uh-who-kohl-eek)

Dáme un café para salir / One coffee to go = Äk'äyon junwejt kajpe' jini mi mejlel k päy majlel kik'ot (Uh-kuh-yohn hoon-wehHt kaw-peh hee-nee mee mehH-layl kuh-puh-ee mahH-layl kee-coat)

Tú ere muy hermoso [-a] / guapo [-a] / You are very beautiful / handsome = Jatet t'ojol (Hah-teht tuh-oh-hole)

Tu tiene una cara muy linda / You have a very cute face = A wut t'ojol (Ah woot tuh-oh-hole)

¿Puedo sacar una foto? / I can take a photo? = ¿Mik mejlel ba lok' jump'ejl ejtaläl? (Meek mehH-layl buh lohk hoom-pehH-uhl ehH-tuh-luhl)

¿Puedo tomar una foto aquí o no? / Can I take a photo here or no? = ¿Mik mejlel ba lok' jump'ejl ejtaläl wä'i o mach mejlik? (Meek mehH-layl buh lohk hoom-pehH-uhl ehH-tuh-luhl wuh-ee oh mahch mehH-leek)

¿Hay un dormitorio o hotel aquí? / Is there a dormitory or hotel here? = ¿Am ba jump'ejl Otel wä'i?   (Ahm buh hoom-pehH-uhl Oh-tehl wuh-ee)

Llévame al Dormitorio o Hotel / Take me to the Dormitory or Hotel = Päyon majlel tyi Otel (Puh-yohn mahH-layl tyee oh-tehl)

¿Hay un cuarto disponible en cual puedo quedarme / dormir? / Is there a room available in which I can stay / sleep? = ¿Am ba jump'ejl tsaläl baki mi mejlel k yajñel / k wäyel? (Ahm buh hoom-pehH-ehl bah-key mee mehH-layl kyahH-nyehl / kuh-wuh-yehl)

¿Cuántas noches quieres quedarse? / How many nights do you want to stay? = ¿Bajche' ak'älelob a wom a yajñel wä'i? (BahH-cheh ahk-uhl-lehl-ohb ah wohm ah yahH-nyehl wuh-ee)

Quiero quedarme aquí por uno / dos / tres noches / I want to stay here for one / two / three nights = Kom k yajñel wä'i tyi jump'ejl / cha'p'ejl / uxp'ejl ak'älelob (Kohm kyahH-nyehl wuh-ee tyee hoom-pehH-uhl / chah-pehH-uhl / oosh-pehH-uhl ahk-uhl-lehl-ohb)

¿Cuánto cuesta el cuarto? / How much does the room cost? = ¿Bajche' i tojol jump'ejl tsaläl? (BahH-cheh ee toh-hole hoom-pehH-uhl dzahl-luhl)

¿Puedo ver el cuarto? / Can I see the room? = ¿Mi mejlel ba k'el jini tsaläl? (Mee mehH-layl buh kayl hee-nee dzahl-luhl)

No me gusta / I don't like it = Mach komik (Mahch kohm-eek)

Me gusta, quiero el cuarto / I like it, I'll take the room = Uts tsaläl, kom tsaläl (Oodz dzahl-luhl, kohm dzahl-lahl)

El cuarto es sucio, quiero otro / The room is dirty, I want a different one = Tsaläl bibesäbil, Kom yambä tsaläl (Dzahl-luhl bee-beh-suh-beel, kohm yahm-buh dzahl-luhl)

Todas las sábanas son sucias / All of the sheets are dirty = Pejtel sabanajob ik'sowan

(PehH-tehl suh-bahn-uh-hobe eek-soh-wahn)

¿Durmieron Ustedes bien? / Did you all sleep well? = ¿Tzi' la' wäyel utz? (Dzee-lah wuh-yehl oodz)

No dormí bien / I didn't sleep well = Ma'anix tsak' wäyel utz (Mah-ah-neesh dzahk-wuh-yehl oodz)

¿Porqué? / Why? = ¿Chukoch…? (Chew-coach…)

Había demasiado ruido / There was too much noise = Ma'anik ch'inch'iña ajnibäl (Mah-ah-neek chuh-eench-ee-nyuh aw-knee-buhl)

Quiero salir / I want to leave = Kom lok'el (Kohm loh-kayl)

314

¡Vamos a buscar otro dormitorio / hotel! / Let's look for another dormitory / hotel! = Mi kaj lojon k säklan yambä Otel (Mee kahH loh-hohn kuh-suck-lahn yahm-buh Óh-tehl)

¿Quieres ir conmigo? / Do you want to go with me? = ¿A wom ba majlel kik'ot? (Ah wohm buh mahH-layl key-koht)

No, no puedo ir contigo / No, I can't go with you = Ma', Ma'anix mejli k majlel a wik'ot (Mah, Mah-uh-neesh mehH-lee kuh mahH-layl ah-wee-koht)

No, no quiero ir contigo / No, I don't want to go with you = Ma', Mach komik majlel awik'ot (Mah, Mahch kohm-eek mahH-layl ah-wee-coat)

¿Te puedo ayudar? / Can I help you? =¿Mik mejlel j koltañet? (meek mehH-layl huh-kohl-tahn-yeht)

No te puedo ayudar / I can't help you = Mach mejlik j koltañet (Mahch mehH-leek huh-kohl-tahn-yeht)

Quiero que me ayudes / I want you to help me = Kom jini ma' koltañon (Kohm hee-knee mah kohl-tahn-nyohn)

Si yo tuviera dinero, te ayudaría / If I had money, I would help you = An ku bajkäl tak'in, mi kaj j koltañet (Ahn koo bahH-kuhl tahk-een, mee kahH huh-kohl-tahn-yeht)

Si yo tuviera dinero, me iría / If I had money, I would leave = An ku bajkäl tak'in, mi kaj k lok'el (Ahn koo bahH-kuhl tahk-een, mee kahH kuh lohk-ayl)

¿Porqué me quieres ayudar? / Why do you want to help me? = ¿Chukoch a wom a koltañon? (Chew-coach ah wohm ah kohl-tahn-yohn)

¿Esto es [sustantivo] tuyo? / Is this your [noun]? = ¿Am ba a … jatet? (Ahm buh ah … Hah-teht)

Esto no es [sustantivo] tuyo / This is not your [noun] = Mach'an a … (Mah-chuh-ahn ah …)

315

No es [sustantivo] mío / It's not my [noun] = Ma', ma'anik k/j… (Mah mah-ahn-eek kuh/huh…)

Sí, es [sustantivo] mío / Yes, it's my [noun] = Yomäch, k/j … (yoh-much, kuh/huh…)

Ojalá tengas un buen día / I hope you have a good day = Aniket uts k'in (Ahn-ee-keht oodz keen)

Ojalá puedas venir / I hope you can come = Mejliket tälel (MehH-lee-keht tuh-lehl)

Ojalá yo pueda encontrarlo / I hope I can find it = Mejlikon taj (MehH-lee-kohn tahH)

Ojalá no llueva hoy / Hopefully it doesn't rain today = Ame täliket ja'al (Ah-meh tuhl-ee-keht hah-ahl)

¿Dónde está la iglesia? / Where is the church? = ¿Baki an jump'ejl lesia? (Bah-key ahn hoom-pehH-uhl leh-see-yah)

Llévame a la iglesia / Take me to the church = Päyon majlel tyi jump'ejl lesia (Puh-yohn mahH-layl tyee hoom-pehH-uhl leh-see-yah)

¿Dónde está tu casa? / Where is your house? = ¿Bak an a wotot? (Bahk ahn ah woh-toht)

Dios te bendiga / God bless you = Ch'ujutat mi kaji yäk'et uts (Choo-hoo-taht mee kahH-ee yuck-eht oodz)

Dios los bendiga / God bless you all = Ch'ujutat mi kaji yäk'etla uts (Choo-hoo- that mee kahH-ee yuck-eht-lah oodz)

Vamos a orar por la comida / Let's pray for this food = Mi kaj lak ch'ujiyel tyi jini waj (Mee kahH lahk choo-hee-yell tyee hee-nee-wahH)

Vamos a orarle a Dios y darle gracias / Let's pray to God and give thanks = Mi kaj lak ch'ujiyel yik'ot mi kaj la käk' wokolix a wälä tyi Ch'ujutat (Mee kahH lahk chew-hee-yell yee-coat mee kahH lah cuck-woke-oh-leesh uh wuh-luh tyee chew-hoo-taht)

Dios es muy Bueno / God is good; God is great = Ch'ujutat Uts (Chew-who-taht oodz)

Dios nos ha bendecido con otro día / God has blessed us with another day = Ch'ujutat tsi' yäk'äyon lojon yambä k'iin (Chew-hoo-taht dzee yuck-uh-yohn loh-hohn yahm-buh keen)

Te amo / I love you = Mij k'uxbiñet (MeeH koosh-bean-yeht)

¿Me amas? / Do you love me? = ¿Ma' k'uxbiñon ba? (Mah koosh-bean-nyohn buh)

Te quiero besar / I want to kiss you = Kom k ts'ujts'unet (Kohm kuh dzoohH-dzoohn-eht)

Te quiero abrazar / I want to hug you = Kom k mek'et (Kohm kuh mehk-eht)

Te quiero envolver bien en mis brazos / I want to wrap you in my arms = Kom k pixet tyi j k'äb (Kohm kuh-peesh-eht tyee huh-kuhb)

Te extraño mucho / I miss you very much = An to yom k pusik'al bäjñel jini jatet kik'ot (Ahn toh yohm kuh-poos-ee-kuhl buhH-nyehl hee-nee hah-teht kee-coat)

Nunca te boy a olvidar / I will never forget you = Ma'anix mi kaj k ñajätesañet (Mah-ah-neesh mee kahH kuh-nyah-huht-eh-sah-nyeht)

Solo quiero quedarme a tu lado / I only want to stay at your side = Kom k yajñel tyi a t'ejl (Kohm kuh-yahH-nyehl tyee ah tehH-uhl)

VII)   COMMON COMMANDS [Imperatives]:

¡Vete! ¡Vayase! ¡Vayanse! / Go! – ¡Kuku! [a una persona / to one person] ¡Kukula! [a dos o más gente/ to two or more people] (koo-koo … koo-koo-luh)

¡Ven acá! ¡Venga acá! ¡Vengan acá! / Come here! = ¡La' wä'i! [a una persona / to one person], ¡La'la wä'i! [a dos o más personas / to two or more people] (Lah wuh-ee……Lah-luh wuh-ee)

¡Ven conmigo! ¡Venga conmigo! ¡Vengan conmigo! / Come with me! = ¡La' kik'ot [a una persona / to one person] ¡La'la kik'ot [a dos o más personas / to two or more people] (Lah keek-oht…Lah-luh keek-oht)

¡Vamos!!! ¡Vayamos!!! / Let's go!!! = ¡Konla! (Kohn-lah)

¡Vamos a comer!!! / Let's go eat!!! = ¡Mi lak k'ux!!! (Mee lahk koohsh)

¡Trabajemos!!! / Let's work!!! = ¡Mi lak cha'len e'tel!!! (Mee lahk chah-lehn eh-tehl)

¡Váyase a trabajar!!! / Go to work!!! = ¡Kuku, cha'len e'tel!!! (Koo-koo, chah-lehn eh-tehl)

¡Hágamoslo!!! / Let's do it!!! = ¡Mi lak mel!!! (Mee lahk mehl)

¡Váyase a hacerlo!!! / Go do it!!! = ¡Kuku, Mele / Cha'len!!! (coo-coo, Meh-leh / Chah-lehn)

¡Hágalo!!! / Do it!!! = ¡Cha'len!!! ¡Mele!!! (Chah-lehn, Meh-leh)

¡No lo hagas! / Don't do it! = ¡Mach a mel! (Mahch ah mehl)

318

¡Vamos a hacerlo!!! / Let's do it!!! = Mi kaj lojon k cha'len (Mee kahH loh-hohn kuh-chah-layn)

¡Vamos a hacer leña! / Let's collect firewood! = ¡Me kaj lojon k cha'len si' (Mee kahH loh-hohn kuh-chah-layn see)

¡Vamos a bailar!!! / Let's dance!!! = ¡Mi kaj lojon k cha'len son! (Mee kahH loh-hohn kuh-chah-layn sohn)

¡Dámelo!!! / Give me it!!! = ¡Äk'ä!!! (Ah-kuh)

Dame dos aguardientes, Por favor / Give me two aguardientes [Regional alcoholic beverage], Please = Äk'äyon cha'wejt lembal tak (Ah-kuh-yohn chah-wehHt lehm-bahl tahk)

Dame una botella de agua / una gaseosa / Give me a bottle of water / soda, Please = Äk'äyon jump'ejl limete ja' / refresko (Ah-kuh-yohn Hoom-pehH-uhl lee-meh-teh hah / reh-freh-skoh)

¡Beba! / Drink! = ¡Japä! (Hah-puh)

¡Beba agua! / Drink water! = ¡Japä ja'! (hah-puh hah)

¡No me toques! / Don't touch me! = ¡Mach a täl! (Mahch ah tuhl)

¡Éntrate! ¡Éntrese! ¡Éntrense! / Enter! Come in! = ¡Ochen! ¡Ochenla! (Oh-chehn / Oh-chehn-lah)

Aguárdame aquí / Wait for me here = Pijtañon wä'i (PeehH-tuhn-nyohn wuh-ee)

Llévame al mercado / Take me to the market = Päyon majlel tyi choñonibäl (Puy-yohn mahH-layl tyee choh-nyohn-nee-buhl)

VIII) EMERGENCY PHRASES:

¡Ayúdame! ¡Ayudenme! / Help me!!! – ¡Koltañon!!! [a una persona / to one person], ¡Koltanlayon'!!! [a dos o más personas / to two or more people] (Kohl-tahn-nyohn, Kohl-tahn-lahn-nyohn)

¡Ten Cuidado! ¡Tengan Cuidado! / Be Careful!!! = ¡Tsajin! ¡Tsajinla! (Dzah-heen, Dzah-heen-luh)

¡No te caígas!!! / Don't Fall!!! = ¡Ame yajliket!!! (Mah cot-pah-hee)

¡No me molestes!!! ¡No me chingues!!! / Don't mess with me!!! = ¡Mach a tik'lañon!!! (Mahch ah-teek-lah-nyohn)

¡Llama a la Policia!!! / Call the Police!!! – ¡Päy / Lich'k'äban [signaling] juntikil Polisía!!! (Puh-ee / Leech-kuh-bahn hoon-tee-keel Pohl-ee-sée-yah)

¡Hagálo!!! / Do it!!! = ¡Cha'len!!! (Chah-layn)

Alguién me robó, alguien hurtó mis pertenecías / Someone robbed me, someone stole my things – Juntikil tsi' xujch'iyon (Hoon-tee-keel dzee-shuhH-chee-yohn)

¿Dónde está el hospital? / Where is the Hospital? – ¿Bakii jump'ejl ts'ak ajnibäl [Ospital]? (Bah-key hoom-pehH-uhl dzuh-ahk aw-nee-buhl [Oh-spee-tahl])

Una serpiente me mordió / A snake bit me = Junkojt lukum tsi' ch'ojoyon (hoon-kohHt loo-koom dzee-chohH-oh-yohn)

Un chucho me mordió / A dog bit me = Junkojt ts'i' tsi' ch'ojoyon (hoon-kohHt Dzih dzee-chohH-oh-yohn)

Estoy sangrando mucho / I'm bleeding very bad – Woli' lok'el ch'ich' bäjñel (Woh-leek loh-kayl chuh-each buhH-nyehl)

Necesito beber un poco agua / I need water = Yom mik jap junwejt ja' (Yohm meek hahp hoon-wehHt Hah)

Estoy enfermo / I'm sick = K'amon; Joñon xk'amäjel (Kuh-mohn; Hoh-nyohn shkahm-uh-hayl)

Tengo mucho dolor / I am in a lot of pain = K'ux bäjñel (Kuh-oosh buhH-nyehl)

(...) me duele / My ... hurts = K'ux [...] (Kuh-oosh)

- Example: K'ux k jol [hurts-my head] = Me duele la cabeza /My head hurts

Ak' [Ahk] = Lengua / Tongue

Ya' [Yah] = Pierna / Leg

Ejäl; Yej [EhH-uhl; YehH] = Boca / Mouth

Bäkel ejäl [Buck-uhl ehH-uhl] = Diente / Tooth; Teeth

Pat [Paht] = Espalda / Back

Chuyib; Jo'ñal; Ñäk'; Chuyo' (Choo-yeeb; Hoh-nyahl; Ñuhk; Choo-yoh) [pahn] = Estomago / Stomach

Wut [woot] = Cara; Rostro / Face

K'äbäl [Kuh-uh-buhl] = Brazo; Mano / Arm; Hand

Ok [Ohk] = Pie / Foot

Yal la kok [Yahl lah kohk] = Dedo de pie / Toe

Kejlo' [kehH-low] = Hombros / Shoulders

Pächälel la kej [Puh-chuhl-ayl lah kehH] = Labio / Lip(s)

Ni' [knee] = Nariz / Nose

Wut [woot] = Ojo / Eye

Jol [hole] = Cabeza / Head

Chikin [Cheek-een] = Oreja / Ear

Ch'uyit [chuh-oo-yeet] = Trasero / Buttocks

Tengo diarrea / I have diarrea = An tukñäk' (Ahn tewk-nyuhk)

Tengo diarrea y vomitos = An tukñäk' yik'ot xej (Ahn tewk-nyuhk yee-coat shehH)

Tengo miedo / I'm afraid = An bäken tyi k pusik'al (Ahn buh-cane tyee kuh-poos-ee-kuhl)

Tenía miedo, Tuve miedo / I was afraid = An bäken tyi k pusik'al wajalix (Ahn buh-cane tyee kuh-poos-ee-kuhl wah-huh-leesh)

No tengas miedo / Don't be afraid = Ame aniket bäken (Ah-meh ah-nee-keht buh-cane)

Llévame al hospital / Take me to the Hospital – Päyon majlel tyi ts'ak ajnibäl (Puh-yohn mahH-layl tyee dzuh-ahk aw-nee-buhl)

D) YUCATEC

Language name: MAAYAT'AAN

Region / Country: LA PENÍNSULA DE YUCATÁN, MÉXICO & PARTS OF BELIZE AND QUINTANA ROO

Quantity of native speakers: 900,000+

YUCATEC VOCABULARY:

FOOD – O'OCH / WAAJ

ACHIOTE [SPICE] = K'UXU' / K'IWI'

AGAVE = KI

AGUARDIENTE [LIQUOR] = AANIS

ATOL = SA'

ATOL = SAKSA'

AVOCADO = OON

BANANA = JA'AS

BEAN, LIMA = IIB

BEANS = BU'UL

BEER = CHEBA

BEER, FERMENTED HONEY = BAALCHE'

BREAD = WAAJ

BROTH = K'AAB / K'AA' / K'OOL

CACAO = KAKAW

CACTUS = PAAK'AM

CANDY = CH'UJUK

CATFISH = LU'

CHICKEN = KAAX

CHICKEN, BAKED = PIIBIL KAAX

CHICKEN, FRIED = TZAJBIL KAAX

CHILE = IIK

CHOCOLATE = CHUKWA'

CIGAR = SAAK'

CIGARETTE = CHAMAL

CITRUS FRUIT = PAK'AAL

COFFEE = BOXJA'

COFFEE = KAAPE

CORN = IXIM

CORN = XI'IM

CORNMEAL = SAKAN

COW = WAKAX

CRAB = BAB

EGG = JE'

FISH = KAY

FLOUR, CORN [MASA] = SAKAN

FOOD = JAANAL

FOOD = O'OCH

FOOD = WAAJ

FRUIT = CH'UJUK

GUAVA = PICHI'

HONEY = KAAB

ICE = BAT

JICAMA [EDIBLE ROOT] = CHI'IKAM

MANGO = MAANKO

MEAL = JAANAL

MEAT = BAK'

MEAT, FRESH = AAK' BAK'

MEAT, GRILLED = K'A'BIL BAK'

MEAT, GRILLED = POK CHUK

MILE = LEECHE

ORANGE = CHIINA

ORANGE JUICE = K'AAB CHIINA

PAPAYA = PUUT

PEANUT BUTTER = MANIIYA

PEPPER = IIK

PIG = AK

PLUM = ABAL

PORK, ROASTED = PIIBIL K'EEK'EN

POSOL [CORN GRUEL] = K'EYEM

PUMPKIN = K'UUM

RICE = AROS

SALT = TA'AB

SAPOTE [REGIONAL FRUIT] = YA'

SEEDS [PEPITA] = SIKIL

SOURSOP [CUSTARD APPLE] = OOP

SQUASH = K'UUM

STEW = K'OOL

SUGAR = ASUKAAR

SWEET POTATO / YAM = IIS

TOBACCO = K'UUTZ

TOMATO = P'AAK

TORTILLA = WAAJ

TURKEY = TZ'O'

TURKEY = JTZ'O'

TURKEY = TZUN

TURKEY = ULUM

TURKEY = TUX

VENISON = KEEJ

WATER = JA'

ANIMALS – BA'ALCHE' / ALAK'

ALLIGATOR = AAYIN

ANIMAL, DOMESTIC = AALAK'

ANIMAL, WILD = BA'ALCHE'

ARMADILLO = IBACH

ARMADILLO = WECH

BAT = SOOTZ'

BAT, VAMPIRE = CHIKOOP

BEDBUG = PIK

BEE = KAAB

BIRD = CH' IICH'

BLUE JAY [BIRD] = CH' EL

BOA CONSTRICTOR = OCH KAAN

BOAR = KITAM

BULL = WAKAX

BUTTERFLY = PEEPEM

CAIMAN = AAYIN

CAT = MIIS

CATFISH = LU'

CHICKEN = KAAX

COW = WAKAX

COYOTE = CH'AMAK

COYOTE = CH'OMAK

COYOTE = JWAYU

CRAB = BAB

CROCODILE = AAYIN

DEER = KE

DEER, SMALL = YUUK

DOG = PEEK'

DOVE = XUUKUM

EAGLE = MEN

EEL = KAANILJA'

FALCON = KOOS

FISH = KAY

FLY = XYA'AXKAACH

FOX = CH'AMAK

FOX = CH'OMAK

FROG = MUUCH

GNAT = US

GOAT = JTAMAN

GRASSHOPPER = SAAK'

HEADLICE = UK'

HERON, WHITE = SAK BOK

HORSE = TZIIMIN

HUMMINGBIRD = TZ'UNU'UN

IGUANA = JOOJ

JAGUAR = BAALAM

JAGUAR = BAALAN

JAGUAR = CHAKMO'OL

JAGUAR = KO

LICE = UK'

LIZARD = IXMECH

LIZARD = JOOJ

LIZARD, SMALL = TOOLOK

LOCUST = SAAK'

LOUSE = UK'

MACAW = MO'

MONKEY = TUUCHA

MONKEY, HOWLER = BAATZ'

MONKEY, IN GENERAL = MA'AX

MOSQUITO = K'AXOL

MOSQUITO = K'OXOL

MOUNTAIN LION = KO

MOUSE = CH'O'

OWL = BUUJ

OWL = TUNKULUUCHU

OX = WAKAX

PACA, LARGE RODENT = JAALEB

PARROT = XT' UUT'

PECCARY, WILD PIG = KITAM

PIG = AK

PORCUPINE = K'I'IX PECH OOCH

PUMA = KO

QUAIL = BEECH'

QUETZAL [BIRD] = K'UK'

RABBIT = T'U'UL

RACCOON = K'ULU'

RAT = CH'O'

RATTLESNAKE = TZAA'KAAN

RATTLESNAKE = TZAAB'KAAN

ROOSTER = T'EEL

SCORPION = SIINA'AN

SHEEP = JTAMAN

SKUNK = PAAYOOCH

SNAIL = UURICH

SNAKE = KAAN

SPIDER = AM

SQUIRREL = KU'UK

TARANTULA = CHIIN WOL

TICK [INSECT] = PEECH

TOUCAN = PIITORLEEYAAL

TURKEY = TUX

TURKEY = TZ'O'

TURKEY = JTZ'O'

TURKEY = TZON

TURKEY, DOMESTICATED = UULUM

TURKEY, WILD = KUUTZ

TURTLE = AAK

VULTURE = CH'OOM

WASP = XUUX

WEASEL = OOCH

WOLF = KABKO

WORM = KAAN

WORM = NOK'OL

PEOPLE – WIINIKO'OB

BABY = CHAAMPAL

BOSS = NOOJOCHIIL

BOY = PAAL

BOY = XI'IPAL

BROTHER (BY BLOOD) = LAAK'TZIIL

BROTHER (OLDER) = SUKU'UN

BROTHER (YOUNGER) = IITZ'IIN

BROTHER (YOUNGER) = JT'UUP

CHIEF = JOLIIL

CHILD = CHAAMPAL

CHILD = PAAL

CHILD, BLONDE = CHAN CH'EL

CHILD, BLONDE OR RED-HAIRED = CHAN CH'EL

CURER = JMEEN

DEMON (MALE) = JTAABAY

DEMON (MALE) = JTABAAY

DEMON = XTAABAY

DEMON = XTABAAY

DEVIL = KISIN

DOCTOR (FEMALE) = XTZ'AAK

DOCTOR (MALE) = JTZ'AAK

DREAMER (FEMALE) = XWAYAK'

DREAMER (MALE) = JWAYAK'

DUMMY = JNUUM

EVIL MAN = JK'AAS

EVIL WOMAN = XK'AAS

FARMER = KOOLNAAL

FATHER = PAAPA

FATHER = TAAT

FATHER = YUUM

FIGHTER = JBA'TE'EL

FOREIGNER (FEMALE) = XUNAAN

FOREIGNER = TZ'UUL

FOREST SPIRIT = YUNTZIL

FRIEND = AAMIGO

FRIEND = ET'OOL

FRIEND = UK'UNAJ WIINIK

GAY (HOMOSEXUAL) = XCH'UUPUL XIB

GENTLEMAN = YUUM

GHOST (FEMALE) = XTAABAY

GHOST (FEMALE) = XTABAAY

GHOST (MALE) = JTAABAY

GHOST (MALE) = JTABAAY

GIRL = XCH'UUPAL

GOD = DYOS

GOD = K'U

GOD = YUUM

GODS = K'UJO'OB

GRANDCHILD = AABIL

GRANDFATHER (AGED) = MAM

GRANDFATHER = NOJOCH PAAPA

GRANDFATHER = NOJOCH TAAT

GRANDFATHER = NOJOCH TAATA

GRANDMOTHER = CHIICH

HELPER = AANTAJ

HOMOSEXUAL = XCH'UUPUL XIB

HUNTER = TZ'ONERO

HUNTER = TZ'ONNAAL

HUSBAND = IICHAM

HUSBAND = JWICHAM

IDIOT = JNUUM

IGNORANT PERSON = JNUUM

IMBECIL = JNUUM

INDIAN = JMAYABIIL

INDIAN = MAASEWAAL

INDIGENOUS PERSON = JMAYABIIL

INDIGENOUS PERSON = MAASEWAAL

INFANT = PAAL

INJURED MAN = JLOOB

INJURED WOMAN = XLOOB

LADY = XUNAAN

LAZY MAN = JOYKEEP

LOCAL PERSON = WAYILE'

MAIDEN = SUJUY PAAL

MALE = XIIB

MAN = MAAK

MAN = WIINIK

MAN = XIIB

MEDICINE MAN = JMEEN

MEXICAN (FEMALE) = XWAACH

MEXICAN (MALE) = JWAACH

MINOR = PAAL

MOTHER = MAAM

MOTHER = NA'

NATIVE = WAYILE'

OLD MAN = NOJOCH WIINIK

OLD MAN = NUXIIB

OLD WOMAN = NOJOCH KO'OLEL

OLD WOMAN = XNUUK

OWNER = YUUM

PARENT = LAAK

PERSON = MAAK

PERSON = WIINIK

POPE = PAAPA

PRIEST = AJK'IIN

PRIEST = JK'IIN

QUEER (HOMOSEXUAL) = XCH'UUPUL XIIB

RELATIVE = CHILANKABIL

RELATIVE = LAAK'

SAINTS = K'UJO'OB

SALESMAN = KOONOL

SALESWOMAN = XKOONOL

SHAMAN = JMEEN

SIBLING (FEMALE) = LAAK'TZIIL

SIBLING (MALE) = JK'EBAN

SISTER (OLDER) = KIIK

SISTER (YOUNGER) = IITZ'IIN

SISTER (YOUNGER) = XT'UUP

SOLDIER = JK'ATUN

SOLDIER = K'ATUN

SOLDIER = WAACH

SOMEONE = WAAJ MAAX

SON = PAAL

SPEAKER (FEMALE) = XT'AN

SPEAKER (MALE) = JT'AN

SPOUSE = LAAK'

STEP-FATHER = MAJAN YUUM

STRANGER (FEMALE) = XUNAAN

STRANGER (MALE) = TZ'UUL

STUPID MAN = JNUUM

STUPID WOMAN = XNUUM

TEACHER = KA'ANSAJ

VENDOR (FEMALE) = XKOONOL

VENDOR (MALE) = KOONOL

VIRGEN (WOMAN) = SUJUY PAAL

VIRGIN = SUJUY

WHITE MAN = TZ'UUL

WHITE WOMAN = XUNAAN

WIFE = ATAN

WITCH = XWAAY

WIZARD = JWAAY

WOMAN = KO'OLEL

WOMAN = XCH'UUP

WORKER = JMEYAJ

WRITER (FEMALE) = XTZ'IIB

WRITER (MALE) JTZ'IIB

YOUNG WOMAN = SUJUY PAAL

YOUTH = XI'IPAAL

PLACES – KAAJTALO'OB

BANK = BAANKO

BATHROOM = BAANYO

CHURCH = IGLEESYA

CHURCH = YOTOCH DYOS

FIELD = KOL

FOREST = K'AAX

HEAVEN = KA'AN

HOME = OTOCH

HOUSE = KAJTAL

HOUSE = OTOCH

JAIL = KARSA

JAIL = KARSE

LAND = KAAB

LAND = LU'UM

MOUNTAINS = WITZOB

PLACE = KAJTAL

RESTROOM = BAANYO

ROAD = BEEL

SKY = KA'AN

TOWN = KAJ

TOWN = NOJKAJ

VALLEY = K'OM

VALLEY = K'OP

VILLAGE = KAJ

VILLAGE = NOJKAJ

WORLD = KAAB

NATURE – LE LU'UMO'

AIR = IIK'

AREA = BAANDA

BARK (TREE) = SOOL

CEIBA [REGIONAL TREE] = YAXCHE'

CLOUD = MUNYAL

CYCLONE = CHAKIK'AT

DAWN = SAASTAL

DAY = K'IIN

DEW = YEEB

DUSK = BIN KA AK'ABTAL

EARTH = KAAB

EARTH = LU'UM

EAST = LAK'IN

FIELD = KOL

FIRE = K'AAK'

FIREWOOD = SI'

FLOWER = LOOL

FLOWER = NIKTE'

FOG = YEEB

FOREST = K'AAX

FOUNTAIN = SAYAB

HAIL = BAT

HILL = MUUL

LAGOON = AAK'AL

LAKE = JA'

LANDMARK = XU'UK

LEAF = LE'

MIST = YEEB

MOON = UW

MOUNTAIN = WITZ

MOUNTAINS = WITZOB

NIGHT = AK'AB

NORTH = XAMAN

NORTH WIND = XAMAN KA'AN

PLANT = PAK'AL

RAIN = CHAAK

RAIN = JA'

RIVER = BEKAN

ROCK = TUUNICH

ROOT = MOOTZ

ROSE = LOOL

SOIL = LU'UM

SOUTH = NOJOL

STONE = TUUNICH

SUN = K'IIN

SWAMP = AAK'AL

THUNDER = JUUM CHAAK

TREE = CHE'

TREE, CEIBA [REGIONAL TREE] = YAXCHE'

TWIG = CH'ILIB

VALLEY = K'OM

VALLEY = K'OP

VINE = AAK'

VIRGIN FOREST = SUJUY K'AAX

WEED = K'AAX

WEST = CHIK'IN

WIND = IIK'

WOOD = CHE'

WORLD = KAAB

WORLD = LU'UM

OTHER IMPORTANT WORDS – LAAK' K'A'ANA'AN T'AANOB

ABILITY = PAT

ACCIDENT = LOOB

AFFAIR = BEEL

AGE = JA' ABIIL

ALTAR = KA'ANCHE'

AX = BAAT

BAG = SAABUKAAN

BALL = PELOOTA

BASE = CHUUN

BASE = IIT

BASE = JAAL

BASKET, LARGE = XUUX

BASKET, SMALL = XAAK

BEAUTY = JATZ'UTZIIL

BEGINNING = CHUUN

BIT = XEET'

BLOW [WITH FIST] = LOOBIIL

BOAT = CHEEM

BOOK = JU'UN

BOX = PIIX

BROOM = MIIS

BUCKET = CH'OOY

BUILDING = NAJIIL

BURDEN = KUUCH

CANDLE = KIB

CANOE = CHEM

CAR = KAARO

CASE = PIIX

CHARCOAL = CHUUK

COLD MEDICINE = TZ'AAK SE'EN

COMB = XAACHE'

COTTON = TAMAN

DANCE = OOK'OT

DIGNITY = SU'TAL

DISTANCE = NAACHIIL

DOLL = AALNOOK'

DREAM = WAYAK'

DYE = BON

EDGE = CHI'

EDGE = EJ

EDGE = JAAL

EMBARASSMENT = SU'UTAL

END = TZ'OOK

END = XUUL

ENERGY = OOL

ENGLISH LANGUAGE = INGLES

ENTRANCE = JOOL

ERRAND = TUS BEEL

ERROR = SI'IPIIL

ERROR = SIIP

EXCREMENT = TA'

EXPLANATION = NU'UKUL

FALSEHOOD = TUUS

FART = KIIS

FAULT (BLAME) = KUUCH

FAULT (BLAME) = SI'IPIIL

FAULT (BLAME) = SIIP

FAVOR = UTZIIL

FEAR = SAJKIIL

FECES = TA'

FIGHT = BA'TE'EL

FIRE = K'AAK'

FIREWOOD = SI'

FLATULENCE = KIIS

FLINT = TOK' TUUNICH

FLUTE = PIITO

FOAM = YOON

GIFT = SIIJBIL

GOD = YUUM

GODS = K'UJO'OB

GOLD = TAAK'IN

GOODNESS = JATZ'UTZIIL

GUN = TZ'OON

HAMMOCK = K'AAN

HATCHET = BAAT

HOUR = K'IIN

HOUR = OORA

ILLNESS = K'OJA'ANIIL

INCLINE = NIIX

INJURY = LOOB

IRON = MAASKAB

ITCH = SAAK'

KEY = YAABE

KITCHEN = K'OOBEN

LABOR = MEYAJ

LANGUAGE = T'AAN

LAUGHTER = CHE'EJ

LIE = TUUS

LIFE = KUXTAL

LIGHT = K'AAK'

LIGHT = SAASIL

LOAD = KUUCH

LORD = YUUM

LOVE = YAAMAJ

MACHETE = MAASKAB

MARIJUANA = K'UUTZ

MASONRY = PAK'

MATTER = BEEL

MEDICATION = TZ'AAK

MEDICINE = TZ'AAK

MILL = JUCH'

MIRROR = NEEN

MISFORTUNE = LOOB

MONEY = TAAK'IN

MOVEMENT = PEEK

MUSIC = K'AAY

NAME = K'ABA'

NAPKIN = JAAY

NEEDLE = PUUTZ'

NEST = K'U'

NIGHTMARE = K'AAS WAYAK'

NOTHING = MIXBA'AL

OBLIGATION = KUUCH

ODOR = CH'E'J

OMEN = TAMAX CHI'

OPENING = CHI'

OPENING = JOOL

PAIN = K'I'INAM

PAINT = BON

PAPER = JU'UN

PIECE = XEET'

PILLAR = OKOM

PILLOW = XK'AANJO'OL

POINT = U YEJ

POLE = CHE'

PORTION = XEET'

POST = OKOM

PRICE = TOJOL

PROBLEM = BA'TE'EL

PYRAMID = MUUL

REASON = NU'UKUL

RESERVOIR = AAK'AL

ROAD = BEEL

ROOF = U JO'OL NAJ

ROOF = U POOL NAJ

ROPE = SUUM

RUST = ITZ

SAINTS = K'UJO'OB

SAP = ITZ

SHADE = BO'OY

SHADOW = BO'OY

SHAME = SU'UTAL

SHELL (EGG) = SOOL

SHIT = TA'

SHOTGUN = TZ'OON

SHOW = CHA'AN

SICKNESS = K'OJA'ANIIL

SIN = K'EBAN

SIN = SI'IPIIL

SIN = SIIP

SINKHOLE = TZ'OONO'OT

SITUATION = BEEL

SIZE = NOJOCHIIL

SLOPE = NIIX

SMELL = BOK

SMOKE = BUUTZ'

SNARE = PEETZ'

SONG = K'AAY

SOUND = JUUM

SOURCE = SAYAB

SPANISH LANGUAGE = KAXLANT'AAN

SPARK = XIKIN K'AAK'

SPECTACLE = CHA'AN

SPEECH = T'AAN

STAR = EEK'

STEM = CHUN

STICK = CHE'

STING = AACH

STOOL = K'AANCHE'

STORM = CHIICHIK'

STRAP = K'AXAB NAK'

STRAW = SIIT

STRENGTH = MUUK'

TABLE = MEESA

THICKNESS = POOLKIIL

THING = BA'AL

THORN = K'I'IX

THOUGHT = TUUKUL

TIME = K'IIN

TOBACCO = K'UUTZ

TOOL = NU'UKUL

TOOTHPICK = CH'ILIB

TOWEL = TWAAYA

TRAP = PEETZ'

TRASH = SOJOL

TRUTH = JAAJIIL

URINE = WIIX

UTENSIL = NU'UKUL

VALUE = TOJOL

VOICE = KAAL

VOMIT = XEJ

WART = AAX

WASHTUB = CHEEM

WEEK = SAMAANA

WHISTLE = PIITO

WILL = OOL

WINDOW = WENTANA

WOOD = CHE'

WORK = MEYAJ

WORK = OOBRA

WOUND = LOOB

WRITING = TZ'IIB

YEAR = AANYO

YEAR =JA'ABIIL

COMMON ADJECTIVES

ACCUSTOMED = SUUK

ACIDIC = PAJ

ALIVE = KUXA'AN

ANCIENT = UUCHBEN

ANGERED = P'UJUUL

ASHAMED = SU'LAK

BAD = K'AAS

BEAUTIFUL = JATZ'UTZ

BIG = NOJOCH

BITTER = K'AAJ

BLIND = CH'OP

BOTHERED = P'UJUUL

BROKEN = KAACHA'AL

BUSTED = KAACHA'AL

CAPTURED = CHUKA'AN

CHANGED = K'EEXEL

CHEAP = MA' KO'OJI'

CLEAN = JAANIL

CLEAN = SAK

CLEAR = SAAS

CLOUDY = NOOKOY

COLD = SIIS

CONSUMED = XUUPUL

CONTENT = KI'IMAK OOL

CONVENIENT = KI'

COOKED = TAK'AN

CROSSED = K'AATAL

CROWDED = BABAJKIL

CUTE = JATZ'UTZ

DANGEROUS = JACH K'AAS U BIN

DARK = EE'JOCH'E'EEN

DEAD = KIMEN

DEAF = KOOK

DEEP = TAAM

DELICATE = LUKUM

DIFFERENT = JEEL

DIFFERENT = JELA'AN

DIFFICULT = YAJ

DIRTY = EEK'

DISTANT = NAACH

DISTINCT = JELA'AN

DONE = TZ'OKA'AN

DRIED = JAYK'INTA'AN

DRUNK = KALA'AN

DRY = TIKIN

DUMB = TZ'U'UY POOL

EMBARASSED = SU'LAK

ENOUGH = JACH YA'AB

EVIL = K'AAS

EXCHANGED = K'EEXEL

EXPENSIVE = KO'OJ

EXPLODED = WAAK'AL

EXTENDED = TIINIL

FADED = POOS

FAIR (PERSON) = CHAKXICH'

FAIR (COMPLEXIONED) = CH'EL

FAT = POLOK

FILLED = CHUUPUL

FINE = LUKUM

FINISHED = CHUKA'AN

FINISHED = TZ'OKA'AN

FIRST = YAAXIIL

FIXED = JETZ'A'AN

FLAT = PEK'A'AN

FORCEFUL = JELA'AN

FRACTURED = KAACHA'AL

FRIED = TZAJBIL

FRIGHTENED = P'UUJUL

FULL = CHUUP

GOOD = MA'ALOB

GOOD = UTZ

GOOD-LOOKING = KI'ICHPAM

GOOFY = NUUM

GOOFY = TZ'U'UY POOL

GRILLED = K'A'BIL

GROUND (UP) = JUCH'BIL

HALF = CHUMUK

HANDSOME = JATZ'UTZ

HANDSOME = KI'ICHPAM

HAPPY = KI'IMAK OOL

HARSH = K'A'AM

HEATED UP = K'IINAL

HEAVY = AL

HIGH = KA'ANAL

HOARSE = MA'A KAAL

HOLLOW = POOS

HOT (FOOD; SPICY) = PAAP

HOT (WEATHER) = K'IILKAB

HOT = CHOKOJ

HOT = K'IINAL

HUMBLE = UMIILDE

HUNGRY = WI'IJ

IGNORANT = NUUM

IMPORTANT = K'A'ANA'AN

INDIGENOUS = MAASEWAAL

INTACT = SUJUY

INTOXICATED = KALA'AN

JUST = UTZ

LARGE (PLURAL) = NUKUCH

LARGE = NOJOCH

LAZY = NUUM

LEATHERY = TZ'U'UY

LEFT = TZ'IK

LIGHT = SAAL

LITTLE = CHAN

LITTLE = MA' YA'ABI'

LITTLE = MEJEN

LIVING = KUXA'AN

LONG = CHOWAK

LOST = SAATAL

LOUD = CH'E'EJ

LOW = KAABAL

MANY = YA'AB

MANY = YA'AKACH

MARRIED = TZ'OKA'AN BEEL

MATURE = TAK'AN

MOIST = CH'UUL

MUDDY = PUUK

NAKED = CHAKNUL

NARROW = KOOM

NEAR = NAATZ'

NEW = TUMBEN

NICE = JATZ'UTZ

NICE = KI'

NICE = LUKUM

NICE, VERY = SEN UTZ

NOISY = CH'E'EJ

OBSCURE = EE'JOCH'E'EEN

OLD = CH'IJA'AN

OLD = NOJOCH

OLD = NUXIB

OLD = UUCHBEN

OPENED = JE'AN

OPENED = JE'IK

OPENED = JEBAN

OTHER = JEEL

OTHER = LAAK'

OVERCAST = NOOKOY

PAINFUL = YAJ

PAINTED = BO'ON

PAINTED = BOONOL

PREGNANT = YO'OM

PRETTY = JATZ'UTZ

PRETTY = KI'ICHPAM

QUICK = SEEBAK

RICH = AYIK'AL

RICH = TAAK'INAL

RIPE = K'AN

RIPE = TAK'AN

ROASTED = K'A'BIL

ROUND = WOLIS

SCRAMBLED = PUUK'

SEATED = JETZ'A'AN

SEATED = KULA'AN

SECONDHAND = ASBE'EN

SECURED = JETZ'A'AN

SETTLED = JETZ'A'AN

SHAVEN = TZ'IKA'AN

SICK = K'OJA'AN

SILLY = NUUM

SINGLE = JUN

SKINNY = TZ'OYA'AN

SLICED = TAAJAL

SLIPPERY = JAJALKIL

SLOW = CHAAMBEEL

SMALL = CHAN

SMALL = CHICHAN

SMALL = MEJEN

SMOOTH = JOJOLKIL

SMOOTH = TAAX

SOUR = PAJ

SPICY = PAAP

SPILLED = WEEJEL

SPILLED = WEEKEL

SPLIT = KAACHA'AL

STIFF = T'IINIL

STILL (NOT MOVING) = WA'BAL

STOLEN = OOKOLBIL

STOPPED = WA'BAL

STRAIGHT = TOJ

STRANGE = JELA'AN

STRONG = CHICH

STRONG = K'A'AM

STUPID = NUUM

STUPID = TZ'U'UY POOL

SUBMERGED = T'UBUKBAL

SUBMERGED = T'UUBAL

SUBSTITUTED = K'EEXEL

SUFFICIENT = JACH YA'AB

SUNKEN = T'UBUKBAL

SUNKEN = T'UUBAL

SUPER = SEN MA'ALOB

SURPRISING = JAK'OOLAL

SWEET = CH'UJUK

SWOLLEN = CHUUP

TAME = SUUK

TASTY = KI'

TENSE = T'IINIL

THICK = PIIM

THICK = POLOK

THIN (PAPER / CLOTHES) = JAAY

THIN = BEK'ECH

THIRSTY = UK'AJ

TILTED = NIIXIL

TIRED = KA'ANA'AN

TOASTED = POKBIL

TOO MANY = JACH YA'AB

TOUGH = CHICH

TOUGH = TZ'U'UY

TRUE = JAAJ

UNTIDY = LOOB

USED = ASBE'EN

USED UP = XU'UPI

USELESS = NUUM

VERY = JACH

WASHED = P'O'A'AL

WEALTHY = AYIK'AL

WET = CH'UUL

WIDE = KOOCH

WILD = K'O'OX

WRONG = K'EBAN

THE BODY – LE WIINKILO'

ANUS = IIT

ARM = K'AB

BACK = PAACH

BEAK (BIRD) = KO

BEARD = ME'EX

BELLY = NAK'

BONE = BAK

BOSOM = IIM

BREAST = IIM

BUTT = BAK'EL IIT

BUTT = P'U'UKIL IIT

BUTTOCKS = BAK'EL IIT

BUTTOCKS = P'U'UKIL IIT

CALLUS = T'AAJAM

CHIN = K'O NO'OCH

CLAW (ANIMAL) = IICH'AK

CLITORIS = AK'

EAR = XIKIN

EXCREMENT = TA'

EYE = ICH

FACE = ICH

FANG (ANIMAL) = TZ'A'AY

FAT = TZAATZ

FEATHERS (BIRD) = K'U'UK'UM

FINGER = AAL K'AB

FINGER = U YAAL K'AB

FINGERNAIL = IICH'AK

FLESH = BAK'

FOOT = OOK

HAIR = JO'OL

HAIR = TZO'OTZ

HAIR = U TZO'OTZ A JO'OL

HAND = K'AB

HEAD = JO'OL

HEART = OOL

HEART = PUKSI'IK'AL

HEEL = TUUNKUY

HORN (ANIMAL) = BAK

INTESTINES = CHOOCH

KNEE = PIIX

LIPS = BOOX

LIVER = TAAMAN

MOUSTACHE = ME'EX

MOUTH = CHI'

MUCUS = SIIM

NAIL = IICH'AK

NECK = KAAL

NERVE = XIICH'

NOSE = NI'

PENIS = TOON

PENIS = XIIBIL

PUS = TZ'IIK

RUMP = BAK'EL IIT

SHOULDER = KELEMBAL

SINEW = XIICH'

SKIN = K'EEWEL

SOUL = PIXAAN

STOMACH = NAK'

TAIL (ANIMAL) = NE

TEAT = IIM

TENDON = XIICH'

TESTICLES = U YE'EL TOON

THROAT = KAAL

TOE = AAL OOK

TONGUE = AK'

TOOTH; TEETH = KO

URINE = WIIX

VOICE = KAAL

VOMITE = XE

WING (BIRD) = XIIK'

CLOTHING – NOOK'

BELT = K'AXAB NAK'

CAPE = JAAY

CLOAK = JAAY

CLOTH = NOOK'

CLOTHES = NOOK'

CLOTHING = NOOK'

FABRIC = NOOK'

FOOTWEAR = XANAB

HAT = P'OK

HAT, MADE FROM STRAW = XA'ANIL P'OK

HUIPIL [TRADITIONAL DRESS FOR WOMEN] = IIPIL

LEATHER = K'EEWEL

PANTS = EEX

SANDAL = XANAB

SHAWL = BOOCH'

SHIRT = KAMIISA

SHOE = XANAB

SHOES = XANAB

T-SHIRT = KAMIISA

UNDERWEAR = EEX

COLORS – KOLORILO'OB

BLACK = BOX

BLACK = EEK'

BLUE = YA'AX

BROWN = MORENO

GREEN = YA'AX

ORANGE = ANARANJADO

PINK = CHAKPOSE'EN

PURPLE = MORADO

RED = CHAK

WHITE = SAK

YELLOW = K'AN

YUCATEC VERBS

EXAMPLE: LOVE = YAKUNTIK

NOTES:

-VERBS WITH THE -IK SUFFIX ATTACHED TO THE ROOT ARE ALWAYS TRANSITIVE VERBS

-VERBS WITHOUT A SUFFIX ATTACHED TO THE ROOT ARE ALMOST ALWAYS INTRANSITIVE

-VERBS WITH THE -TAL ENDING, WILL RECEIVE -TAL VERB CONJUGATION (SEE VERB SECTION GRAMMAR)

ABANDON = NAK'

ACCEPT A PROPOSITION = KETIK

ADD = TZAKBESAJ

ADJUST = NUUKBESAJ

ADORN = SENBESAJ

 AGE = CH'IIJ

ALLOW = CHA'

ALLOW = CHA'IK

AMUSE = BAAXAL

ANSWER = NUUKIK

APPROACH = NAATZ'AL

APPROACH = NAATZ'IK

ARISE = LIIK'IL

ARRIVE = K'UCHUL

ASK FOR = K'AATIK

ATTAIN = CHUKIK

AWAKEN = AJAL

BAKE = TAJAL

BATHE = ICHKIIL

BE = YAAN

BE ABLE TO = PAAJTAL (*AUXILIARY*)

BE BORN = SIIJIL

BE HUNGRY = WI'IJ- + SET B AFFIX

BE LATE = XANAL

BE MARRIED = TZ'OKA'AN BEEL

BE SUSPENDED = CH'UUYUL

BE THIRSTY = UK'AJ- +SET B AFFIX

BEAT (MIXING INGREDIENTS) = P'UUCH

BEAT (WITH FISTS) = JATZ'IK

BECOME ACCUSTOMED = NAPTZAAJ

BECOME CLOUDY = NOOKOYTAL

BECOME DENSE = SU'UTAL

BECOME DRUNK = KAALTAL

BECOME HOT = CHOKOTAL

BECOME ILL = K'OJA'ANTAL

BECOME OVERCAST = NOOKOYTAL

BECOME PREGNANT = YO'OMCHAJTAL

BECOME WET = CH'ULCHAJTAL

BEGIN = CHUUNIK

BEGIN = KAAJSIK

BEND = WUTZ'IK

BITE = CHI'IBAL

BLESS = BENDISYONTIK

BLOCK (ROAD) = SUP'IK

BLOW (WITH MOUTH) = USTIK

BOIL = TAJAL

BOTHER = P'U'UJSIK

BOUNCE = SIIT'

BREAK (LONG THINGS) = KACHIK

BREAK (OUT IN RASH) = IXBAL

BREAK SOMETHING = PA'IK

BREAK SOMETHING = XIKIK

BREAKFAST (TO HAVE BREAKFAST) = UK'UL

BREATHE = CH'A'IIK

BREATHE = CH'A'IK IIK

BRING = TAASIK

BRUISE = PUCH'IK

BURN = ELEL

BURN = TOK

BURN = TOOKIK

BURST = XIKIK

BUY = MANIK

CAN (TO BE ABLE) = KU' PAAJTAL

CAN = JU' CHABALE

CARE FOR = KANANTIK

CARRY (SOMETHING ON BACK) = KUCHIK

CATCH = CHUKIK

CHANGE = K'EXIK

CHAT = TZIKBAL

CHAT = TZIKBATIK

CHEW SOMETHING = JACH'IK

CLEAN = MISTIK

CLEAN = UTZKINTIK

CLEAR = PAAK

CLIMB = NA'AKAL

CLOSE = K'ALIK

CLOSE = SUP'IK

COLLECT (FIREWOOD) BEETIK SI'

COMB (ONE'S HAIR) = XAACHTIK

COME = TAAL

COME = TAALEL

COME OUT = JOOK'OL

COMPLETE = CHUKBESIK

COOK = TAJAL

COPULATE = TZ'IIS

COUGH = SE'EN

COUNT = XOK

COUNT = XOKIK

COVER = TO'IK

CRACK = XIKIK

CROSS = K'AATEL

CRUSH = PUCH'IK

CRY = OK'OL

CURSE = MALDISYONTIK

CUT (FRUIT OR LEAVES ON A STEM) = T'OKIK

CUT = XOTIK

CUT FIREWOOD = XOTIK SI'

CUT IT WITH ONE SWING = CH'AKIK

CUT WITH SCISSORS = K'OSIK

DANCE = OK'OT

DECEIVE = KECHTIK

DECEIVE = TUUS

DECEIVE = TUUSIK

DELAY = XAANTAL

DELIVER = K'UBIK

DESCEND = EEMEL

DESIRE = TAAK (*AUXILIARY*)

DESIRE = TZ'IIBOLTIK

DETAIN = PETZ'IK

DETEST = P'EKTIK

DIE = KIIMIL

DIG = PAANIK

DIMINISH = JATZIK

DISAPPEAR = SATPAJAL

DISCUSS = TZIKBATIK

DISLIKE = P'EKTIK

DISROBE = PITIK

DISTRIBUTE = T'OXIK

DIVIDE = JATZIK

DO = BEETIK

DOMESTICATE = AALAK'TIK

DREAM = NAAY

DREAM = WAYAK'

DRENCH = CH'ULIK

DRESS ONESELF = BUUKINTIK

DRINK = UK'UL

DRY = TIIJIL

DRY = TIJSIK

EAT = JAANAL

EAT SOMETHING = JAANTIK

EMBRACE = MEEK'IK

ENTER = OOKOL

ESCAPE = PUUTZ'UL

EXCHANGE = K'EXIK

EXPECT = PA'ATIK

EXPLAIN = TZOLIK

EXPLODE = XIKIK

EXPOSE = WAK

EXTEND = SATZ'IK

EXTINGUISH = TUPIK

EXTRACT = JO'OSIK

FALL = LUUBUL

FART = KIIS

FEED = TZEENTIK

FEEL = U'UYIK

FIGHT = BA'TE'EL

FILL = BUT'IK

FILL = CHUPIK

FIND = KAXTIK

FIND OUT = OJELTIK

FINISH = CHUKBESIK

FINISH = TZ'O'OKSIK

FIX = UTZKIINTIK

FLATTEN = MACH'

FLATTEN = PAK'ACHTIK

FOLD = WUTZ'IK

FOLLOW = TZAYNEJ

FOOL SOMEONE = KECHTIK

FORGET = TU'UB

FORGET = TU'UBSIK

FORGET = TU'UBUL

FRACTURE (LONG THINGS) = KACHIK

FREE = CHA'

FREEZE = SIISKUNTIK

FRY = TZAJIK

GATHER = T'OKIK

GET AWAY = PUUTZ'UL

GET DRUNK = KALTAL

GET IN SOMETHING = NA'AKAL

GET ON SOMETHING = NA'AKAL

GIVE = TZ'IIK

GIVE AS A GIFT = SIIJIK

GIVE BACK = SUUTIK

GO = BIN (IRREGULAR)

GO = JOOK'OL

GO = XIIMBAL

GO ACROSS = K'AATEL

GO OUT = JOOK'OL

GRAB = MACHIK

GRASP = MACHIK

GRILL = K'A'ATIK

GRIND = PUCH'IK

GRIND SOMETHING = JUCH'IK

GROW = AALAK'TIK

HANG = CH'UYTAL

HANG SOMETHING = CH'UUYUL

HAPPEN = UUCHUL

HARVEST = JOOCHIK

HATE = P'EKTIK

HAVE = YAAN

HEAL = TZ'AKIK

HEAR = U'UYIK

HEAT = CHOKOKUNTIK

HELP = AANTAJ

HELP SOMEONE = AANTIK

HIDE = TA'AKIK

HIT = JATZ'IK

HUG = MEEK'IK

HUMILIATE ONESELF = TA'IK U BA

HUNT = TZ'ONIK

HURRY = SEEB

HURRY = SEEKUNTIK

HURT (INJURE) = KINBESIK

HURT = CHI'IBAL

HURT ONESELF = KINPAJAL

IGNITE = T'ABIK

IMAGINE = TZ'IIBOLTIK

IMPROVE = UTZKIINTIK

INSERT = OKSIK

INTRODUCE = OKSIK

JOKE; TELL JOKES = BAAXAL

JUMBLE = XA'AK'TIK

KEEP = KIINSIK

KISS = TZ'U'UTZ'IK

KNOW SOMEONE = K'AAJOOL

KNOW SOMEONE = K'AAJOOLTIK

KNOW SOMETHING = KANIK

KNOW SOMETHING = OOJELTIK

KNOW SOMETHING = WOJEL

LAUGH = CHE'EJ

LEAN = TOKIK

LEARN = KANIK

LEAVE = JOOK'OL

LEAVE = LUK'UL

LEND = MAJAANTIK

LET = CHA'

LIE [TELL LIES] = TUUS

LIE DOWN = CHILTAL

LIE TO SOMEONE = TUUSIK

LIFT = U'UYIK

LIVE = KAAJTAL

LOOK = PAKTIK

LOOK FOR = KAXTIK

LOOSEN = CHA'

LOSE = SATIK

LOVE = YAKUNTIK

LOWER = EENSIK

MAKE (BY HAND) = MAK'ANTIK

MAKE = BEETIK

MAKE = MENTIK

MAKE BETTER = UTZKIINTIK

MAKE READY = LI'SIK

MAKE TORTILLAS = PAK'ACH

MAKE TORTILLAS = PAK'ACHTIK

MARRY = TZ'O'OKOL BEEL

MASH = PUCH'IK

MATURE = TAJ

MEASURE = P'ISIK

MEND = UTZKIINTIK

MIX UP = XA'AK'TIK

MOISTEN = CH'ULIK

MOVE = PEEKSIK

MOVE ONESELF = PEEK

NEED = YAAN + SET A AFFIX + VERB

NOTICE = OOJELTIK

NOURISH = TZEENTIK

OFFER = WAK

OPEN = JEEB

OPEN = JEEBIK

ORDER = TUSBELTIK

ORDER; PUT IN ORDER = TZOLIK

OVERTAKE = CHUKPACHTIK

PACK = BUT'IK

PAINT = BONIK

PASS = MANSIK

PASS BY = MAAN

PASS THROUGH = POTIK

PAY = BO'OTIK

PENETRATE = POTIK

PERCEIVE = U'UYIK

PERMIT = CHA'IK

PISS = BEETIK WIIX

PLACE; PUT = TZ'IIK

PLANT = PAK'AL

PLANT = PAK'IK

PLAY = BAAXAL

PALY = BAAXTIK

POLISH = YUULTIK

POUND = PAK'ACHTIK

PRAY = BO'OTIK DYOS

PREPARE = LI'SIK

PROTECT = TA'AKIK

PULL = KOOLIK

PULL = PAAYTIK

PUNCH = LOXIK

PURSUE = CHUKPACHTIK

PUT = TZ'IIK

PUT CLOTHES ON = BUUKINTIK

PUT IN ORDER = TZOLIK

PUT OUT (FIRE, LIGHT) = TUPIK

RAIN = BEETIK CHAAK

RAIN = BEETIK JA'

RAISE (CHILD) = TZEENTIK

RAISE (LIFT) = LI'ISIK

READ = XOKIK

READ = XOOK

REAR (CHILD) = TZEENTIK

RECEIVE = K'AMIK

RECOGNIZE = K'AAJOOLTIK

RECOUNT = TZIKBATIK

RELEASE = CHA'

RELIEVE = UTZKIINTIK

REMAIN; STAY = P'AATAL

REPAIR = UTZKIINTIK

REPRIMAND = K'EYIK

RESIDE = KAAJTAL

REST = JE'ELEL

RETURN = SUUT

RETURN SOMETHING = SUUTIK

RIPEN = TAJ

RISE = LIIK'IL

ROAST = K'A'ATIK

ROB = OKLIK

ROB = OKOOL

ROLL = KOPIK

ROLL UP = TO'IK

RUB = YUULTIK

RUN = AALKAB

SALT = TA'ABIK

SAVE = TA'AKIK

SAY = A'AL

SAY SOMETHING = T'ANIK

SAY SOMETHING TO SOMEONE = A'ALIK

SCARE = P'U'UJSIK

SCOLD = K'EYIK

SCRAPE = PAANIK

SCREW = KOPIK

SEARCH = KAXTIK

SEE = ILIK

SEEK = KAXTIK

SELL = KONIK

SEND = TUUXTIK

SEW = CHUUY

SHAKE = PEEKSIK

SHAKE = TIIT

SHAKE = TIITIK

SHARE = T'OXIK

SHAVE ONESELF = TZ'IKIK

SHIT = BEETIK TA'

SHOOT = TZ'ONIK

SHOW = E'ESIK

SHOW ONESELF = E'ESIK U BA

SHUCK CORN = OXO'ONTIK

SIGNAL (WITH HAND) = PAAYK'AB

SING = K'AAY

SIT = KULAL

SIT DOWN = KULTAL

SLEEP = WENEL

SLICE = TAJ

SMASH = PETZ'IK

SMELL = U'UYIK

SMOKE A CIGARETTE OR CIGAR = TZ'U'UTZ'IK

SOW = PAK'AL

SOW = PAK'IK

SPEAK = T'AAN

SPEAK = T'AANIK

SPEAK TO SOMEONE = TZIIKBATIK

SPILL = WEKIK

SPILL WATER = WEKIK JA'

SPY = CH'UUK

STAND = WA'AK U BA

STAND UP = WA'AL

START (A FIGHT) = KETIK

STARTED; GET STARTED = CHUNPAJAL

STAY = P'AATAL

STEAL = OKLIK

STEAL = OOKOL

STICK AROUND = XAANTAL

STOP = WA'AL

STRETCH = SATZ'IK

STRIKE = JATZ'IK

STUDY = XOKIK

SUBMERGE = T'UBIK

SUBSTITUTE = K'EXIK

SUCK = TZ'U'UTZ'

SUCK = TZ'U'UTZ'IK

SUPPORT = TZEENTIK

SUSPEND = CH'UYTAL

SWALLOW = LUUK'

SWEEP = MIISTIK

SWIM = BAAB

TAKE (CARRY SOMETHING) = BIISTIK

TAKE A PHOTO = MENTIK POTO

TAKE AWAY = JATZIK

TAKE CARE OF = KANANTIK

TAKE OUT = JO'OSIK

TEACH = KA'ANSIK

TELL JOKES = BAAXAL

TELL JOKES = BAAXTIK

THERE IS / ARE = YAAN

THICKEN = SU'UTAL

THINK = TUUKUL

THROB = PEEK

THROW = CH'INIK

THROW STONES = CH'INIK

TIE = K'AXIK

TILT = NIIXIK

TIRE = KA'ANAL

TRICK = KECHTIK

TWIST = KOPIK

UNDERSTAND = NA'ATIK

UNDERSTAND = OOJELTIK

UNTIE = WACH'IK

URINATE = WIIX

USE = BAAXTIK

USE = CH'A'IK

VISIT = XIIMBATIK

VOMIT = XEJ

WAIT = PA'AT

WAIT FOR = PA'ATIK

WALK = XIIMBAL

WANT = K'AAT (*AUXILIARY*)

WASH = P'O'IK

WAVE (WITH HAND) = PAAYK'AB

WEAVE = WAK'IK

WEED; PULL WEEDS = PAAK

WEED; PULL WEEDS = PAAKTIK

WEEP = OK'OL

WEIGH = P'ISIK

WHIP = JATZ'IK

WHISTLE = XUUXUB

WISH = TZ'IIBOLTIK

WORK = MEYAJ

WORK FAST = AALKAB MEYAJ

WRAP = TO'IK

WRINKLE = CH'UKIK

WRITE = TZ'IIB

WRITE = TZ'IIBTIK

YUCATEC PHRASES:

 * The order of the phrases are as follows: Spanish / English – Yucatec Maya

 *Remember that the 'j' is pronounced like in Spanish like a rough 'h'

  VII) **Hello's and Goodbye's**

 ¡HOLA! / HELLO! = ¡OOLA!

¿QUÉ TAL? ¿QUÉ ONDA? / WHAT'S UP? WHAT'S GOING ON? = ¿TU'UX KA BIN? [LITERALLY: WHERE ARE YOU GOING?]

¿CÓMO ESTÁS? ¿CÓMO ESTÁN USTEDES? / HOW ARE YOU? = ¿B'IX A BEEL? [SINGULAR] ... ¿B'IX A BEELE'EX? [PLURAL]

¿CÓMO ESTÁS? ¿CÓMO ESTÁN USTEDES? / HOW ARE YOU? = ¿B'IX YAANIKEECH? [SINGULAR] ... ¿B'IX YAANIKE'EX? [PLURAL]

¿CÓMO ESTÁS? / HOW ARE YOU? = ¿BA'AX KA WA'ALIK? [LITERALLY: WHAT DO YOU SAY?]

¡ADIÓS! / GOODBYE! = ¡TAK SAAMAL!

¡NOS VEMOS! / SEE YOU AGAIN SOON! = ¡TAK SAAMAL!

¡ADIÓS! / BYE! = ¡KA XI'IK TEECH UTZIIL!

¡BUENA SUERTE! / GOOD LUCK! MAY IT GO WELL
WITH YOU! = ¡KA XI'IK TEECH JATZ'UTZIIL!

¡DIOS TE PROTEJA! / MAY GOD PROTECT YOU! =
¡KA'AJ DYOS KALAANTEECH!

VIII)   Basic phrases of conversation

SÍ / YES = JAAJ

NO / NO = MA'

¿CÓMO ESTÁS? ¿CÓMO ESTÁN USTEDES? / HOW ARE YOU? = ¿B'IX A BEEL? [SINGULAR] ¿B'IX A BEELE'EX? [PLURAL]

¡ESTOY BIEN, GRACIAS! / I'M WELL, THANK YOU = MA'ALOB / UTZ, JACH DYOS BO'OTIK TEECH/ DYOS BO'OTIK TEECH

VARIANTS:

YU'UM BO'OTIK TEECH / JACH YUUM BO'OTIK TEECH

¿Y TÚ? ¿CÓMO ESTÁS? /AND YOU? HOW ARE YOU? = ¿KUX TEECH? ¿B'IX A BEEL?

ESTOY BIEN / I AM WELL = (JACH) MA'ALOB

DE NADA / YOU'RE WELCOME = MA', DYOS BO'OTIK TEECH [RESPONSE TO THANK YOU]

VARIANTS:

MA', YUUM BO'OTIK TEECH / MA', JACH YUUM BO'OTIK TEECH

ESTÁ BIEN / ALL IS WELL = MA'ALOB

¿CÓMO TE LLAMAS? / WHAT'S YOUR NAME? = ¿B'IX A K'ABA'? ¿BA'AX A K'ABA'?

ME LLAMO… / MY NAME IS… = IN K'ABA'E…

NO TE CONOZCO / I DON'T KNOW YOU = MA' TIN KAJOOLTIKEECH

TÚ NO ME CONOCES / YOU DON'T KNOW ME = MA' TAN KAJOOLTIKEECH

¿DE DÓNDE ERES? / WHERE ARE YOU FROM? = ¿TU'UX A TAAL?

¿DE DÓNDE ERES? / WHERE ARE YOU FROM? = ¿TU'UX A KAAJAL?

SOY DE LOS ESTADOS UNIDOS / I'M FROM THE UNITED STATES = LUK'EN LOS ESTADOS UNIDOS

¿CUÁNTOS AÑOS TIENES? / HOW OLD ARE YOU? = ¿JAYP'EL AANYOS YAAN TEECH? ¿JAYP'EL A JA'ABIIL?

*TENGO…AÑOS / I AM…YEARS OLD =

YAAN TEEN…JA'ABIIL

JUN = 1

KA'A =2

OOX = 3

KAN = 4

JO' = 5

WAAK = 6

UK = 7

WAXAK = 8

BOLON = 9

LAJUN = 10

BULUK = 11

LAJKA'A = 12

OOX LAJUN = 13

KAN LAJUN = 14

JO' LAJUN = 15

WAK LAJUN = 16

UK LAJUN = 17

WAXAK LAJUN = 18

BOLON LAJUN = 19

JUN K'AAL = 20

JUN K'AAL JUN = 21

JUN K'AAL KA'A = 22

JUN K'AAL OOX = 23

JUN K'AAL KAN = 24

JUN K'AAL JO' = 25

JUN K'AAL WAK = 26

JUN K'AAL UK = 27

JUN K'AAL WAXAK = 28

JUN K'AAL BOLON = 29

KA' K'AAL = 40

OOX K'AAL = 60

KAN K'AAL = 80

JO' K'AAL = 100

POR FAVOR, DIME ESO EN ESPAÑOL / PLEASE, TELL ME THAT IN SPANISH = ¡A'ANE TEEN TI' LE KAXLANT'AANO'!

¿HABLAS YUCATECO? / DO YOU SPEAK YUCATEC? = ¿KA T'AANIK LE MAAYAT'AANO'?

YO HABLO YUCATECO / I SPEAK YUCATEC = KIN T'AANIK LE MAAYAT'AANO'

NO HABLO YUCATECO / I DON'T SPEAK YUCATEC = MA' TEN T'ANIK LE MAAYAT'AANO'

POR FAVOR, HABLA LENTO / PLEASE SPEAK SLOWLY = ¡T'ANE CHAAMBEEL!

POR FAVOR, DIGÁME ESO OTRA VEZ / TELL ME THAT AGAIN PLEASE = ¡A'ANE TEEN KA'AJ!

¿QUÉ QUIERES QUE YO DIGA? / WHAT DO YOU WANT ME TO SAY? = ¿BA'AX A K'AAT KA'AJ TEN WA'ALIK?

TÚ HABLAS DEMASIADO RÁPIDO / YOU TALK TOO FAST = KA T'AAN JACH SEEB

LO SIENTO / I'M SORRY = MA' TAALI'TEENI'

NO ENTIENDO / I DON'T UNDERSTAND = MA' TIN NA'ATIK TEECH

¿TÚ SABES? / DO YOU KNOW? = ¿M'A WOJLI?

NO, NO SE / NO, I DON'T KNOW = MA', M'IN WOJLI

NO QUIERO SABER LO QUE PASÓ / I DON'T WANT TO KNOW WHAT HAPPENED = M'IN K'AAT IN WOJEL KA'AJ TZ'OK U YUUCHUL

NO QUIERO SABER / I DON'T WANT TO KNOW = M'IN K'AAT IN WOJEL

¡PERDÓNAME! / EXCUSE ME! = ¡PA'ATIKI'!

¡TEN PRISA! ¡TENGA PRISA! ¡APÚRATE! / HURRY! BE QUICK! = ¡SEEKUNTE!

¡VETE! ¡VAYASE! ¡VAYANSE! / GO! = ¡XEN! [TO ONE PERSON] ¡XENE'EX! [TO TWO OR MORE PERSONS]

¡VEN ACÁ! ¡VENGA ACÁ! ¡VENGAN ACÁ! / COME HERE! = ¡KO'OTEN WAYE'! [TO ONE PERSON] ¡KO'OTENE'EX WAYE'! [TO TWO OR MORE PERSONS]

¿CUÁNDO TU LLEGASTE AQUÍ? / WHEN DID YOU ARRIVE HERE? = ¿BA'AX K'IIN K'UCHEECH WAYE'?

YO LLEGUÉ AQUÍ AYER / I ARRIVED HERE YESTERDAY = JO'OLJEYAK K'UCHEEN WAYE'

*THE MAJORITY OF YUCATEC MAYA WORK AS FARMERS OR, IN GENERAL, WITH GROWING CROPS; WHICH NOT ONLY FEEDS THEIR FAMILIES, BUT ALSO MAY PROVIDE EXCESS THAT THEY CAN SELL IN LOCAL MARKETS FOR PROFIT

¿EN QUÉ TÚ TRABAJAS? / WHAT KIND OF WORK DO YOU DO? = ¿MAAKALMAAK MEYAJ KA BEETIK?

SOY UN... / I WORK AS A... = IN MEYAJ...

SOY UN MILPERO / I AM A FARMER = KOOLNAALEEN / KINMEYAJ TI' KOOL

- JEN JOCHIKI = LO COSECHARÉ / I WILL HARVEST IT
- TEN BIN TZ'ON = VOY PARA CAZAR / I AM GOING HUNTING
- TEN BIN XOTIK SI' = VOY PARA CORTAR LEÑA / I AM GOING TO CUT FIREWOOD
- JEN BEETIKI SI' = VOY A HACER LA LEÑA / I WILL SEARCH FOR FIREWOOD

¿ADÓNDE VAS? / WHERE ARE YOU GOING? = ¿TU'UX KA BIN?

¿ADÓNDE FUÍSTE? / WHERE DID YOU GO? = ¿TU'UX BIINEECH?

¿ADÓNDE VAN USTEDES? / WHERE ARE YOU ALL GOING? = ¿TU'UX KA BINE'EX?

¿ADÓNDE FUERON USTEDES? / WHERE DID YOU ALL GO? = ¿TU'UX BIINE'EX?

¿CON QUIÉN FUÍSTE TÚ? / WHO DID YOU GO WITH? = ¿MAAX YETEL BIINEECH?

TENGO QUE IR / I HAVE TO GO = YAAN IN BINEL

TENGO QUE TRABAJAR / I HAVE TO WORK = YAAN IN MEYAJ

TENGO QUE SALIR / I HAVE TO LEAVE = YAAN IN LUK'UL

TENGO QUE HACERLO / I HAVE TO DO IT = YAAN IN BEETIK

VOY A REGRESAR / I WILL RETURN = YAAN IN SUUT

VOY A REGRESAR OTRA VEZ / I WILL RETURN AGAIN = YAAN IN SUUT KA'AJ

VOY A REGRESAR MAÑANA / I WILL RETURN TOMORROW = YAAN IN SUUT SAAMAL

VOY A REGRESAR EN EL PRÓXIMO AÑO / I WILL RETURN NEXT YEAR = JEN SUUTE TI' LAAK' JA'ABIIL

VAMOS A REGRESAR EN EL PRÓXIMO AÑO / WE WILL RETURN NEXT YEAR = JEK SUUTE TI' LAAK' JA'ABIIL

¿DÓNDE ESTÁ EL BANCO? / WHERE IS THE BANK? = ¿TU'UX YAAN LE BAANKO?

LLÉVAME AL BANCO / TAKE ME TO THE BANK = BIISE TEEN TI' BAANKO!

NECESITO CAMBIAR UN POCO DINERO / I NEED TO EXCHANGE SOME MONEY = YAAN IN K'EXIK JUMP'IIT TAAK'IN

QUIERO CAMBIAR [CANJEAR] DINERO / I WANT TO EXCHANGE MONEY = K'AAT IN K'EXIK LE TAAK'INA'

NO TENGO PESOS MEXICANOS / I DON'T HAVE MEXICAN PESOS = MA' YAANI' TEEN PEESOS

QUIERO PESOS MEXICANOS / I WANT MEXICAN PESOS = IN K'AAT PEESOS

¿DÓNDE ESTÁ EL MERCADO [TIENDA]? / WHERE IS THE MARKET [STORE]? = ¿TU'UX YAAN MERKAADO?

LLÉVAME AL MERCADO / TAKE ME TO THE MARKET = BIISE TEEN TI' MERKAADO

NECESITO COMPRAR COMIDA / I NEED TO BUY FOOD = YAAN IN MANIK JAANAL

NECESITO COMPRAR FRUTA / I NEED TO BUY FRUIT = YAAN IN MANIK CH'UJUK

¿QUÉ ES ESO? ¿QUÉ ES ESTO? / WHAT IS THAT? WHAT IS THIS? WHAT IS IT? = ¿BA'AXI?

¿CUÁNTO CUESTA? / HOW MUCH DOES IT [THAT] COST? = ¿BAJUUX U TOJOL?

¿CUÁNTO TE DEBO? / HOW MUCH DO I OWE YOU? = ¿BAJUUX K'AABET IN TZ'IIKEECH?

NO QUIERO COMPRAR ESTO/ I DON'T WANT TO BUY THIS = MA' M'IN K'AAT MANIK LELO'

SÍ, LO QUIERO COMPRAR / YES, I WANT TO BUY IT = JAAJ, K'AAT IN MANIK LELO'

LO SIENTO, NO LO PUEDO COMPRAR / I'M SORRY, I CAN'T BUY IT = MA' TAALI'TEENI', M'IN K'AAT IN MANIK LELO'

¿HAY ALGO MÁS BARATO? / IS THERE SOMETHING A LOT CHEAPER? = ¿YAAN JUMP'EL BA'AL MAAS MA' KO'OJI?

NO TENGO MUCHO DINERO / I DON'T HAVE MUCH MONEY = MA' YAANI TEEN JACH YA'AB TAAK'IN

SI YO TUVIERA DINERO SUFICIENTE, YO LO COMPRARÍA / IF I HAD SUFFICIENT MONEY, I WOULD BUY IT = WAAJ YAANJI TEEN JACH YA'AB TAAK'IN, KU PAAJTAL IN MANIK LELO'

¿TE GUSTA? / DO YOU LIKE IT? = ¿UTZ TAN WICH?

ME GUSTA / I LIKE IT = UTZ TIN WICH

NO, NO ME GUSTA / NO, I DON'T LIKE IT = MA', MA' UTZ TIN WICH

¿DÓNDE ESTÁ UNA TIENDA QUE VENDE…? / WHERE IS THERE A STORE THAT SELLS…? = ¿TU'UX YAAN JUMP'EL MERKAADO KA'AJ KU KONIK…?

NOOK' = ROPA / CLOTHING

KAMIISA = PLAYERA, CAMISA / SHIRT, T-SHIRTS

EEX = PANTALONES / PANTS

XANAB = ZAPATOS / SHOES

O'OCH = COMIDA / FOOD

JAANAL = COMIDA / FOOD

NOOK' = TELA; TEJIDO / BLANKETS; WEAVED FABRICS

JU'UNO'OB = LIBROS / BOOKS

SIIJBILO'OB = REGALOS / GIFTS

P'OKO'OB = SOMBREROS / HATS

WAAJO'OB = TORTILLAS / TORTILLAS

KOOKA = COCA COLA

QUIERO ATRÁVESAR EL RÍO / I WANT TO CROSS THE RIVER = K'AAT IN K'AATIK LE BEKANA'

QUEREMOS ATRÁVESAR EL RÍO / WE WANT TO CROSS THE RIVER = K'AAT IN K'AATIKO'ON LE BEKANA'

¿CUÁNTO CUESTA PARA LLEVARNOS A...? / HOW MUCH DOES IT COST TO TAKE US TO...? = ¿BAJUUX U TOJOL WAAJ TAN BISIKO'ON TI'...?

TODOS MIS COMPAÑEROS QUIEREN IR AL MERCADO PARA COMPRAR / VER LAS COSAS ALLÁ / ALL OF MY FRIENDS WANT TO GO TO THE MARKET TO BUY / SEE THE THINGS THERE =

TULAAKAL IN WAMIIGOJO'OB K'AAT U BINO'OB TI' MERKAADO MANIK / YILIK LE BA'ALO'OBO' TE'ELO'

TENGO HAMBRE / I'M HUNGRY = WI'IJEEN

TENGO SED / I'M THIRSTY = UK'AJEEN

VAMOS A BUSCAR COMIDA / LET'S LOOK FOR FOOD = JEK KAXTIKE O'OCH

NECESITO USAR EL BAÑO / I NEED TO USE THE RESTROOM = YAAN IN BINEL TI' BAANYO

¿DÓNDE ESTÁ EL BAÑO? / WHERE IS THE BATHROOM? = ¿TU'UX YAAN LE BAANYO'O'?

DÁME UN CAFÉ, POR FAVOR / GIVE ME A COFFEE, PLEASE = TZ'A TEEN JUMP'EL BOXJA'

TÚ ERES MUY HERMOSO(A) / GUAPO(A) / YOU ARE VERY BEAUTIFUL /HANDSOME = JATZ'UTZEECH / KI'ICHPANEECH

TÚ TIENE UNA CARA MUY LINDA / YOU HAVE A VERY CUTE FACE = YAAN TEECH JUMP'EL JATZ'UTZ IICH

¿PUEDO SACAR UNA FOTO? / I CAN TAKE A PHOTO? = ¿JU' CHABALE IN MENTIK JUMP'EL POTO?

¿PUEDO TOMAR UNA FOTO AQUÍ O NO? / CAN I TAKE A PHOTO HERE OR NO? = ¿KU PAAJTAL IN MENTIK POTO WAYE' WAAJ MA'?

¿HAY UN HOTEL AQUÍ? / IS THERE A HOTEL HERE? = ¿YAAN JUMP'EL OOTEL WAYE'?

LLÉVAME AL HOTEL / TAKE ME TO THE HOTEL = BISE TEEN TI' OOTEL

¿HAY UN CUARTO DISPONIBLE EN CUAL PUEDO QUEDARME / DORMIR? / IS THERE A ROOM AVAILABLE IN WHICH I CAN STAY / SLEEP? =

¿YAAN JUMP'EL BAANDA KA'AJ JU' PAAJTAL IN P'AATAL / IN WENEL?

¿CUÁNTAS NOCHES QUIERES QUEDARTE? / HOW MANY NIGHTS DO YOU WANT TO STAY? = ¿BAJUUX AK'ABO'OB A K'AAT P'AATAL WAYE'?

QUIERO QUEDARME AQUÍ POR UNO / DOS / TRES NOCHES / I WANT TO STAY HERE FOR ONE / TWO / THREE NIGHTS = K'AAT IN P'AATAL WAYE' JUMP'EL AK'AB / KA'AP'EL AK'ABO'OB / OOXP'EL AK'ABO'OB

¿CUÁNTO CUESTA EL CUARTO? / HOW MUCH DOES THE ROOM COST? = ¿BAJUUX U TOJOL LE BAANDA'A?

¿PUEDO VER EL CUARTO? / CAN I SEE THE ROOM? = ¿JU' PAAJTAL IN WILIK LA BAANDA'O'?

NO ME GUSTA / I DON'T LIKE IT = MA' UTZ TIN WICH

ME GUSTA, QUIERO EL CUARTO / I LIKE IT, I'LL TAKE IT = UTZ TIN WICH, IN K' AAT LE BAANDA' A'

EL CUARTO ES SUCIO, QUIERO OTRO / THE ROOM IS DIRTY, I WANT A DIFFERENT ONE = LE BAANDA' A' JACH EEK', IN K' AAT LAAK' BAANDA

TODAS LAS SÁBANAS SON SUCIAS / ALL OF THE SHEETS ARE DIRTY = TULAAKAL LE SABANA'O'OBO' JACH EEK'

¿DURMIERON USTEDES BIEN? / DID YOU ALL SLEEP WELL? = ¿TZ'OK A WENELE'EX MA'ALOB?

NO DORMÍ BIEN / I DID NOT SLEEP WELL = MA' TZ'OK IN WENELI

¿PORQUÉ? / WHY? = ¿BA'AXTEN…?

HABÍA DEMASIADO MUCHO RUÍDO / THERE WAS TOO MUCH NOISE = YAAN YA'AB JUUM WAYE'

QUIERO SALIR / I WANT TO LEAVE = K'AAT IN LUK'UL

VAMOS A BUSCAR OTRO HOTEL / LET'S LOOK FOR ANOTHER HOTEL = YAAN IN KAXTIKO'ON LAAK' OOTEL

¿QUIERES IR CONMIGO? / DO YOU WANT TO GO WITH ME? = ¿A K'AAT BINEL YETELEEN?

NO, NO PUEDO IR CONTIGO / NO, I CANNOT GO WITH YOU = MA', MU' PATI IN BINEL YETELEECH

NO, NO QUIERO IR CONTIGO / NO, I DO NOT WANT TO GO WITH YOU = MA', M'IN K'AAT BINEL YETELEECH

¿TE PUEDO AYUDAR? / CAN I HELP YOU? = ¿KU PAAJTAL IN WAANTIKEECH?

NO TE PUEDO AYUDAR / I CANNOT HELP YOU = MU' PAATI IN WAANTIKEECH

QUIERO QUE ME AYUDES / I WANT YOU TO HELP ME = IN K'AAT KA'AJ TAN WAANTIKEEN

SI YO TUVIERA DINERO, TE AYUDARÍA / IF I HAD MONEY, I WOULD HELP YOU = WAAJ YAANJI TEEN YA'AB TAAK'IN, JU' PAAJTAL IN WAANTIKEECH

SI YO TUVIERA DINERO, ME IRÍA / IF I HAD MONEY, I WOULD LEAVE = WAAJ YAANJI TEEN YA'AB TAAK'IN, JEN LUK'ULE

¿PORQUÉ ME QUIERES AYUDAR? / WHY DO YOU WANT TO HELP ME? = ¿BA'AXTEN A K'AAT A WAANTIKEEN?

¿ESTO ES TUYO? / IS THIS YOURS? = ¿A TI'AL LELA'?

ESTO NO ES TUYO / THIS IS NOT YOURS = MA'ATI'AAL LELA'

NO ES MÍO / IT IS NOT MINE = M'IN TI'AAL LELO'

SÍ, ES MÍO / YES, IT IS MINE = JAAJ, IN TI'AAL LELO'

OJALÁ TENGAS UN BUEN DÍA / I HOPE THAT YOU HAVE A GOOD DAY = KA'AJ YAAN TEECH JUMP'EL UTZ K'IIN

OJALÁ PUEDAS VENIR / HOPEFULLY YOU CAN COME = KA'AJ TAALAK

OJALÁ PUEDA YO ENCONTRARLO / I HOPE THAT I CAN FIND IT = KA'AJ A KAXTE

OJALÁ NO LLUEVA HOY / HOPEFULLY IT DOES NOT RAIN TODAY = KA'AJ MU' BEETE CHAAK BEJLA'E'

¿DÓNDE ESTÁ LA IGLESIA? / WHERE IS THE CHURCH? = ¿TU'UX YAAN YOTOCH DYOS?

LLÉVAME A LA IGLESIA / TAKE ME TO THE CHURCH = BIISE TEEN TI' YOTOCH DYOS

¿DÓNDE ESTÁ TU CASA? / WHERE IS YOUR HOME? = ¿TU'UX A NAJIIL?

DIOS TE BENDIGA / GOD BLESS YOU = KA'AJ DYOS KU BENDISYONTIKEECH

DIOS LOS BENDIGA / GOD BLESS YOU ALL = KA'AJ DYOS KU BENDISYONTIKE'EX

VAMOS A ORAR POR LA COMIDA / WE SHALL PRAY FOR OUR FOOD = JEK BO'OTIKE DYOS UTI'AL LE O'OCHA'

VAMOS A ORARLE A DIOS Y DARLE GRACIAS / LET'S PRAY TO GOD AND GIVE THANKS = JEK BO'OTIKE DYOS

DIOS ES MUY BUENO / GOD IS GOOD; GOD IS GREAT = DYOS JACH UTZ

DIOS NOS HA BENDECIDO CON OTRO DÍA / GOD HAS BLESSED US WITH ANOTHER DAY = DYOS U TZ'IIKO'ON UTZIIL YETEL TUUMBEN K'IIN

TE AMO / I LOVE YOU = KIN YAKUNTIKEECH

¿ME AMAS? / DO YOU LOVE ME? = ¿KA' YAKUNTIKEEN?

TE QUIERO BESAR / I WANT TO KISS YOU = K'AAT IN TZ'U'UTZ'IKEECH

TE QUIERO ABRAZAR / I WANT TO HUG YOU = K'AAT IN MEEK'IKEECH

TE QUIERO ENVOLVER BIEN EN MIS BRAZOS / I WANT TO WRAP YOU IN MY ARMS = K'AAT IN TO'IKEECH TI' IN K'ABO'OB

TE EXTRAÑARÉ MUCHO / I WILL MISS YOU VERY MUCH = YAAN TEEN XMA'EECH JACH YA'AB

NUNCA TE VOY A OLVIDAR / I WILL NEVER FORGET YOU = MIX B'IKIN KIN TU'UBSIKEECH

SOLO QUIERO QUEDARME A TU LADO / I ONLY WANT TO STAY AT YOUR SIDE = TAAK IN P'AATAL TI' A TZEEL

IX)   COMMON COMMANDS [Imperatives]:

¡VETE! ¡VAYASE! ¡VAYANSE! / GO! = ¡XEN! [TO ONE PERSON] ¡XENE'EX! [TO TWO OR MORE PERSONS]

¡VEN ACÁ! ¡VENGA ACÁ! ¡VENGAN ACÁ! / COME HERE! = ¡KO'OTEN WAYE'! [TO ONE PERSON] ¡KO'OTENE'EX WAYE'! [TO TWO OR MORE PERSONS]

¡VEN CONMIGO! ¡VENGA CONMIGO! ¡VENGAN CONMIGO! / COME WITH ME! = ¡KO'OTEN YETELEEN! [TO ONE PERSON] ¡KO'OTENE'EX YETELEEN! [TO TWO OR MORE PERSONS]

¡LARGATE DE AQUÍ! / GET OUT OF HERE! LEAVE ME IN PEACE! = XEN TE'ELO'!

¡VAMOS! ¡VAYAMOS! / LET'S GO! = ¡KO'ONE'EX!

¡VAMOS A COMER! / LET'S EAT! = ¡JEK JAANALE!

¡TRABAJEMOS! / LET'S WORK! = ¡JEK MEYAJE!

¡VÁYASE A TRABAJAR! / GO TO WORK! = ¡MEYAJ! [SING.] ¡MEYAJE'EX! [PLURAL]

¡HÁGAMOSLO! / LET'S DO IT! = ¡JEK BEETIKE!

¡VÁYASE A HACERLO! / GO DO TI! = ¡BEETE! [SING] ¡BEETE'EX! [PLURAL]

¡HÁGALO! / DO IT! = BEETE!

¡NO LO HAGAS! / DON'T DO IT! = ¡MA' A BEETIK!

HÁGAME UN FAVOR / DO ME A FAVOR, PLEASE = BEETE TEEN JUMP'EL UTZIIL

¡VAMOS A HACERLO! / LET'S DO IT! = ¡JEK BEETIKE!

¡VAMOS A HACER LA LEÑA! / LET'S COLLECT FIRE WOOD! = ¡JEK BEETIKE SI'!

¡VAMOS A BAILAR! / LET'S DANCE! = ¡JEK OK'OTE!

¡DÁMELO! / GIVE ME IT! = ¡TZ'AA TEEN!

DAME DOS CERVEZAS, POR FAVOR / GIVE ME TWO BEERS, PLEASE = TZ'AA TEEN KA'AP'EL CHEBA'O'OB

DAME UNA BOTELLA DE AGUA / UNA COCA COLA / GIVE ME A BOTTLE OF WATER / A COCA COLA = TZ'AA TEEN JUMP'EL SIIS JA' / JUMP'EL KOOKA

¡BEBA! / DRINK! = ¡UK'EN!

¡BEBA AGUA! / DRINK WATER! = ¡UK'EN JA!

¡ÉNTRATE! ¡ÉNTRESE! ¡ÉNTRENSE! / ENTER! COME IN! = ¡OOKEN! [SING] ¡OOKENE'EX! [PLURAL]

¡AGUÁRDAME AQUÍ! / WAIT FOR ME HERE! = ¡PA'ATE WAYE'!

LLÉVAME AL MERCADO / TAKE ME TO THE MARKET = BIISE TEEN TI' MERKAADO

X) EMERGENCY PHRASES:

¡AYÚDAME! ¡AYUDENME! / HELP ME! = ¡Λ'ANTE! [TO ONE PERSON] ¡A'ANTE'EX! [TWO OR MORE PERSONS]

¡NO TE CAÍGAS! / DON'T FALL! = ¡MA' LUUBEN!

¡NO ME MOLESTES! ¡NO ME CHINGUES! / DON'T MESS WITH ME! = ¡MA' P'U'UJSE TEEN!

¡LLAMA LA POLICÍA! / CALL THE POLICE! = ¡PAY / PAYE'EX POLIISYA!

¡HÁGALO! / DO IT! = ¡BEETE!

ALGUIÉN ME ROBÓ / SOMEONE ROBBED ME = JUNTUUL WIINIK TZ'OK U YOKLIKEEN IN BA'ALO'OB

ALGUIÉN HURTÓ MIS PERTENECÍAS / SOMEONE STOLE MY THINGS = JUUNTUL WIINIK TZ'OK U YOKLIK IN BA'ALO'OB

¿DÓNDE ESTÁ EL HOSPITAL? / WHERE IS THE HOSPITAL? = ¿TU'UX YAAN YOTOCH TZ'AAK?

UNA SERPIENTE ME MORDIÓ / A SNAKE BIT ME = JUNTUUL KAAN TZ'OK U CHI'IBALEEN

UN CHUCHO ME MORDIÓ / A DOG BIT ME = JUUNTUL PEEK' TZ'OK U CHI'IBALEEN

ESTOY SANGRANDO MUCHO / I AM BLEEDING VERY BAD = YA'AB K'I'IK' TUN JOK'OOL TEEN

NECESITO BEBER UN POCO AGUA / I NEED TO DRINK WATER = K'AABEET IN WUK'AL JUUMP'IIT JA'

ESTOY ENFERMO / I AM SICK = K'OJA'ANEEN

TENGO MUCHO DOLOR / I AM IN A LOT OF PAIN = YAAN TEEN YA'AB YAAJ

(…) ME DUELE / MY…HURTS = TUN CHI'IBAL […]

AAK' = LENGUA / TONGUE

AAL K'AB = DEDO DE MANO / FINGER

AAL OOK = DEDO DE PIE / TOE

BAK'EL IIT = TRASERO / BUTTOCKS

BOOX = LABIOS / LIPS

CHI' = BOCA / MOUTH

ICH = CARA; ROSTRO / FACE

ICH = OJO / EYE

IIT = ANO / ANUS

JO'OL = CABEZA / HEAD

K'AB = BRAZO; MANO / ARM; HAND

KELEMBAL = HOMBROS / SHOULDERS

KOJ = DIENTE / TOOTH; TEETH

NAK' = ESTOMAGO / STOMACH

NI' = NARIZ / NOSE

OOK = PIE / FOOT

P'U'UKIL IIT = TRASERO / BUTTOCKS

PAACH = ESPALDA / BACK

POOL = CABEZA / HEAD

T'UUP = MEÑIQUE / PINKY FINGER

TOON = PENE / PENIS

XIIBIL = PENE / PENIS

XIKIN = OREJA / EAR

TENGO DIARREA / I HAVE DIARRHEA = YAAN TEEN DIARREA

TENGO DIARREA Y VOMITOS / I HAVE VOMITING AND DIARRHEA = YAAN TEEN XEJ YETEL DIARREA

TENGO MIEDO / I'M AFRAID = YAAN TEEN SAJKIIL

TENÍA MIEDO / I WAS AFRAID = YAANJI TEEN SAJKIIL

NO TENGAS MIEDO / DON'T BE AFRAID = MA' YAANI TEECH SAJKIIL

LLÉVAME AL HOSPITAL / TAKE ME TO THE HOSPITAL = BIISE TEEN TI' YOTOCH TZ'AAK

Made in the USA
Las Vegas, NV
31 August 2021